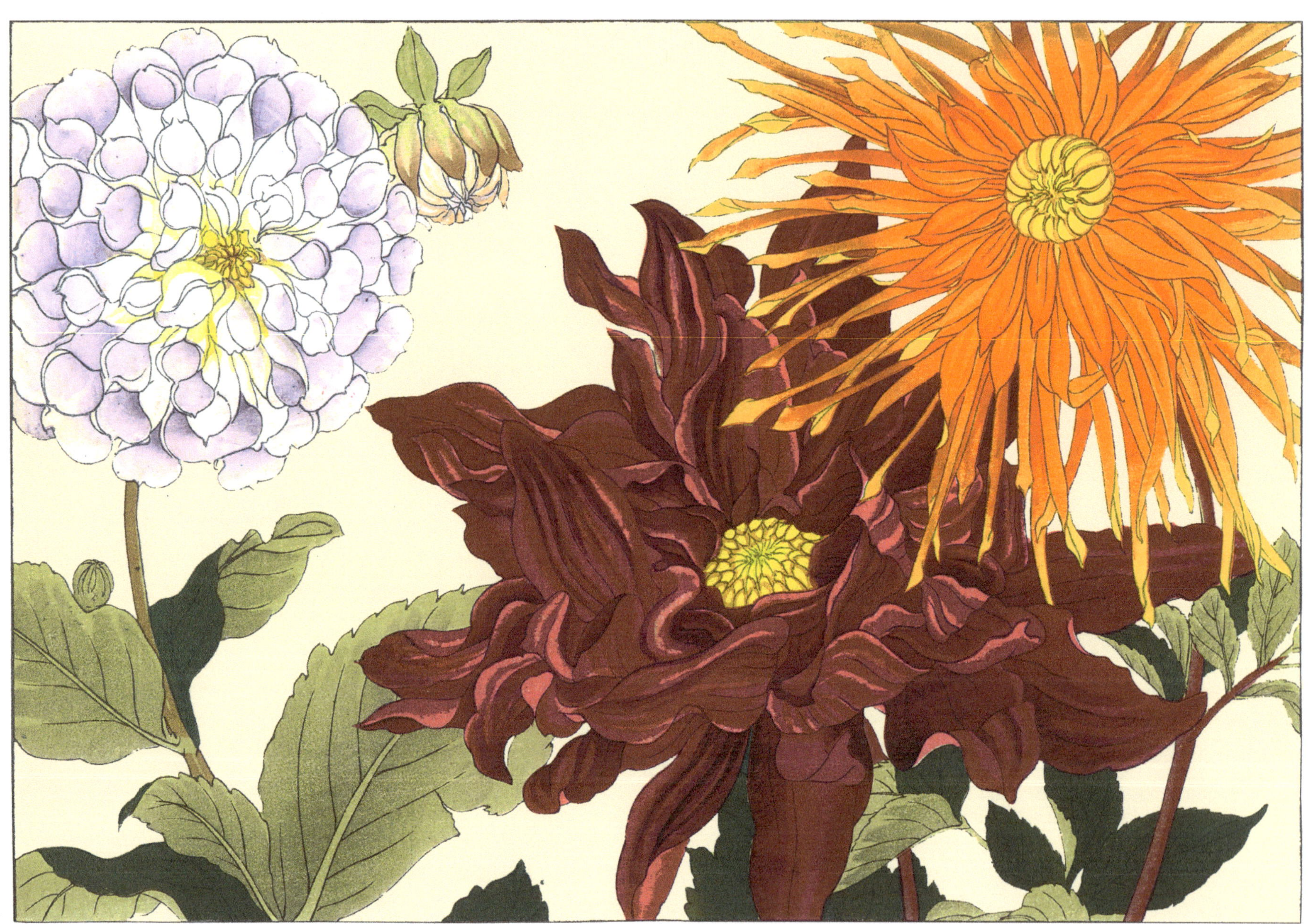

Dahlia

Japanese Woodblock
FLOWER PRINTS

Tanigami Kônan

DOVER PUBLICATIONS
Garden City, New York

This Dover edition, first published in 2008, is a new selection of 120 plates of Japanese woodblock prints from *Seiyô Soka Zufu,* originally published as a five-volume set by Unsôdô, Kyoto, ca. 1917. The Publisher's Note has been specially written for the present edition.

DOVER *Pictorial Archive* SERIES

Library of Congress Cataloging-in-Publication Data

Tanigami, Kônan, 1879–1928.
Japanese woodblock flower prints / Tanigami Kônan. — Dover ed.
p. cm. — (Dover pictorial archive series)
"A new selection of 120 plates of Japanese woodblock prints from Seiyô soka zufu, originally published as a five-volume set by Unsôdô, Kyoto, ca. 1917"—T.p. verso.
ISBN-13: 978-0-486-46442-8
ISBN-10: 0-486-46442-3
1. Tanigami, Kônan, 1879–1928—Catalogs. 2. Flowers in art—Catalogs. I. Tanigami, Kônan, 1879–1928. Seiyô soka zufu. II. Title.

NE1325.T357A4 2008
761'.20952—dc22

2007043047

Printed in Canada
46442307 2026
www.doverpublications.com

Publisher's Note

The present volume reproduces, in full color, a selection of 120 plates from artist Tanigami Kônan's *Seiyô Soka Zufu* (A Picture Album of Western Plants and Flowers), which was originally published as a five-volume set by Unsôdô, Kyoto, ca. 1917. This spectacular work, comprised entirely of authentic Japanese color woodblock prints, depicted a wide variety of lush flowers and exotic plants in full bloom. Organized as a visual record of garden flowers, two volumes each were devoted to the spring and summer seasons. The last volume combined the flowers and plants that flourished in the fall-winter season. In the present edition, the arrangement of the floral plates follows the exact sequence of the original Japanese volumes.

Carefully selected from an extremely rare set of volumes, this new compilation of exquisite illustrations preserves all of the original, richly vivid colors. An assortment of familiar flowers such as daffodils, lilacs, roses, dahlias, poppies, and zinnias are represented in meticulous detail with realistic, vibrant colors. This artistic treasury will delight anyone who appreciates the glorious beauty of Japanese woodblock prints, floral art, and botanicals.

Index of Flowers

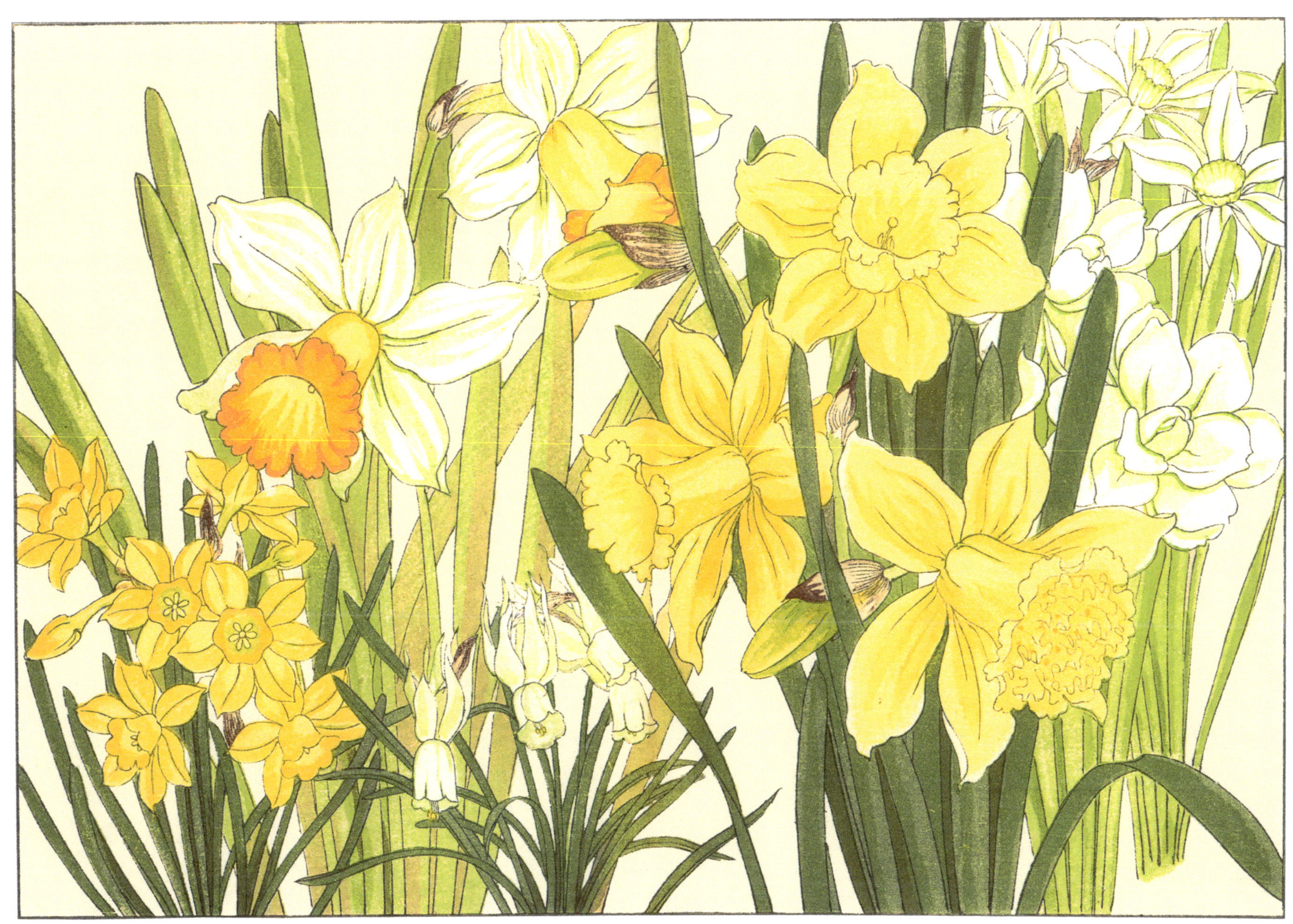

Daffodil

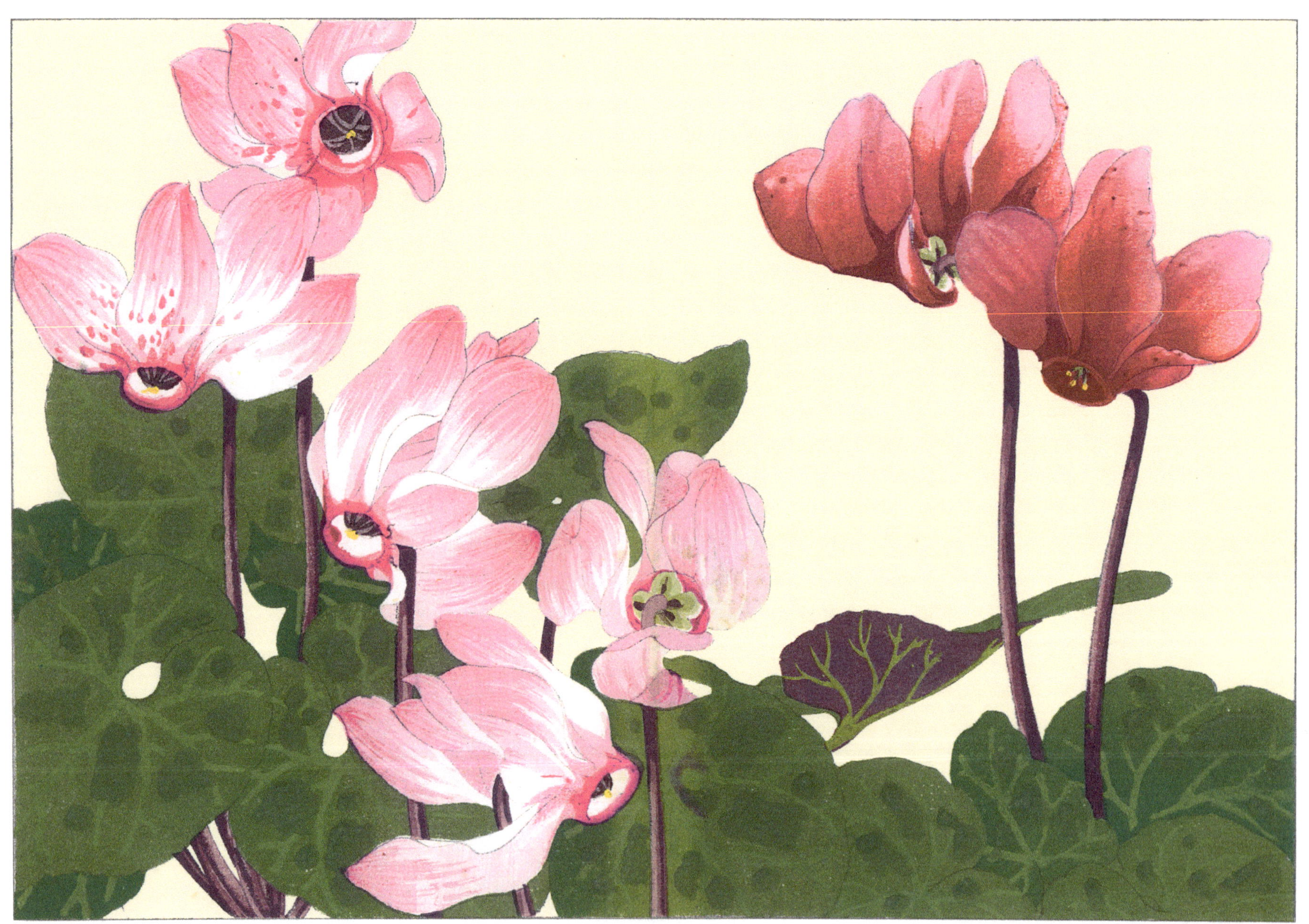

Cyclamen

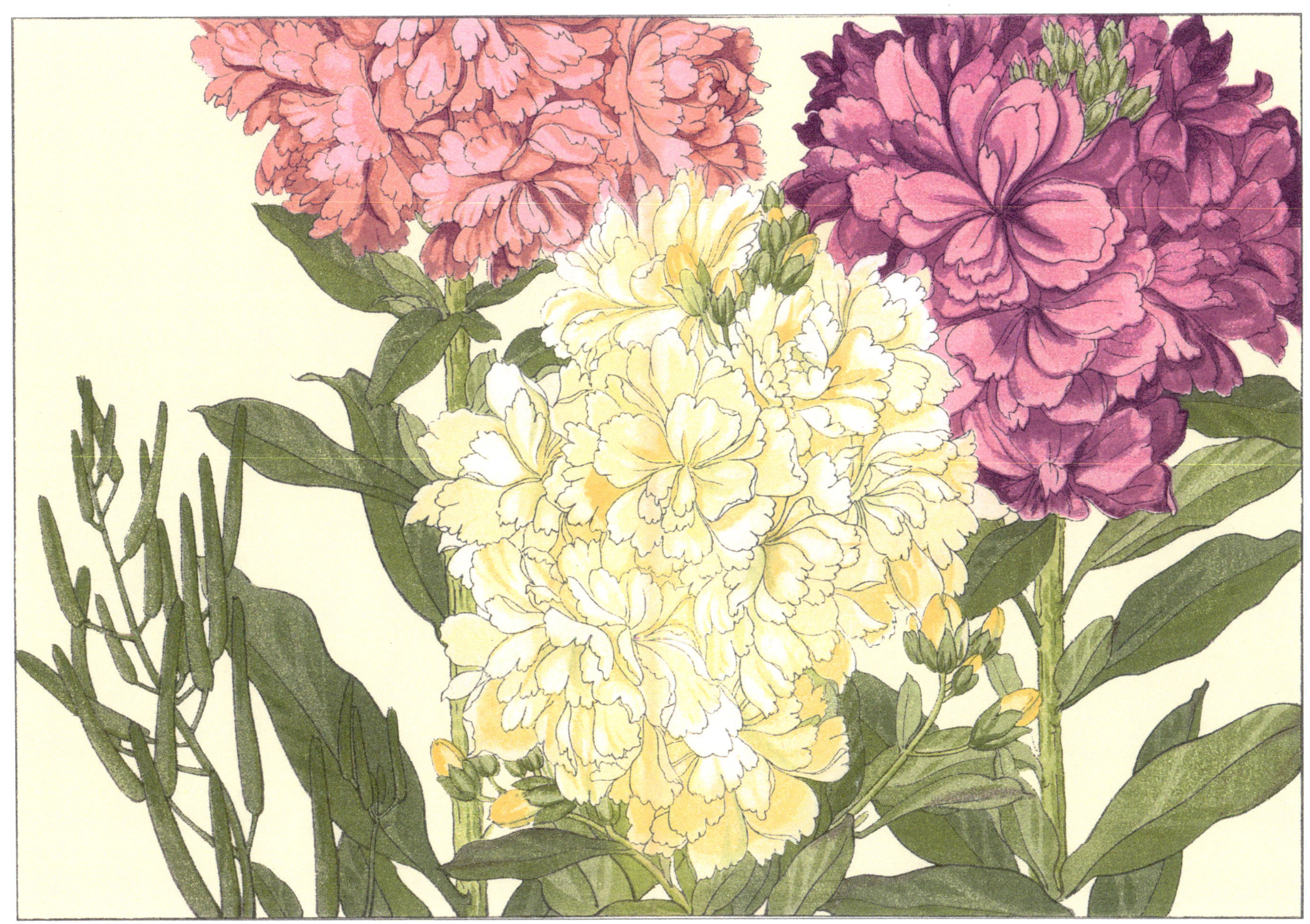

Stock

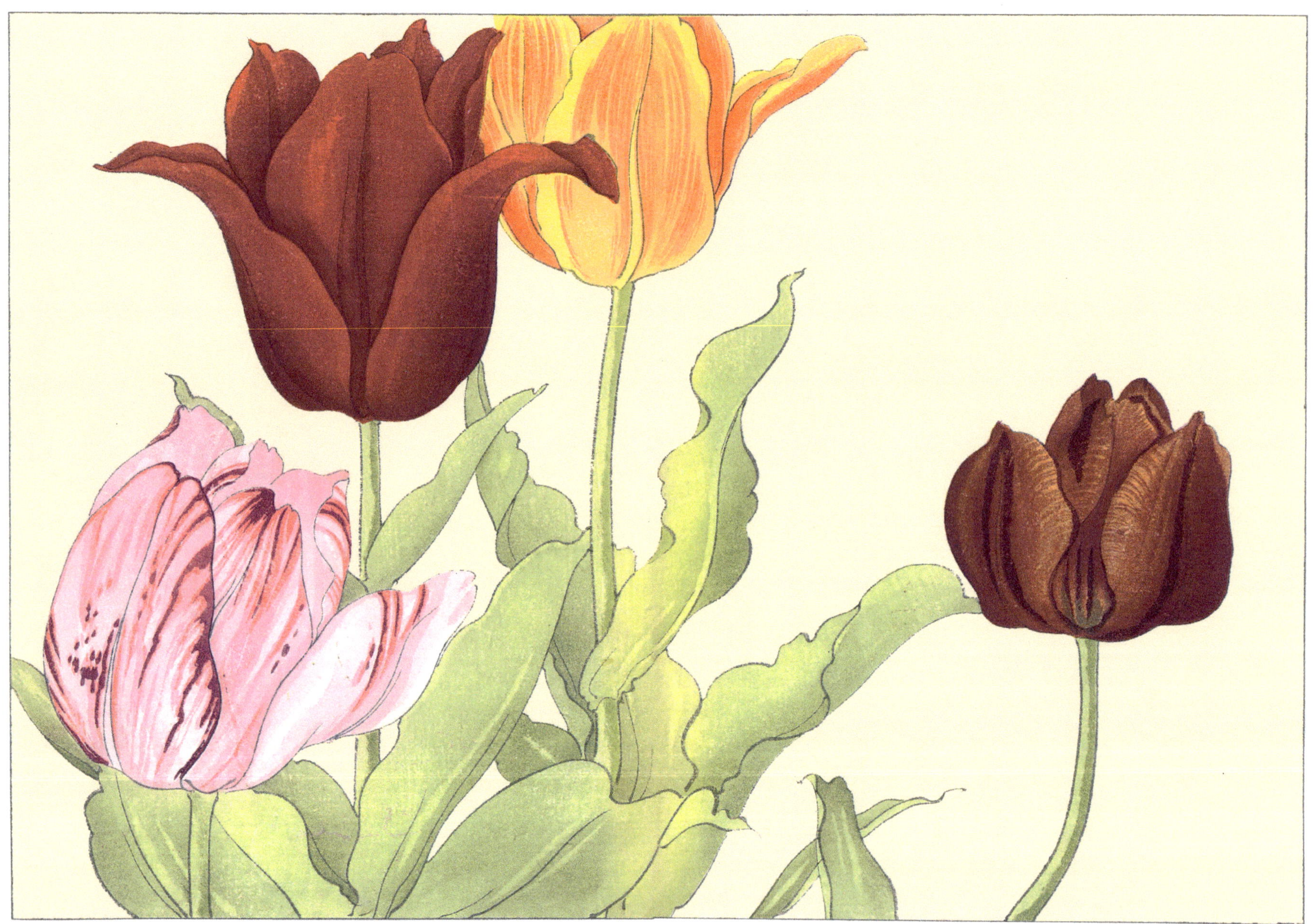

Tulip

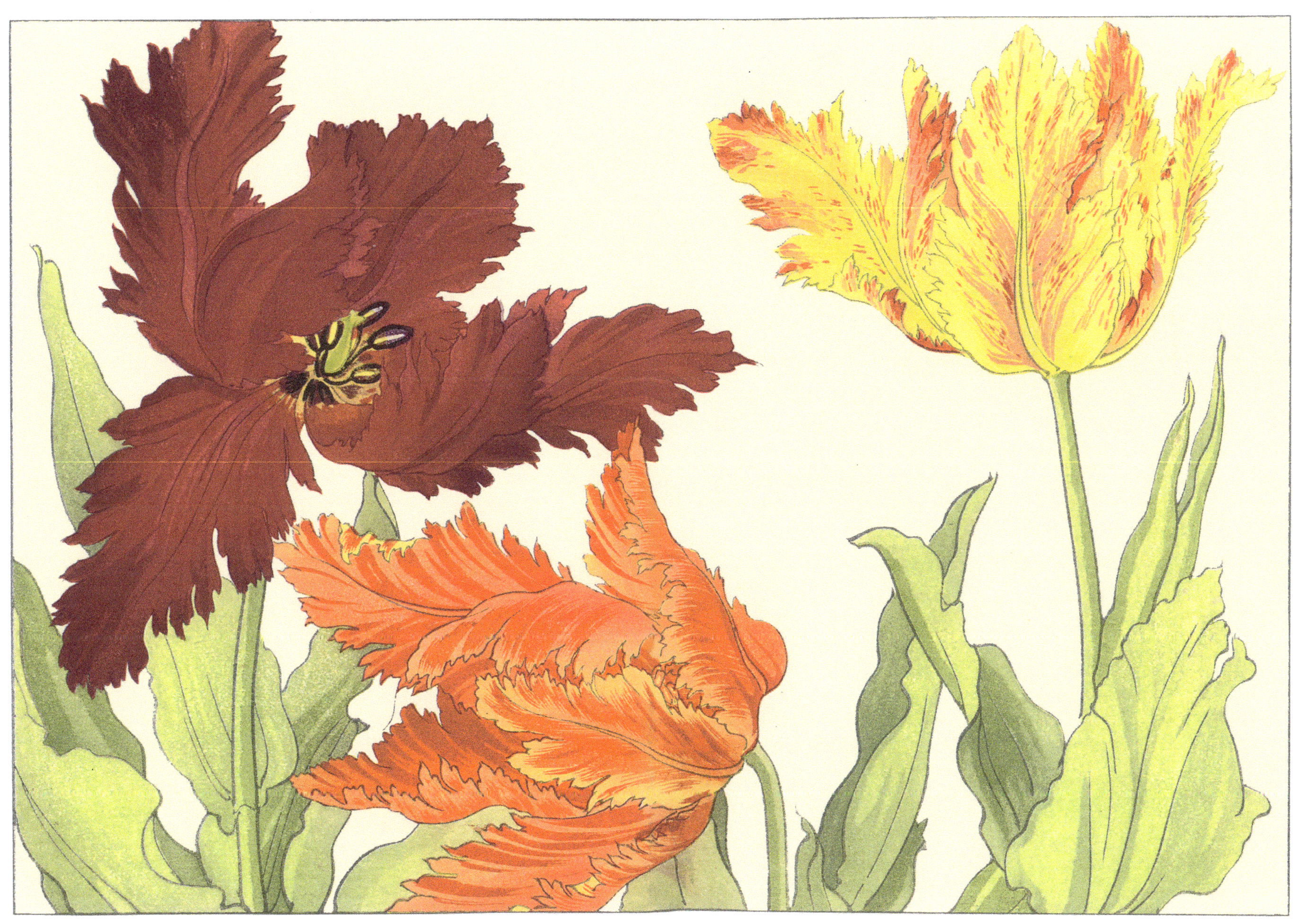

Tulip

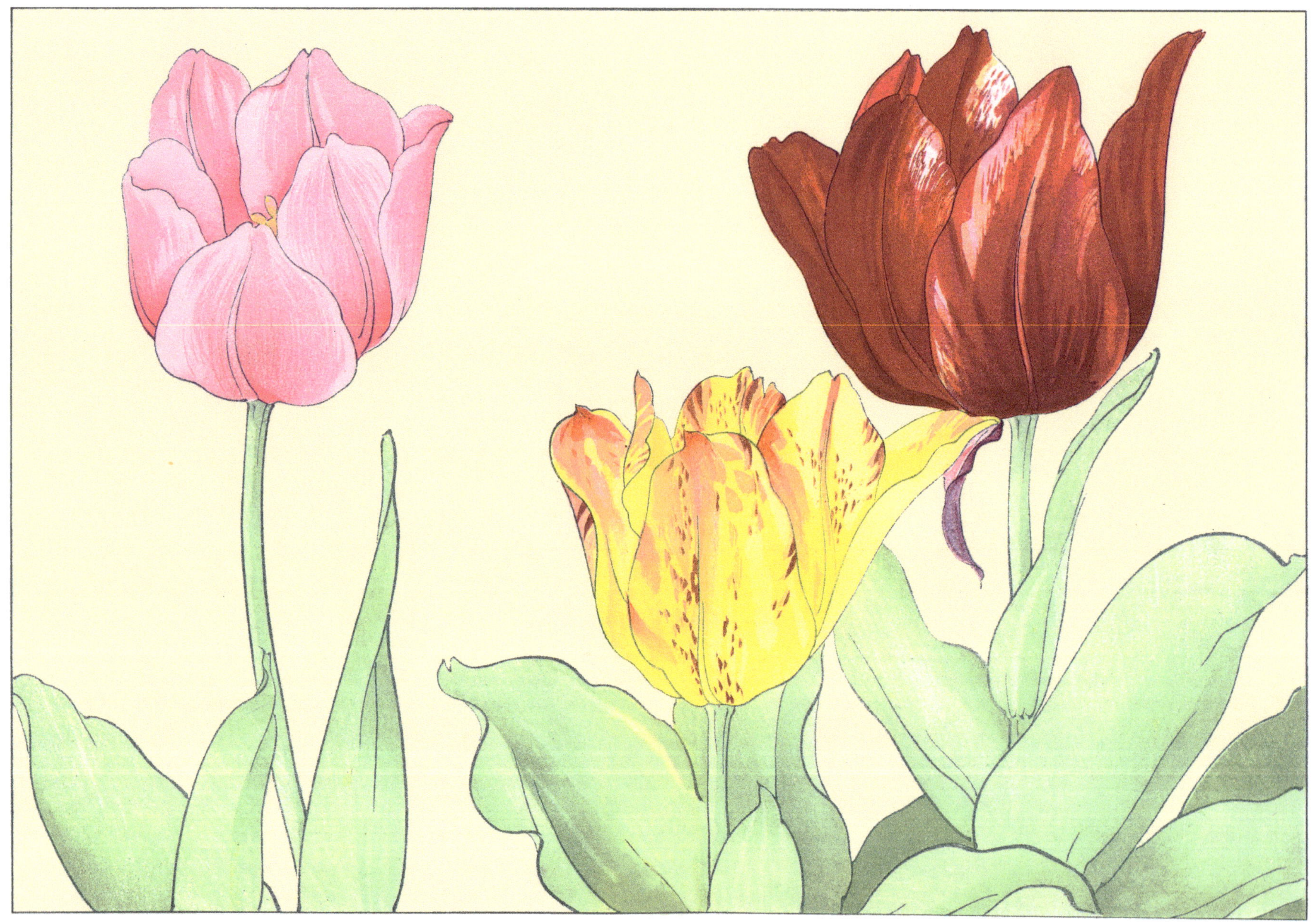

Tulip

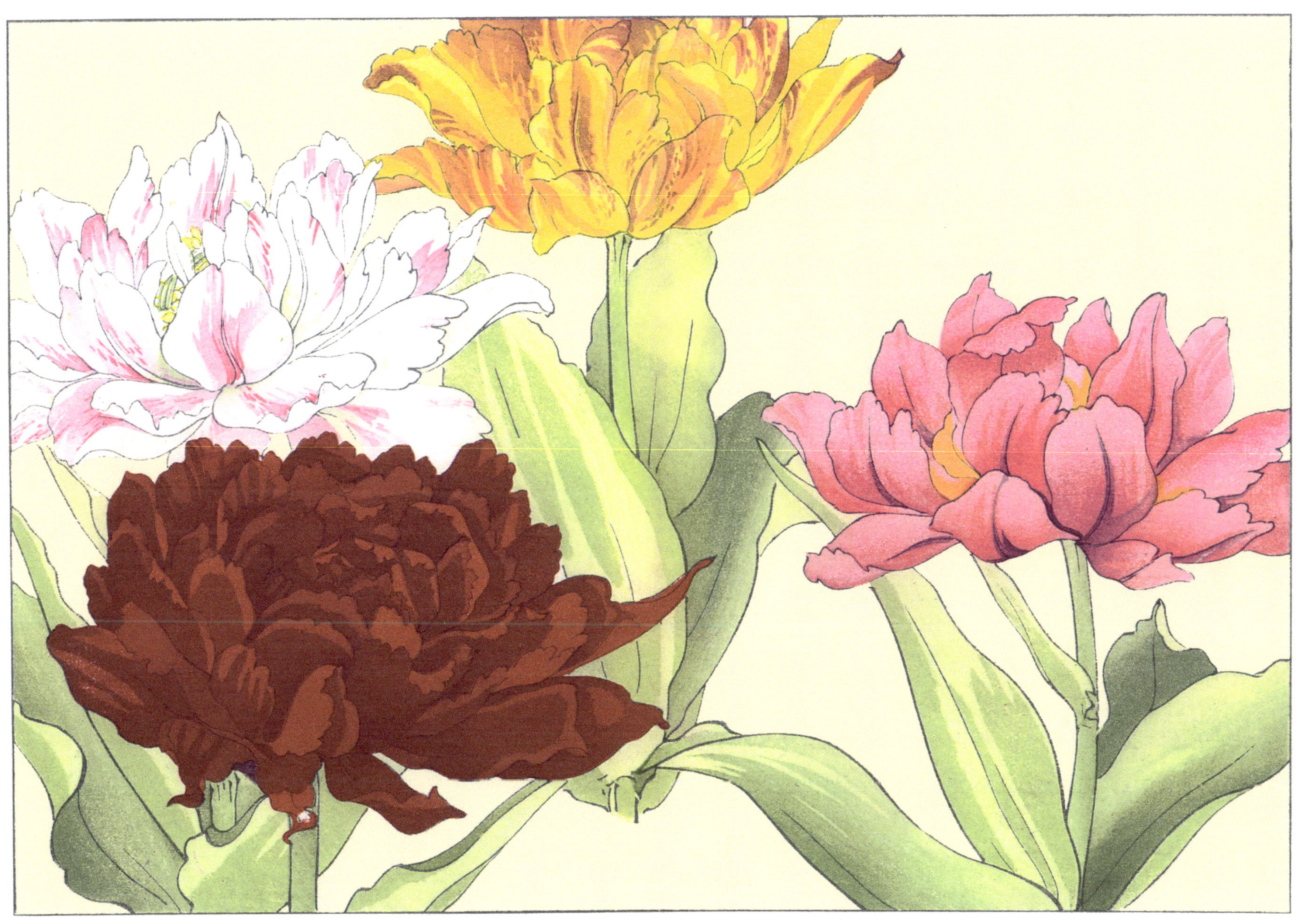

Tulip

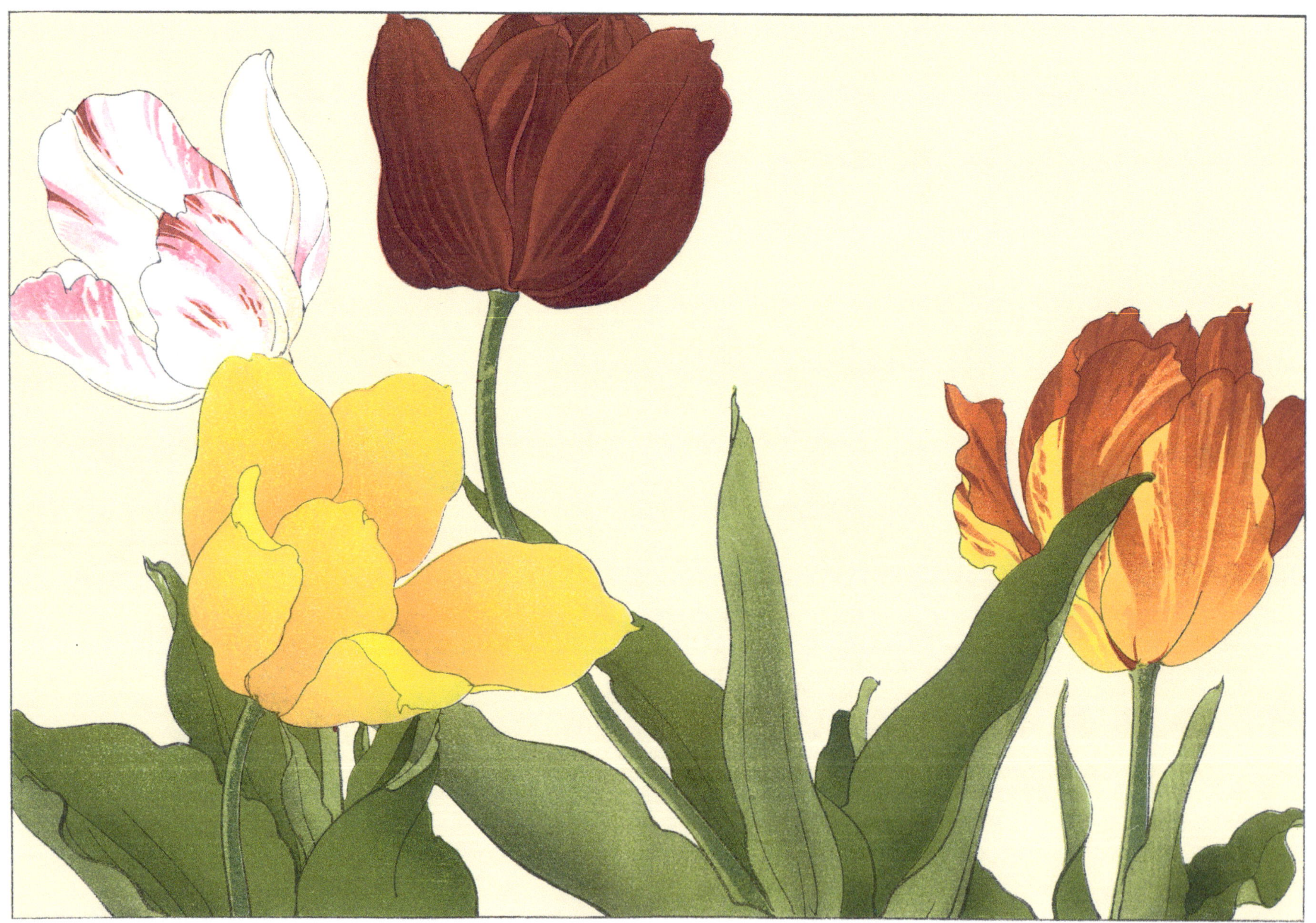

Tulip

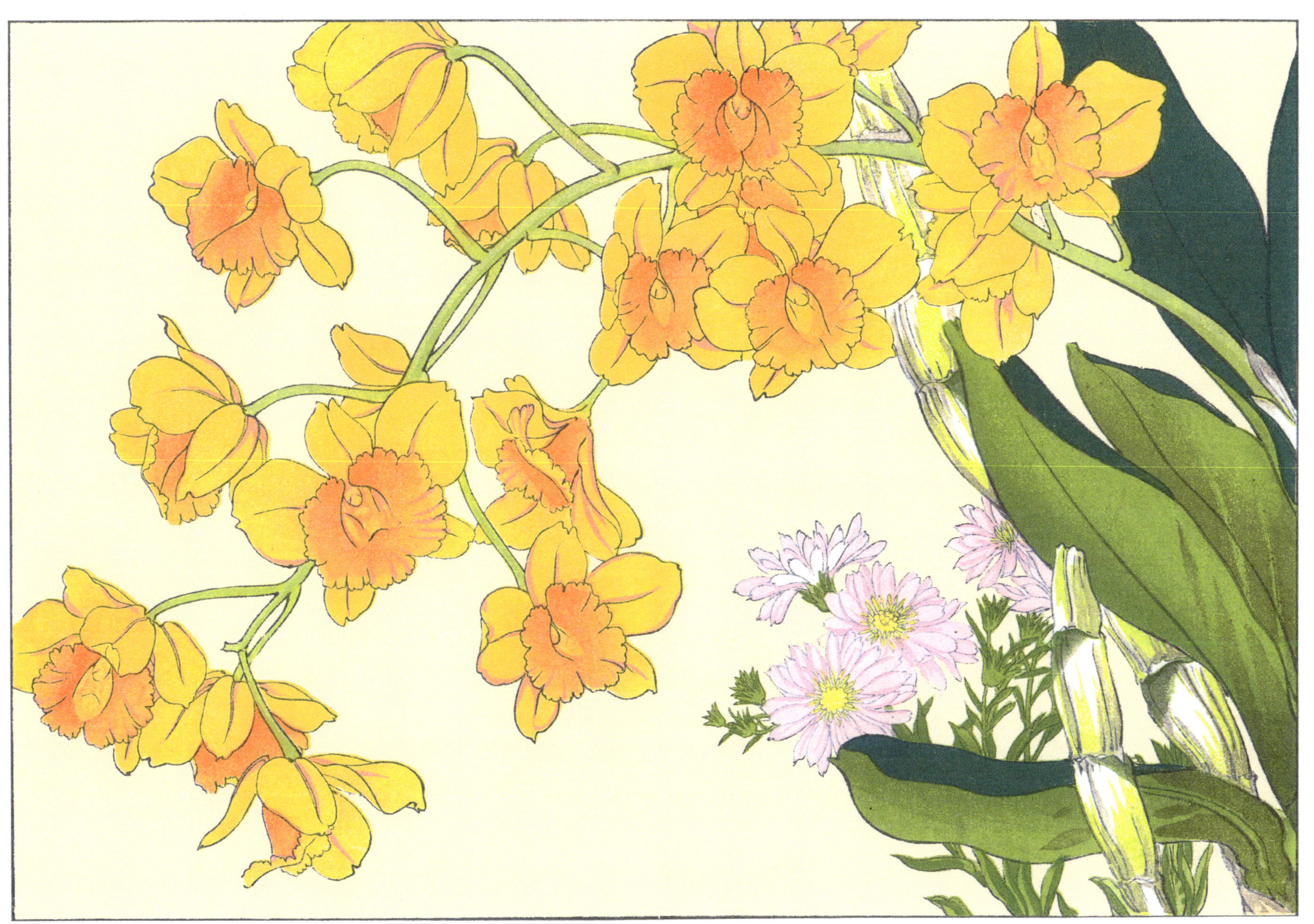

Aster and Dendrobium

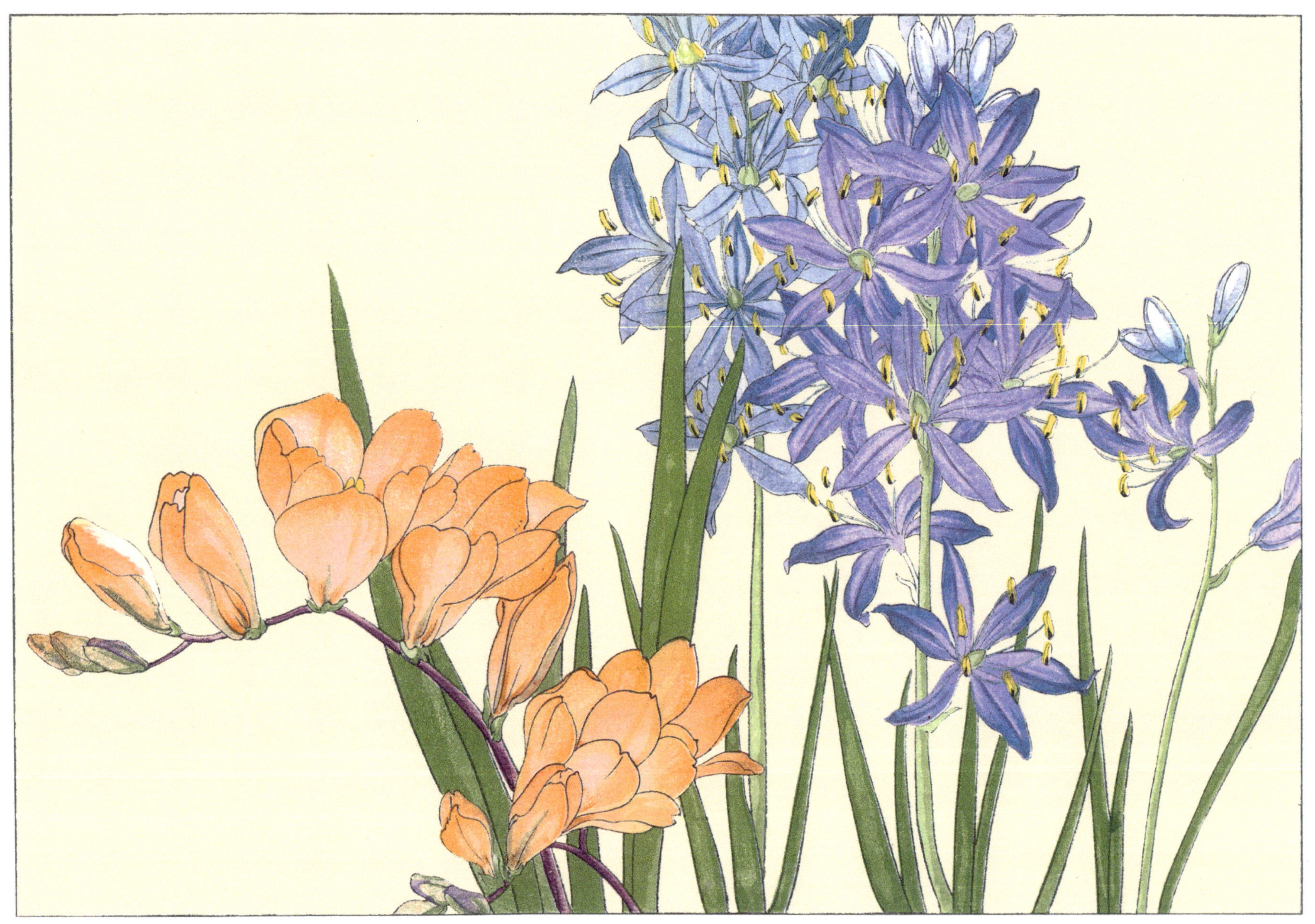

Agapanthus and Freesia

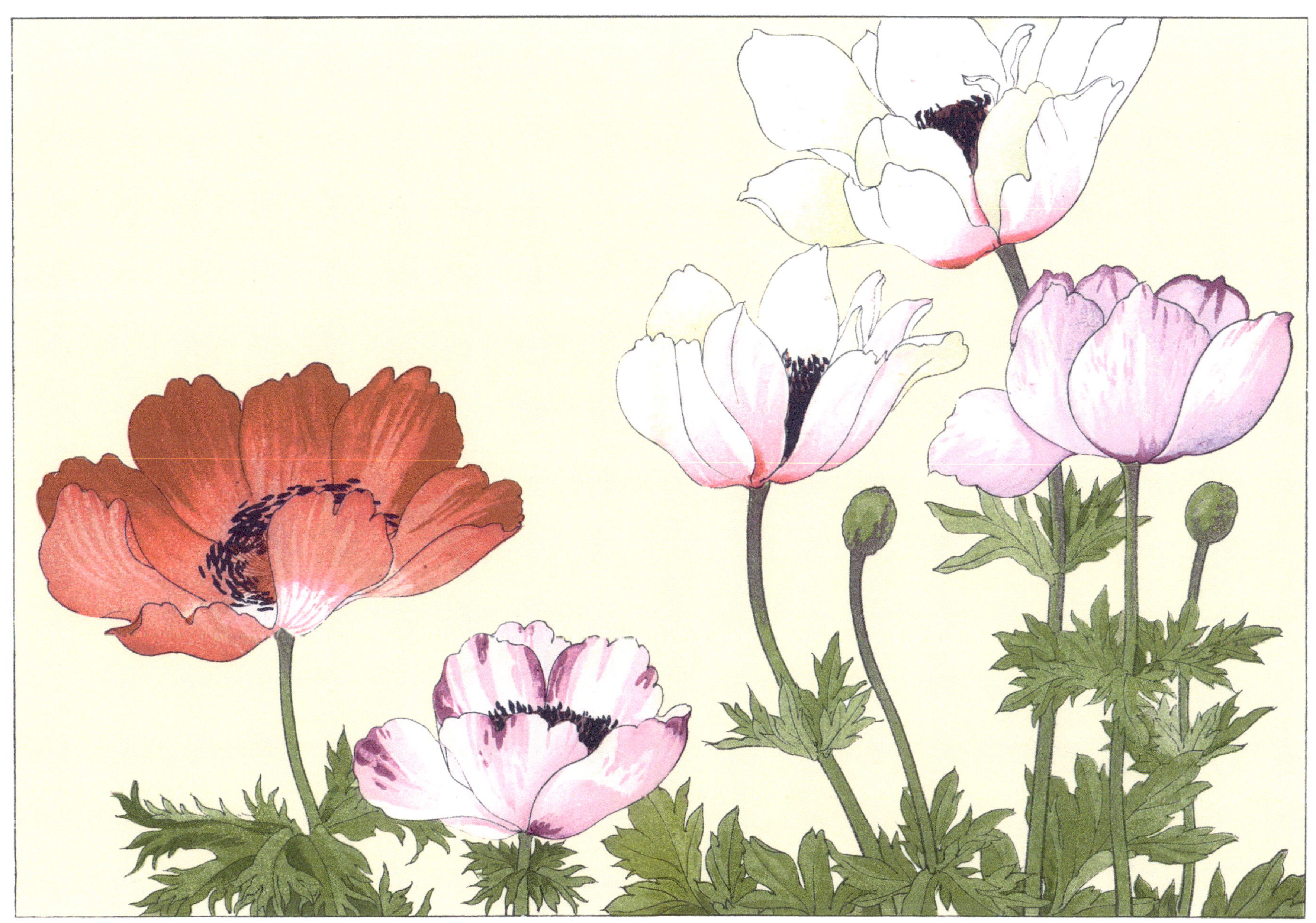

Anemone

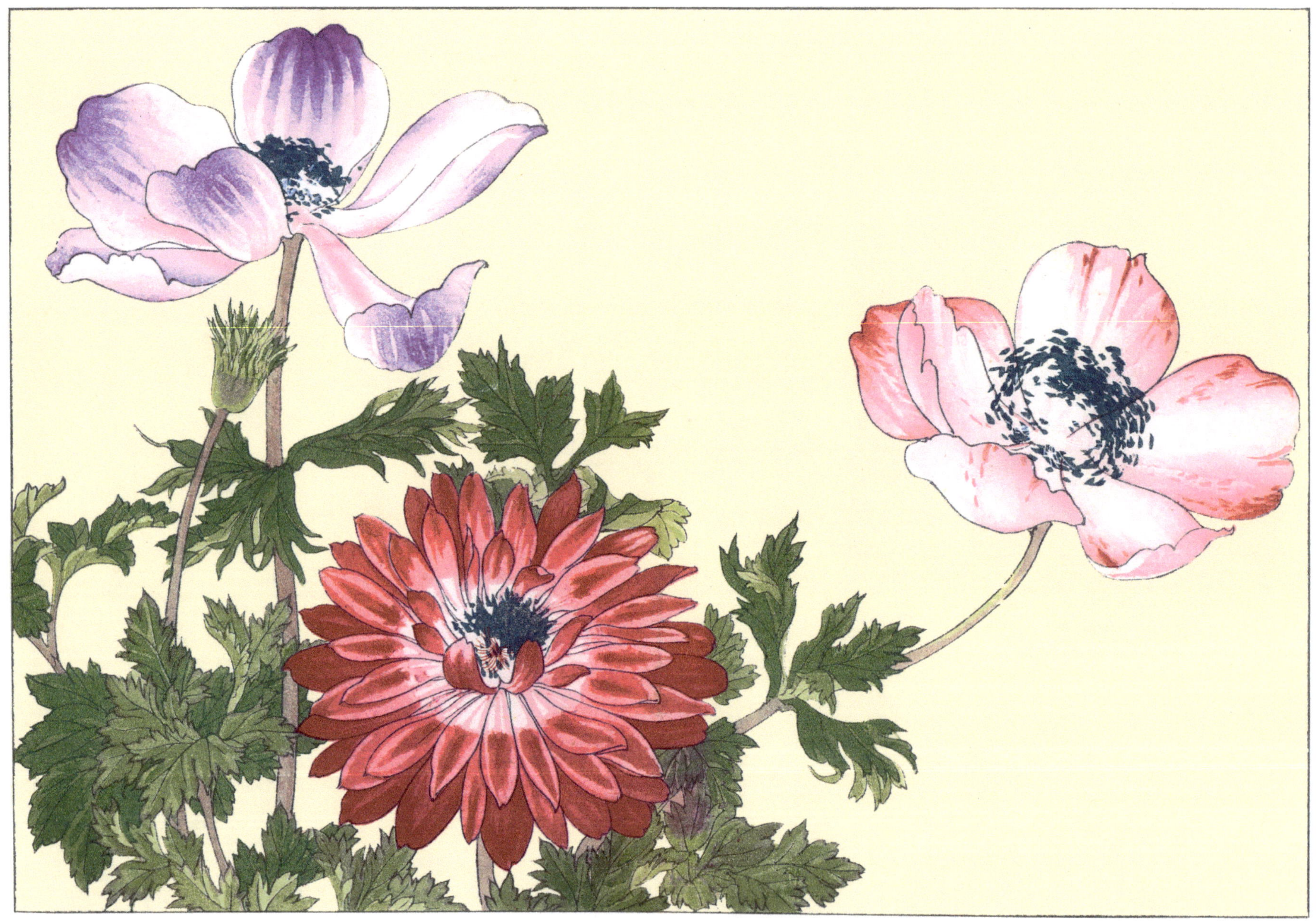

Anemone

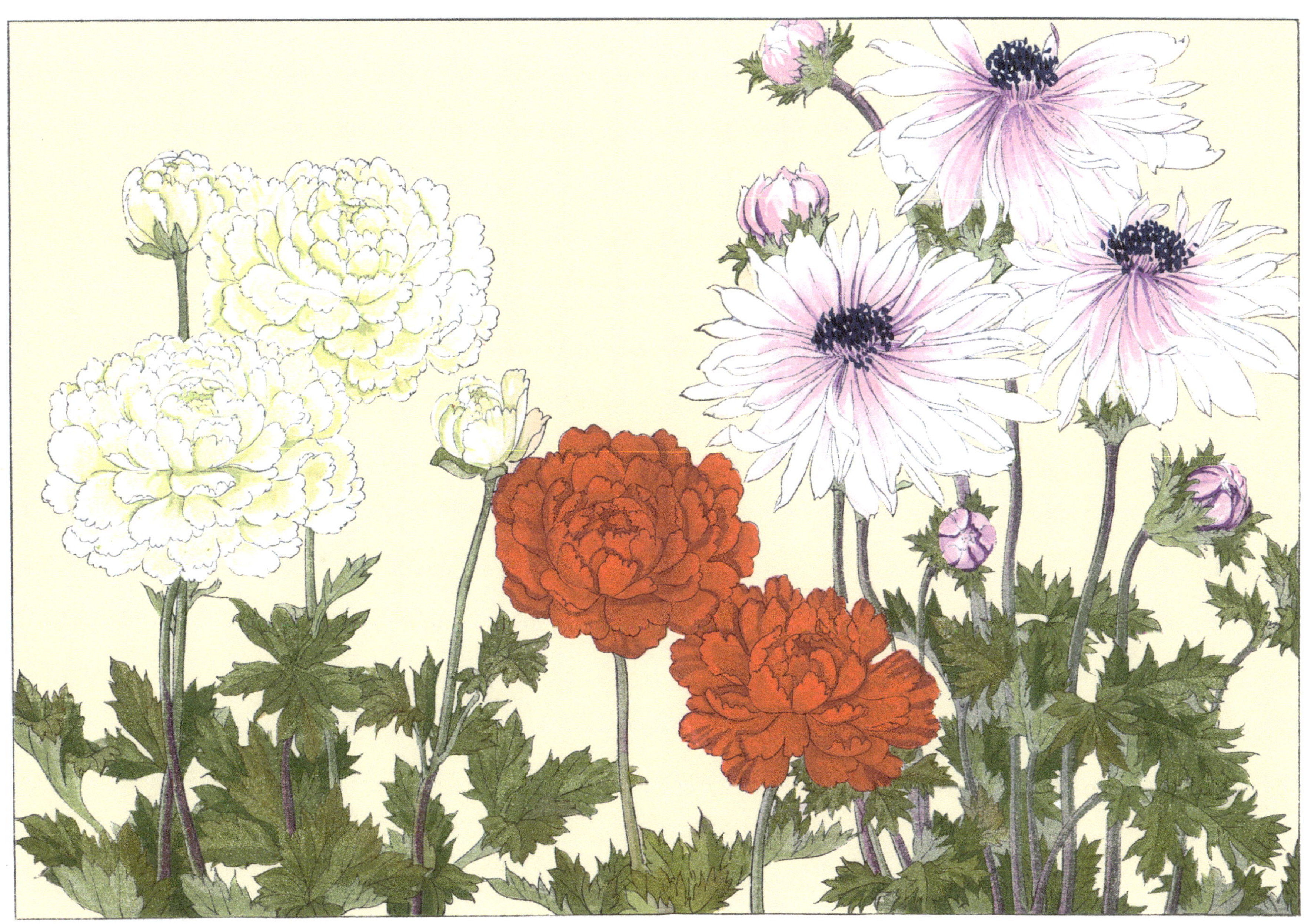

Anemone

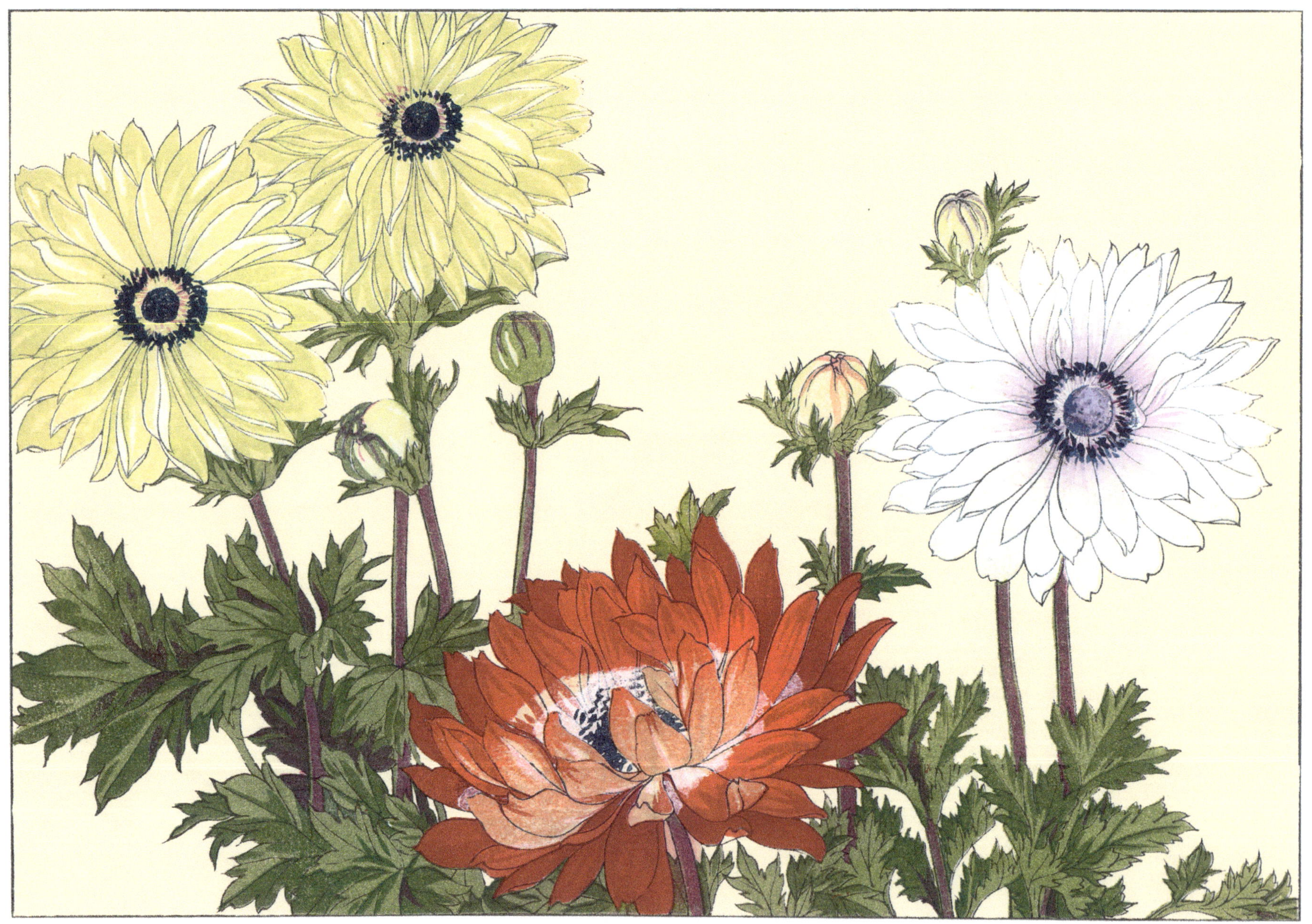

Anemone

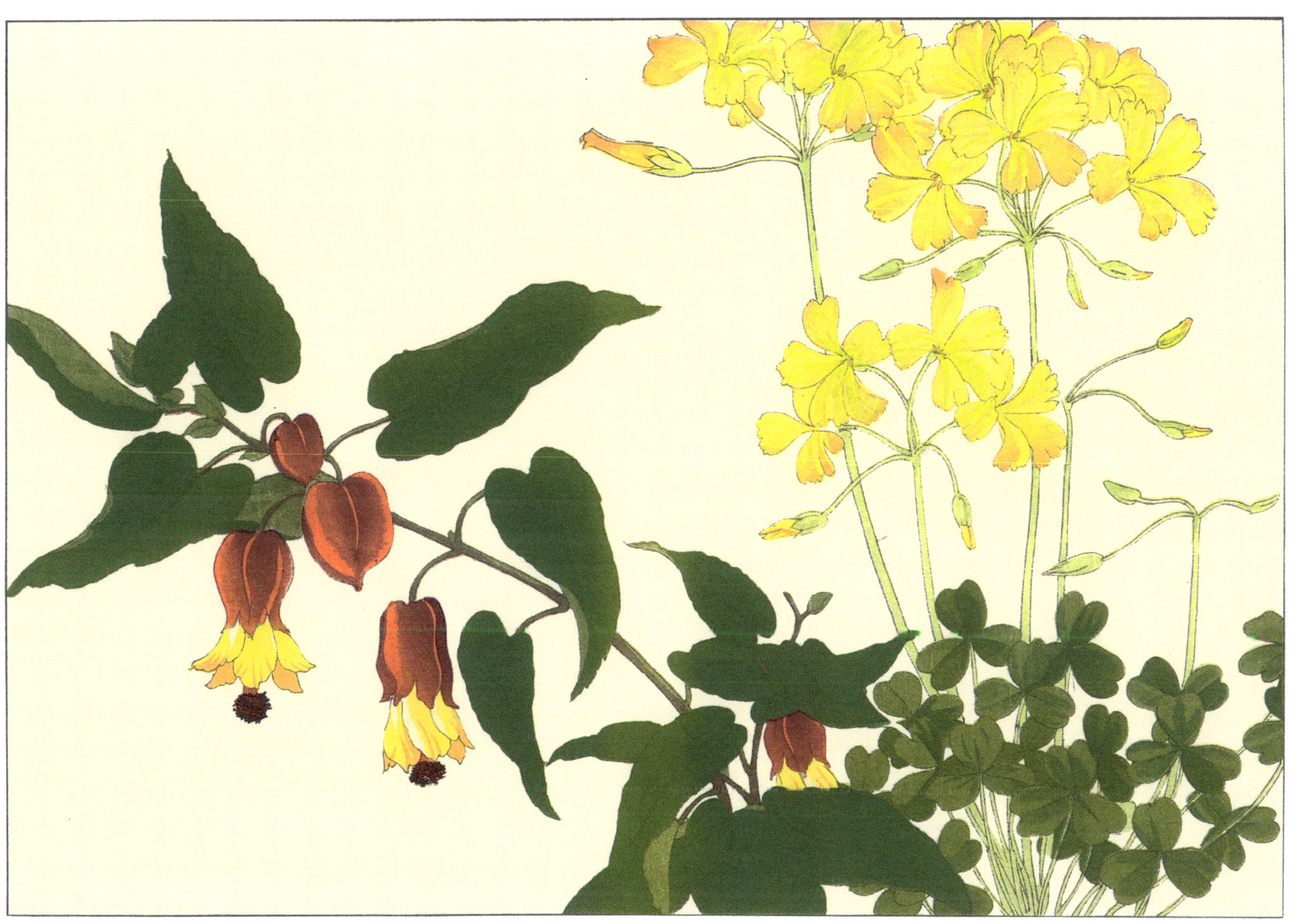

Oxalis and Abutilon

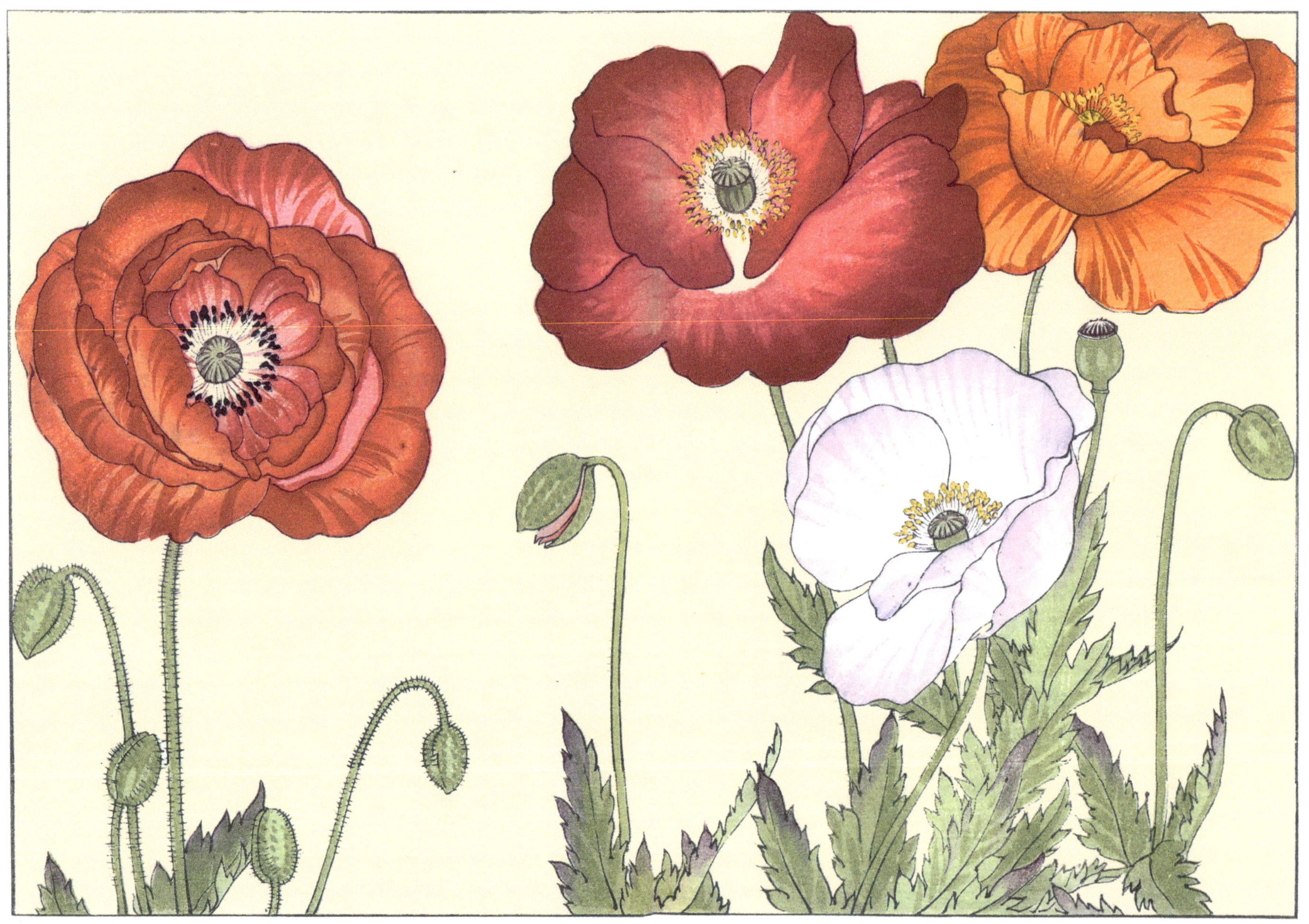

Poppy

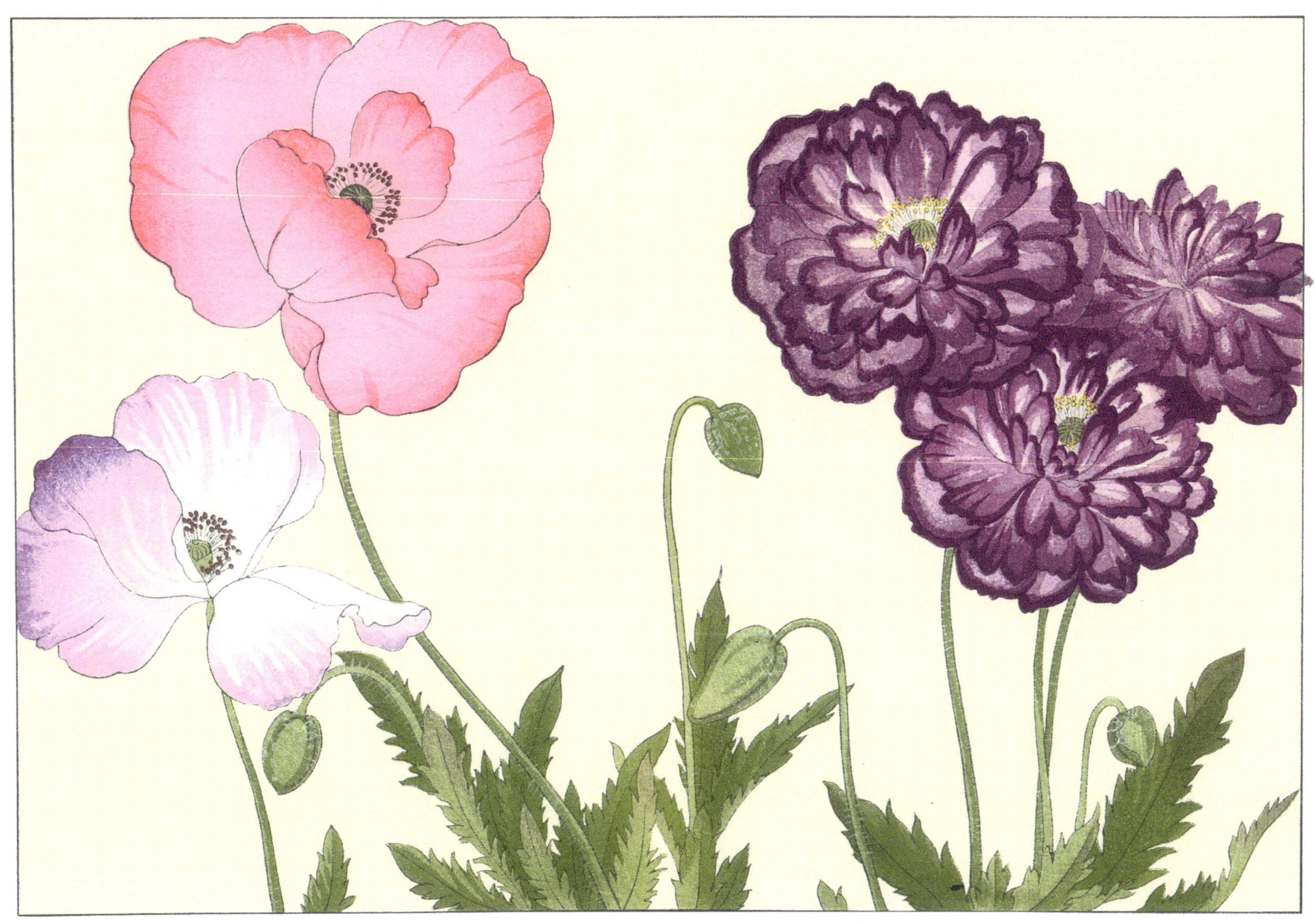

Poppy

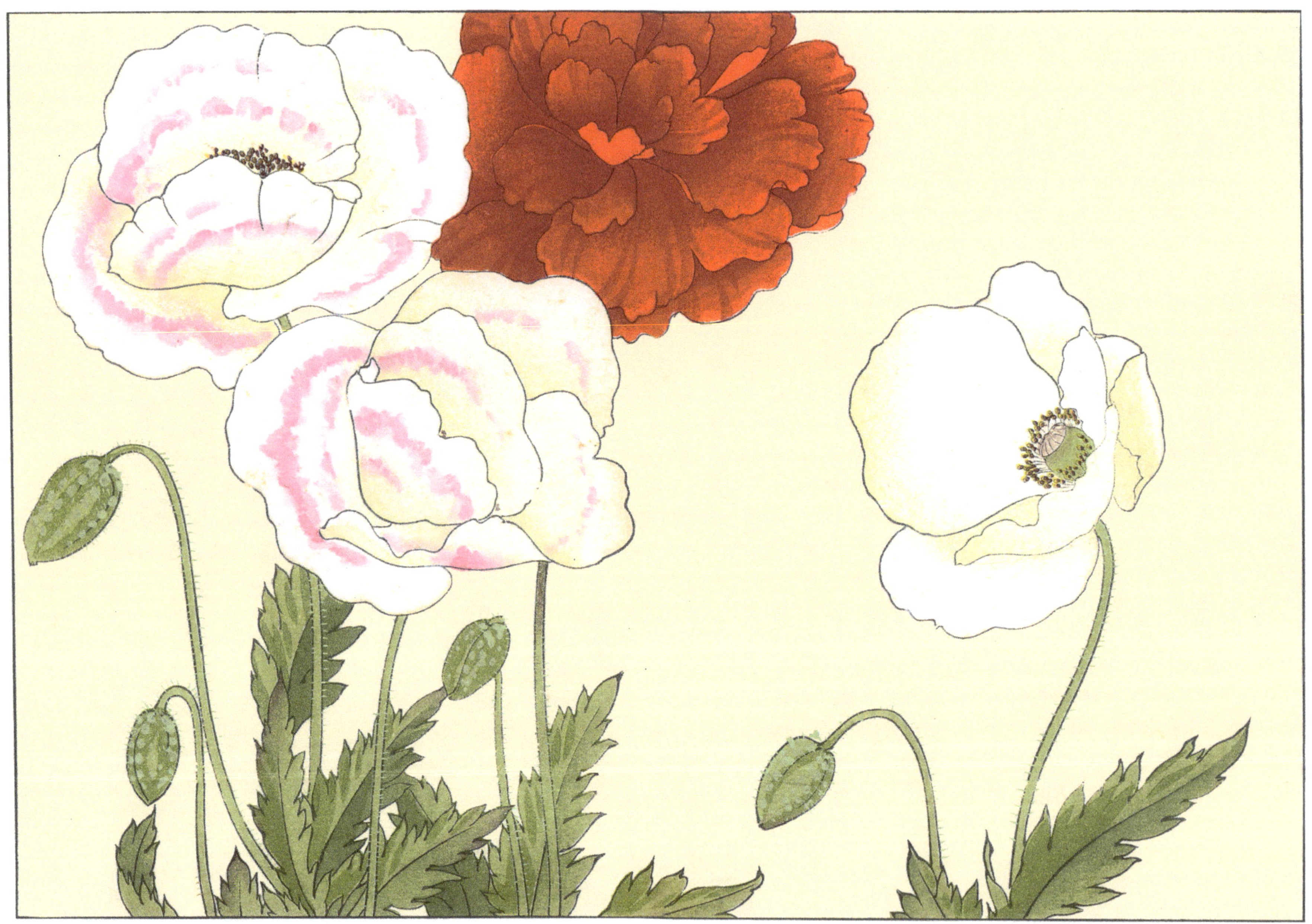

Poppy

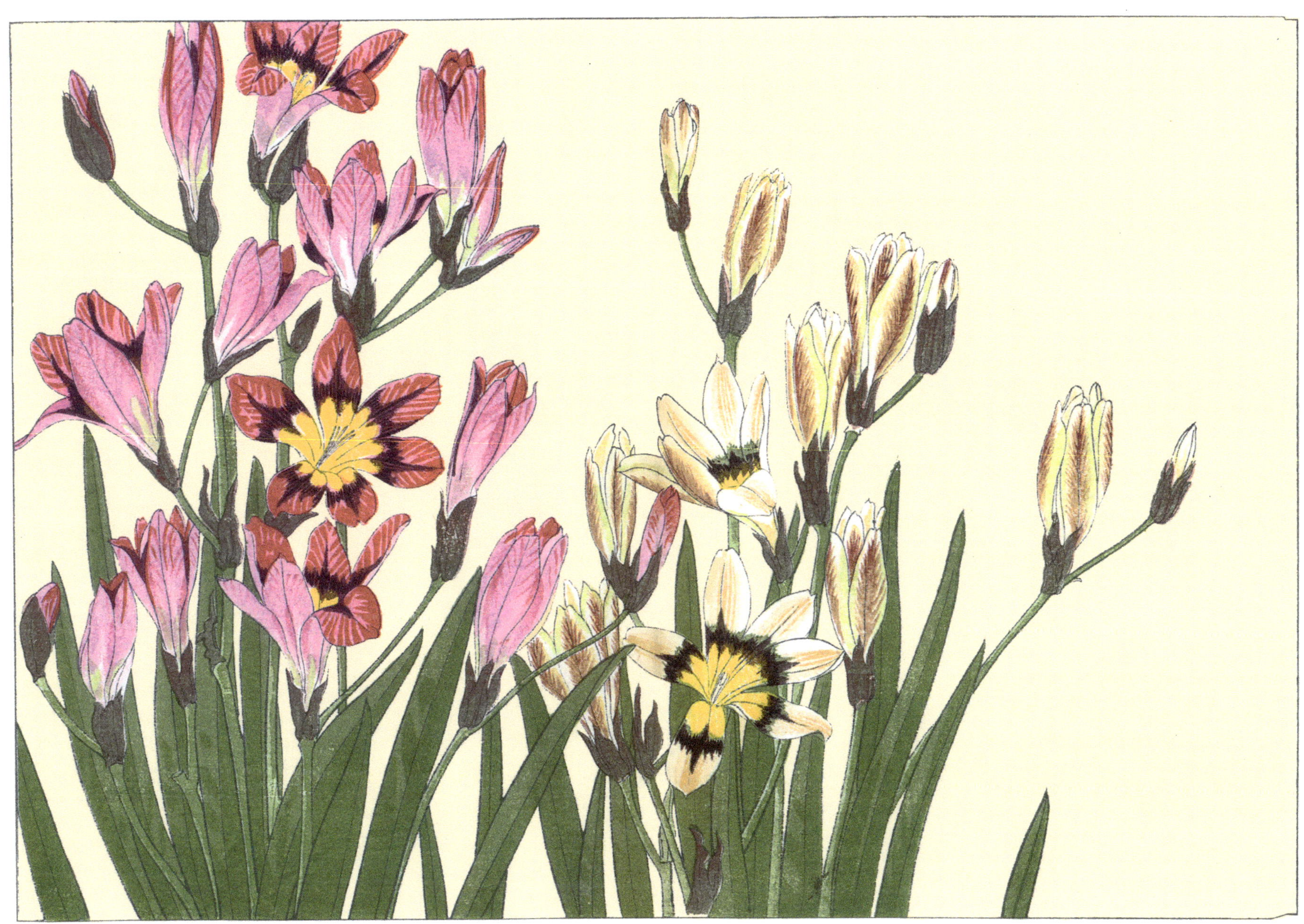

Ixia

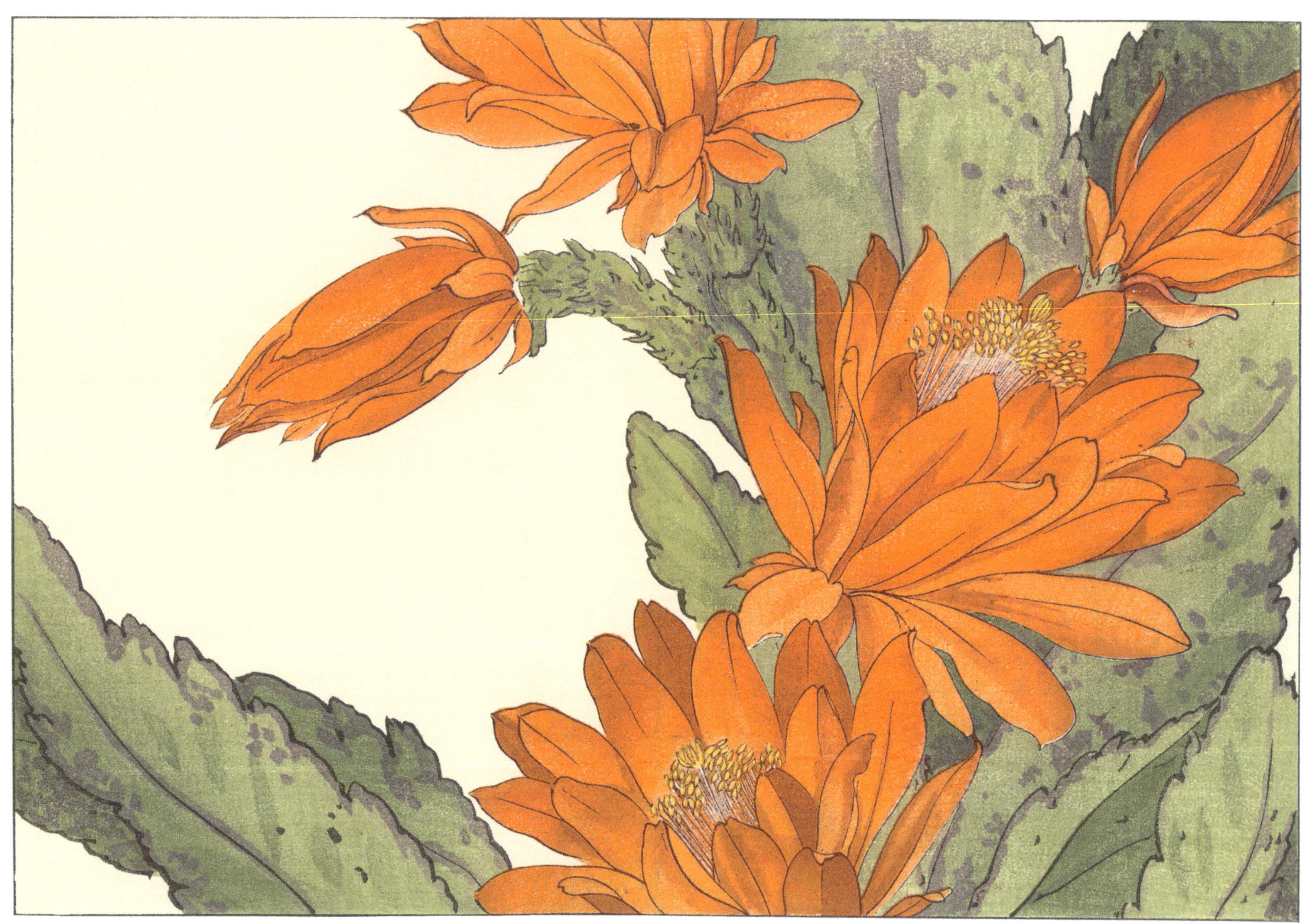

Phyllocactus

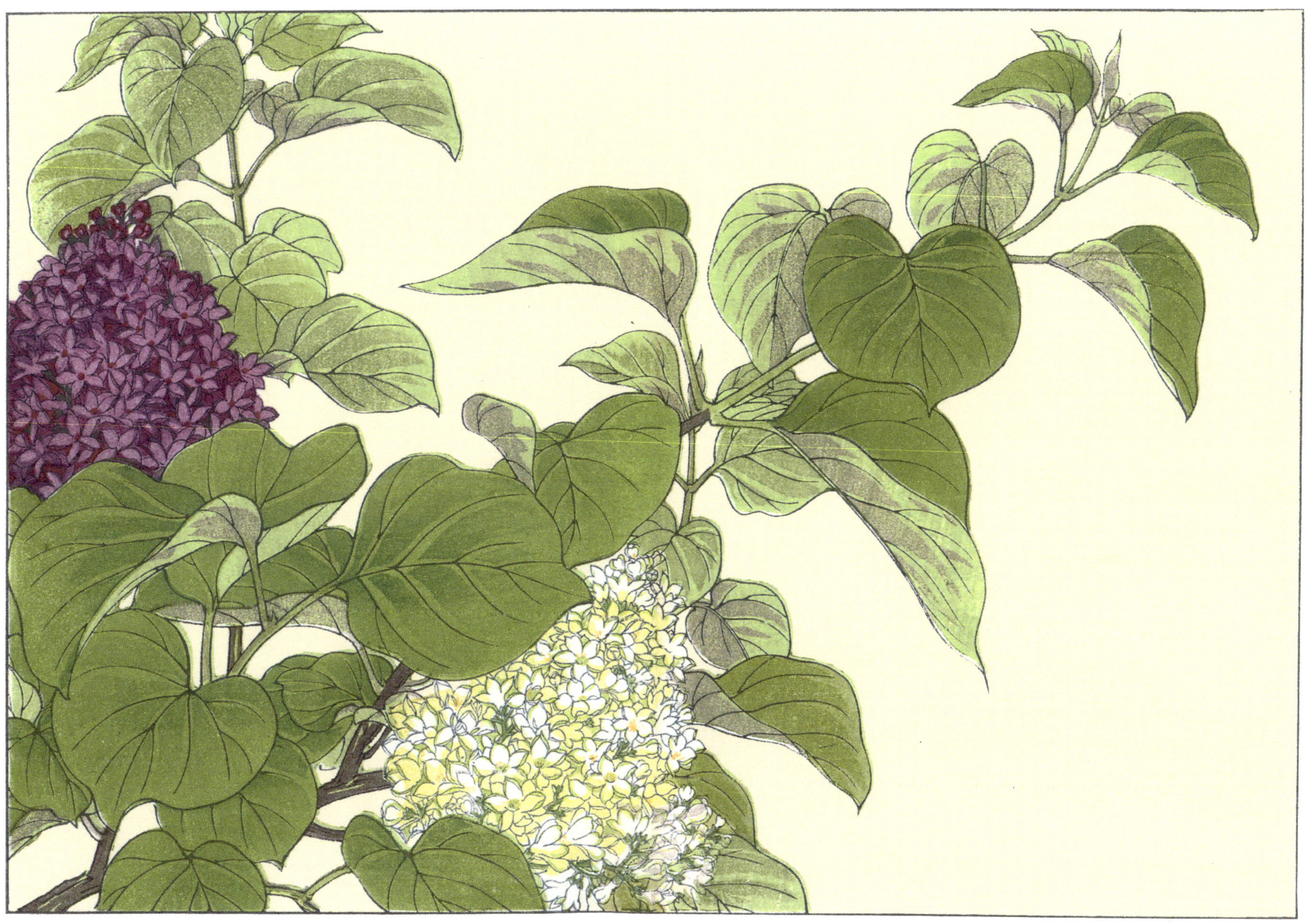

Lilac

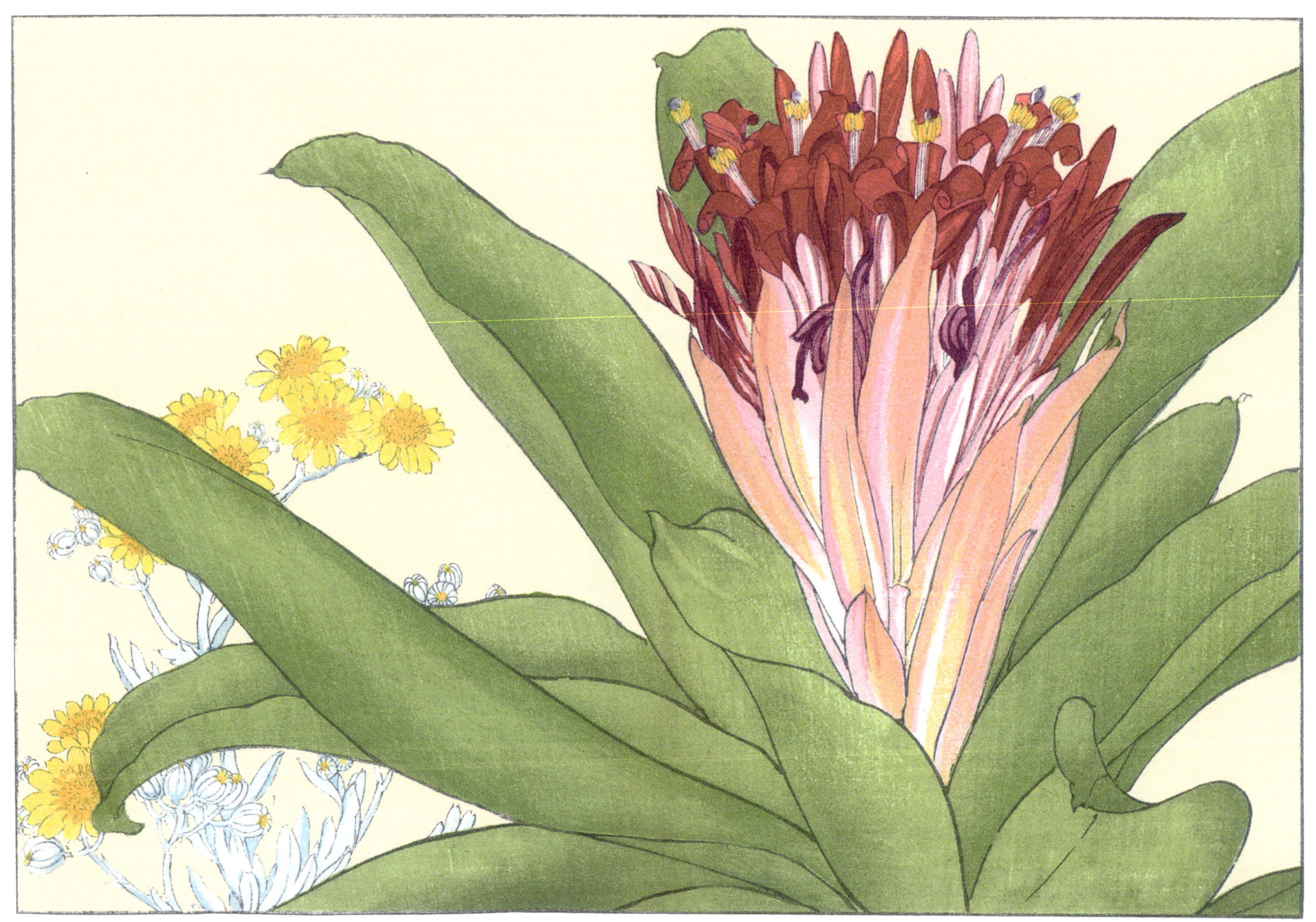

Ananas (or Pineapple) and Cineraria

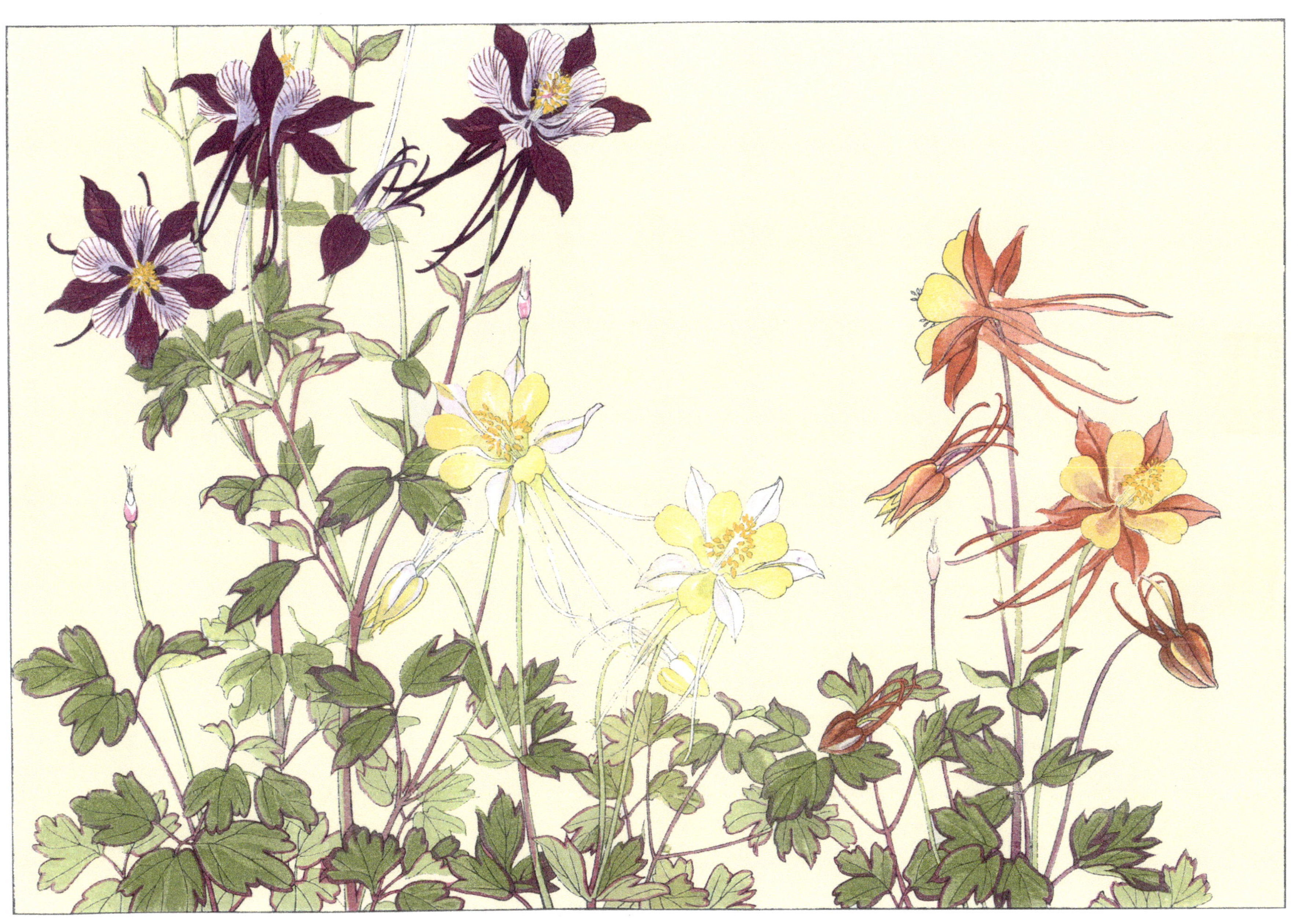

Aquilegia (or Columbine)

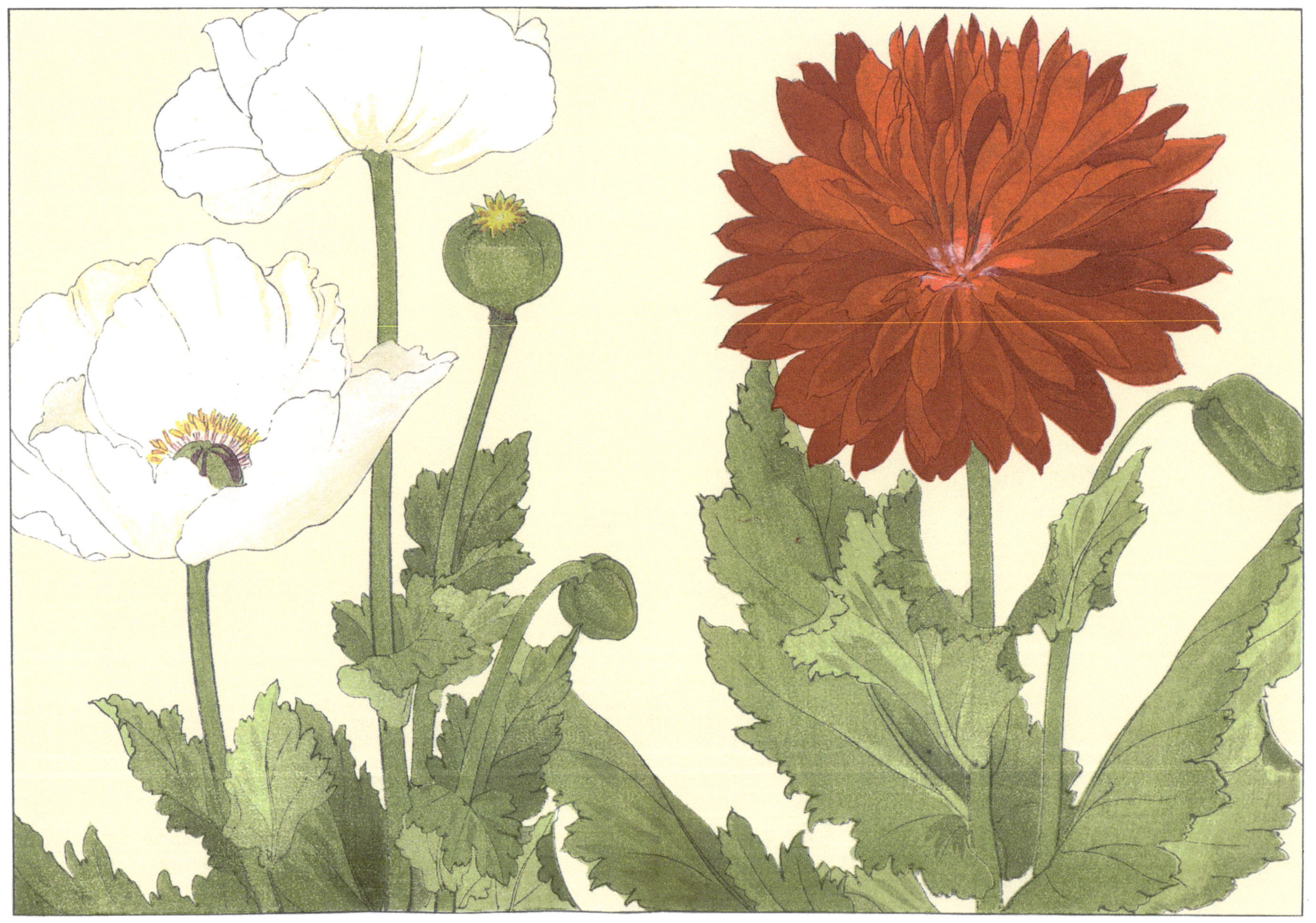

Poppy

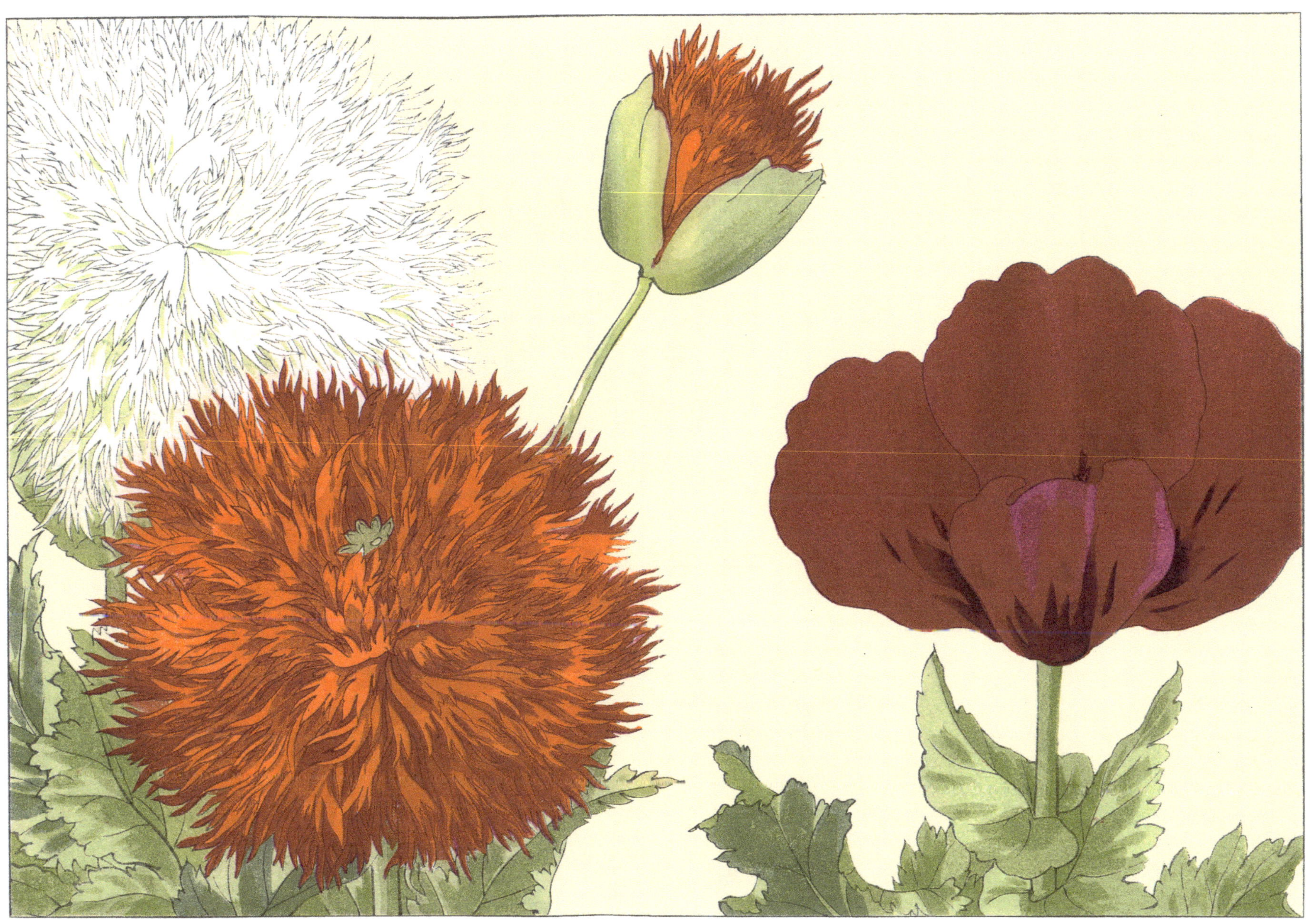

Poppy

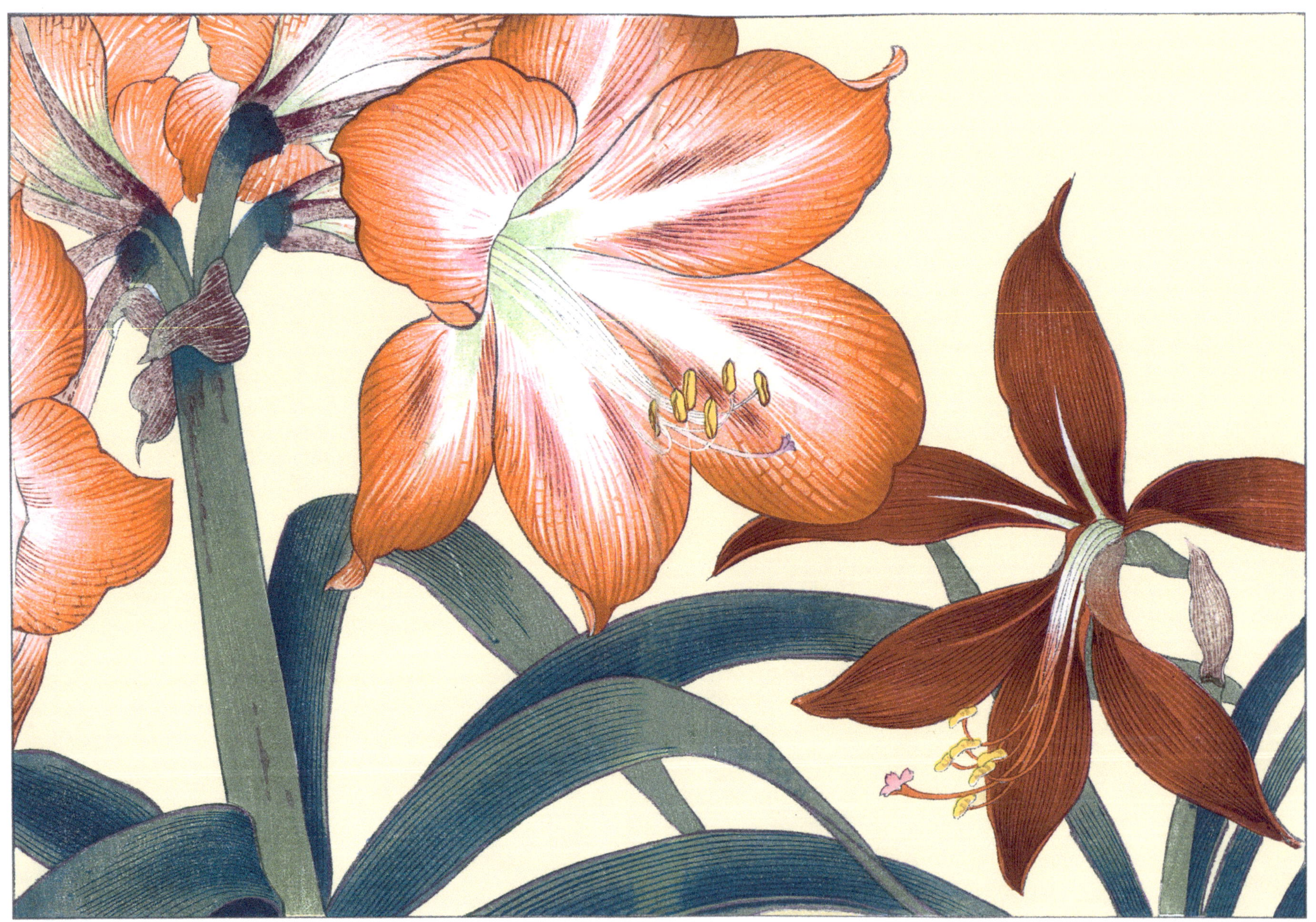

Amaryllis

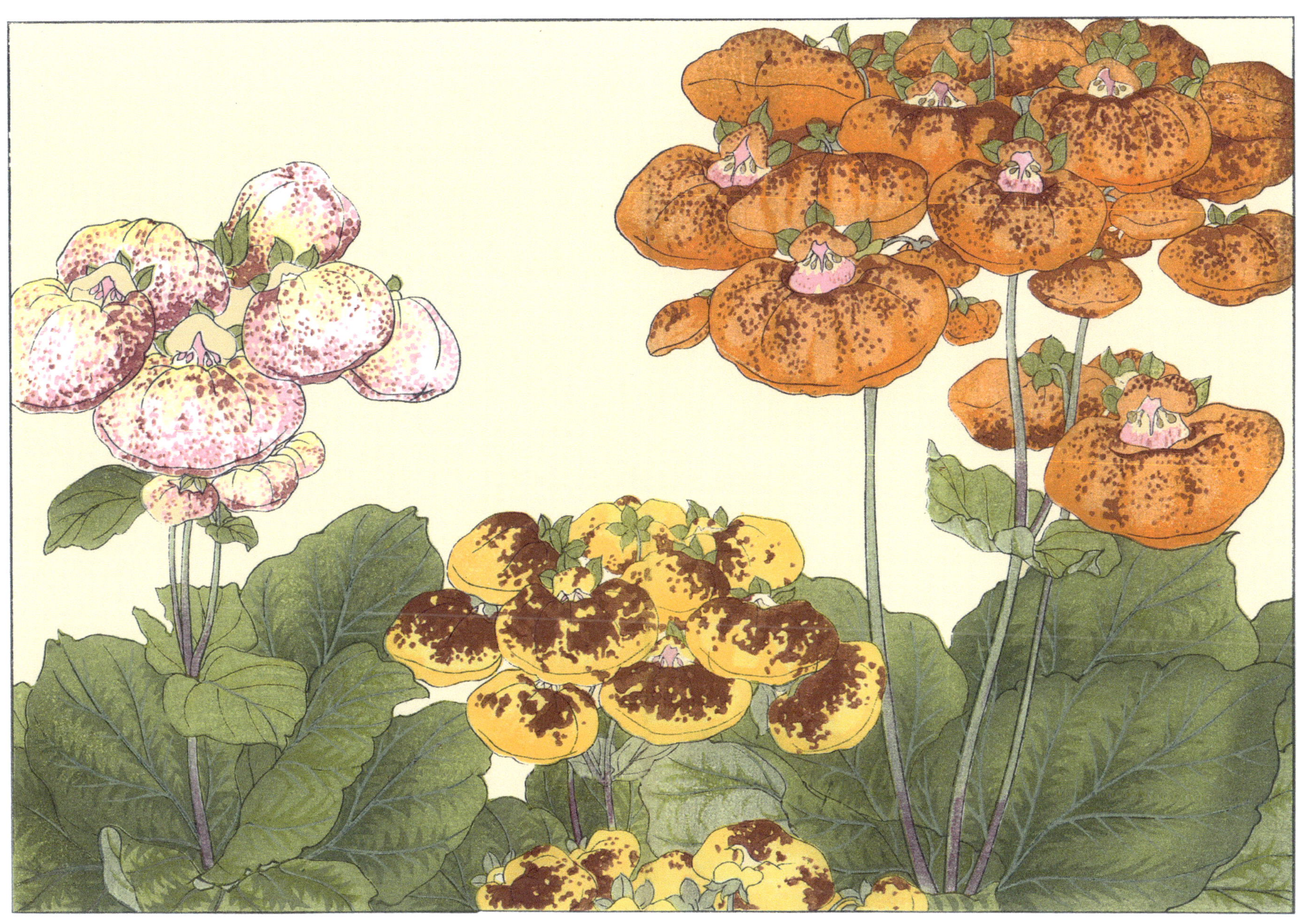

Calceolaria (or Slipperwort)

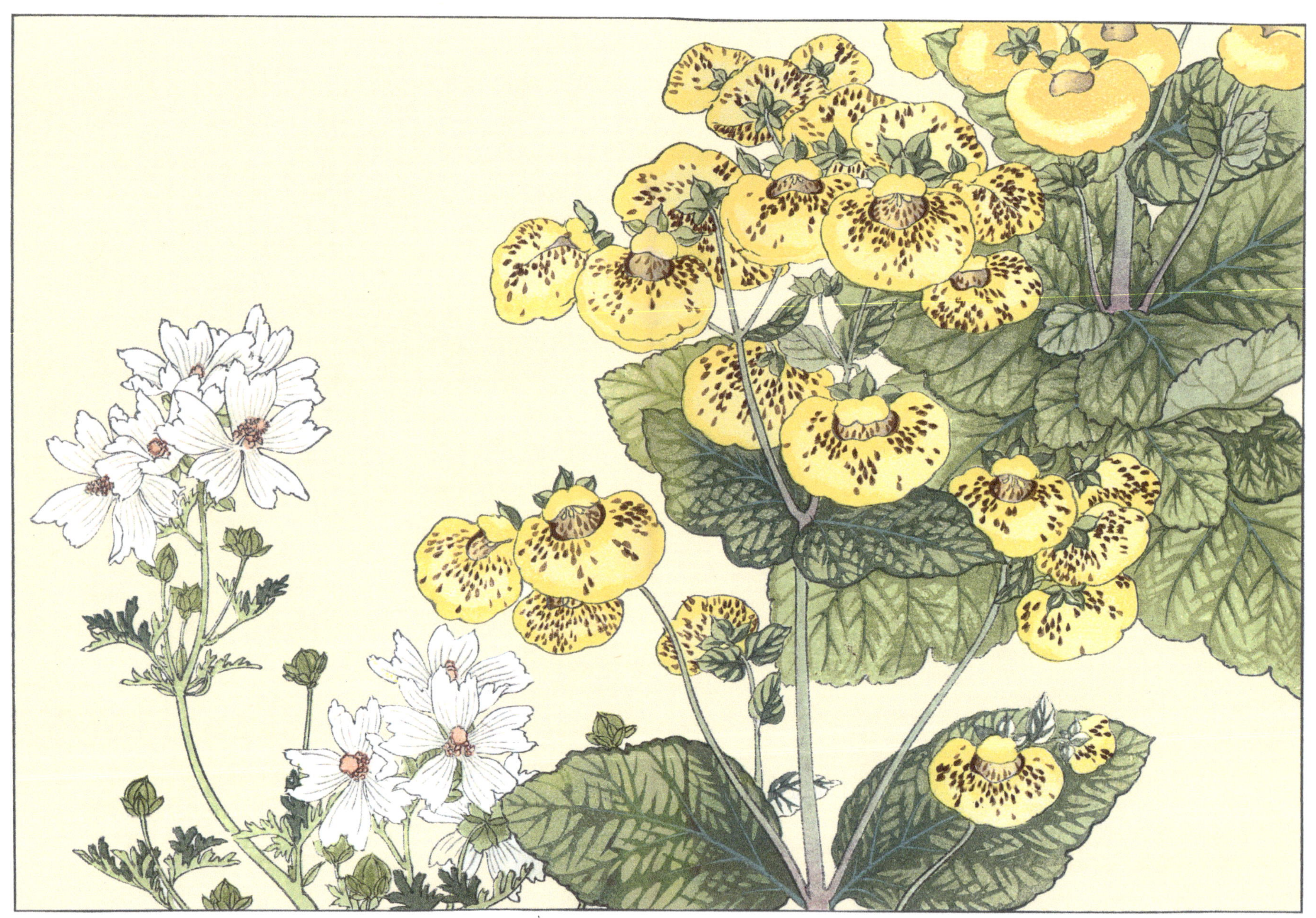

Calceolaria (or Slipperwort) and Lavatera

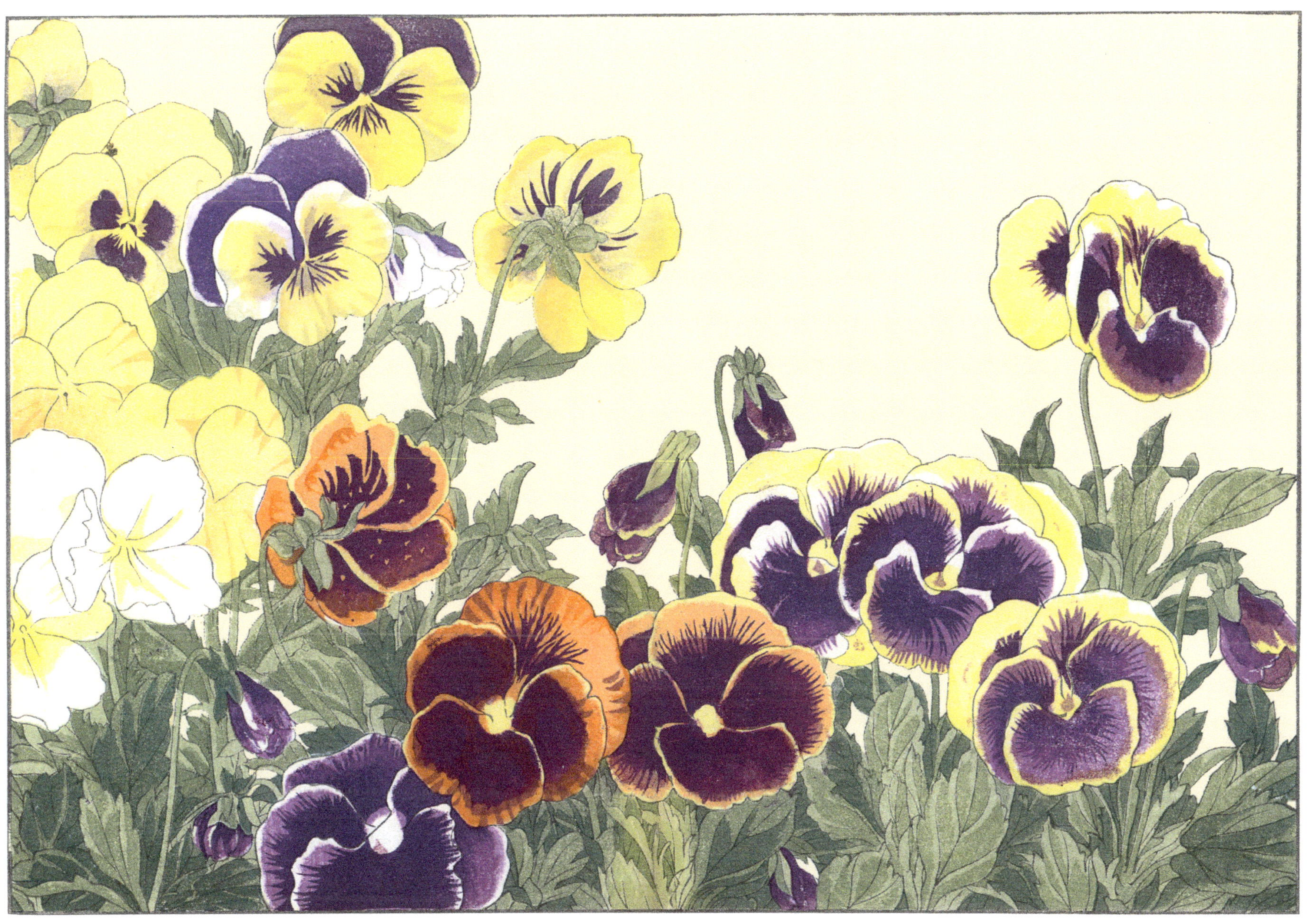

Pansy

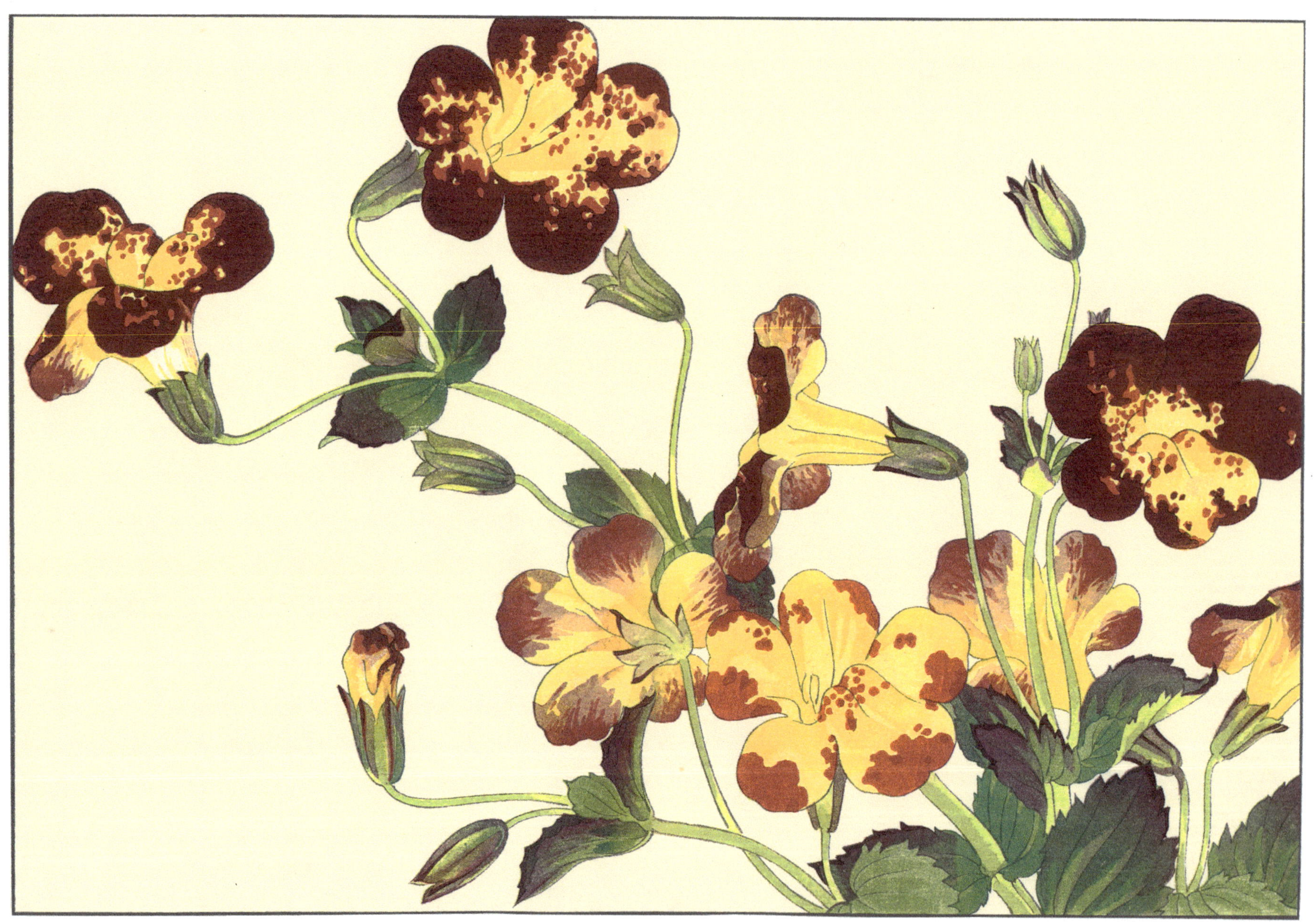

Tulip

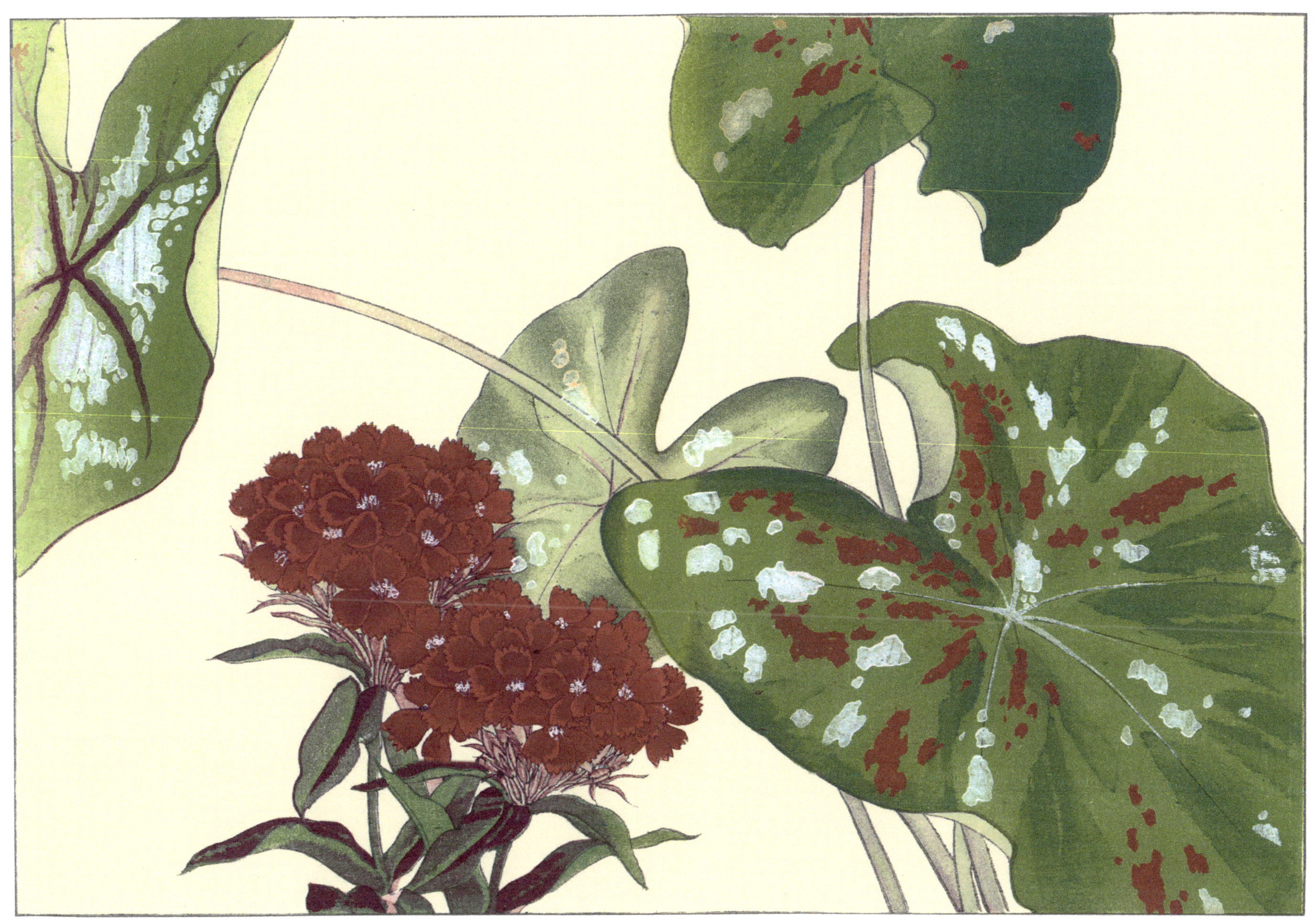

Caladium and Sweet William

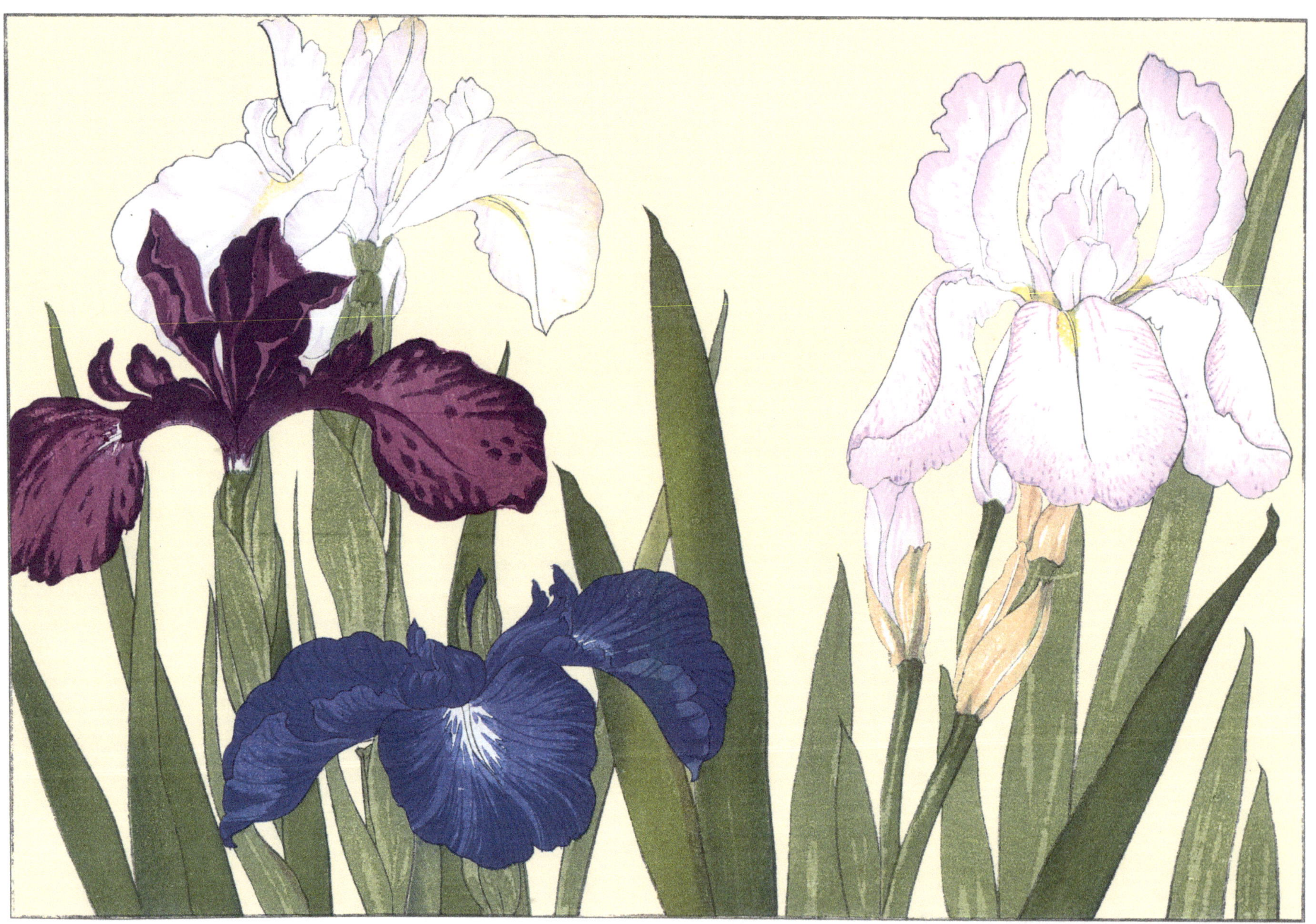

Iris

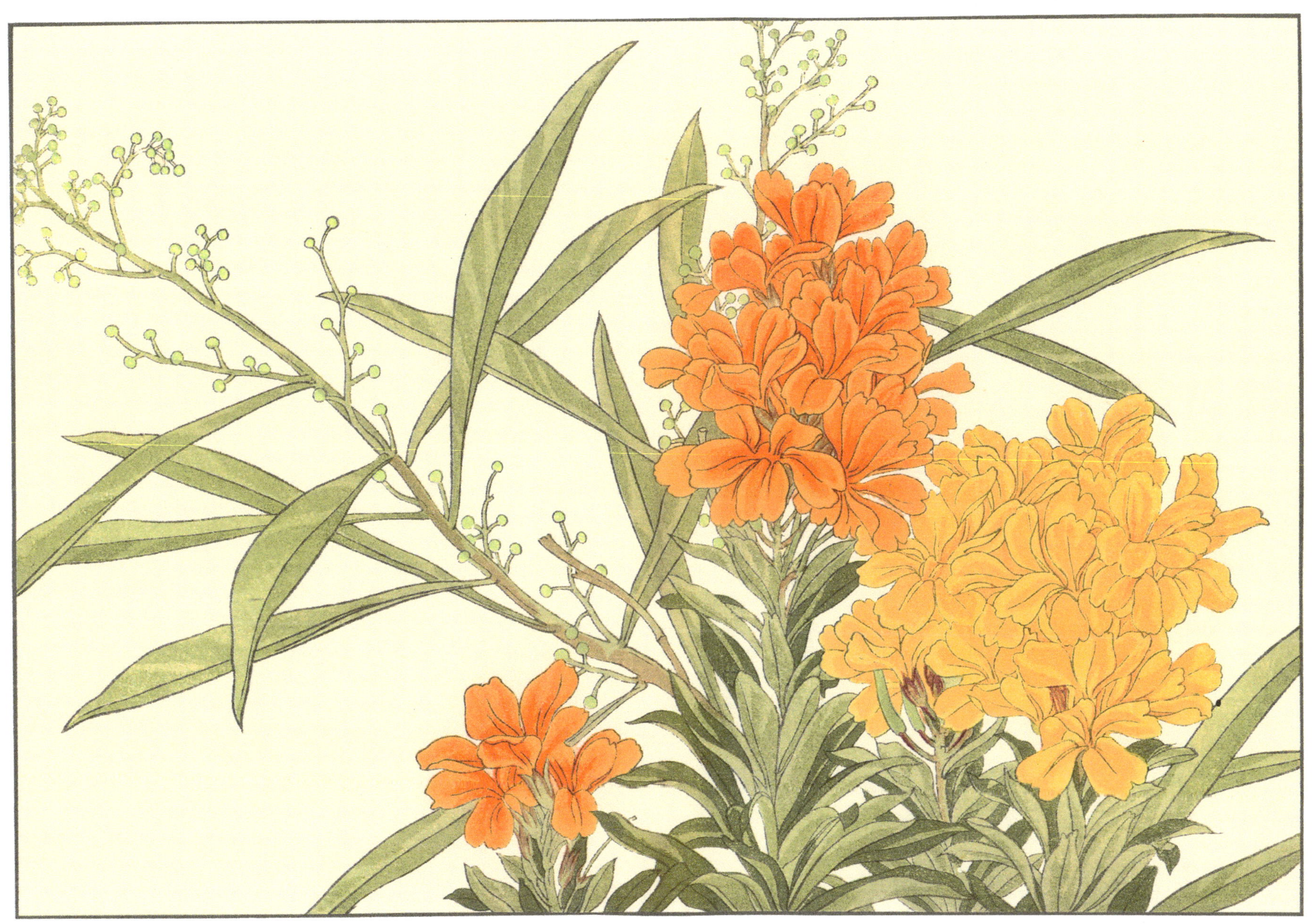

Wallflower

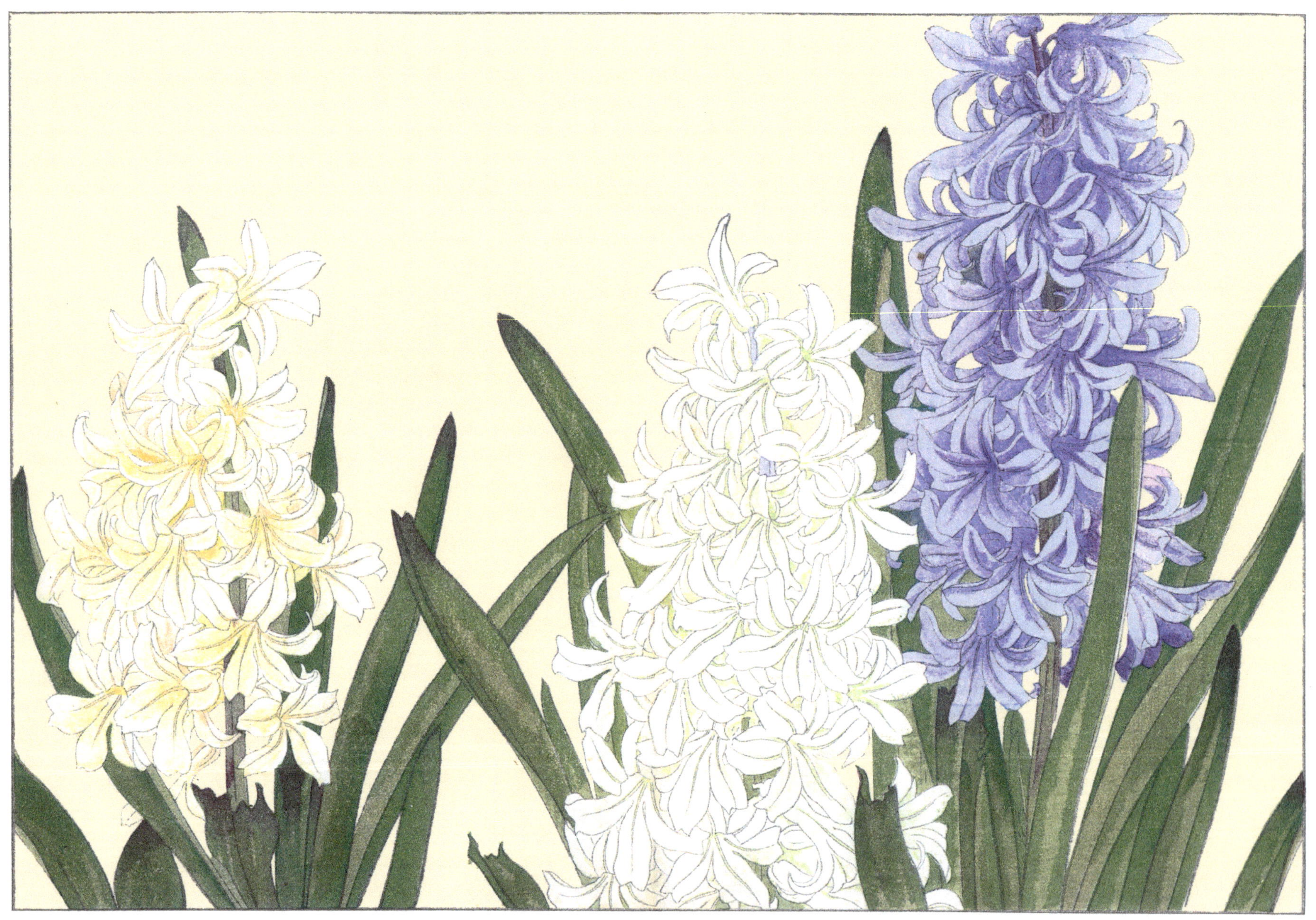

Hyacinth

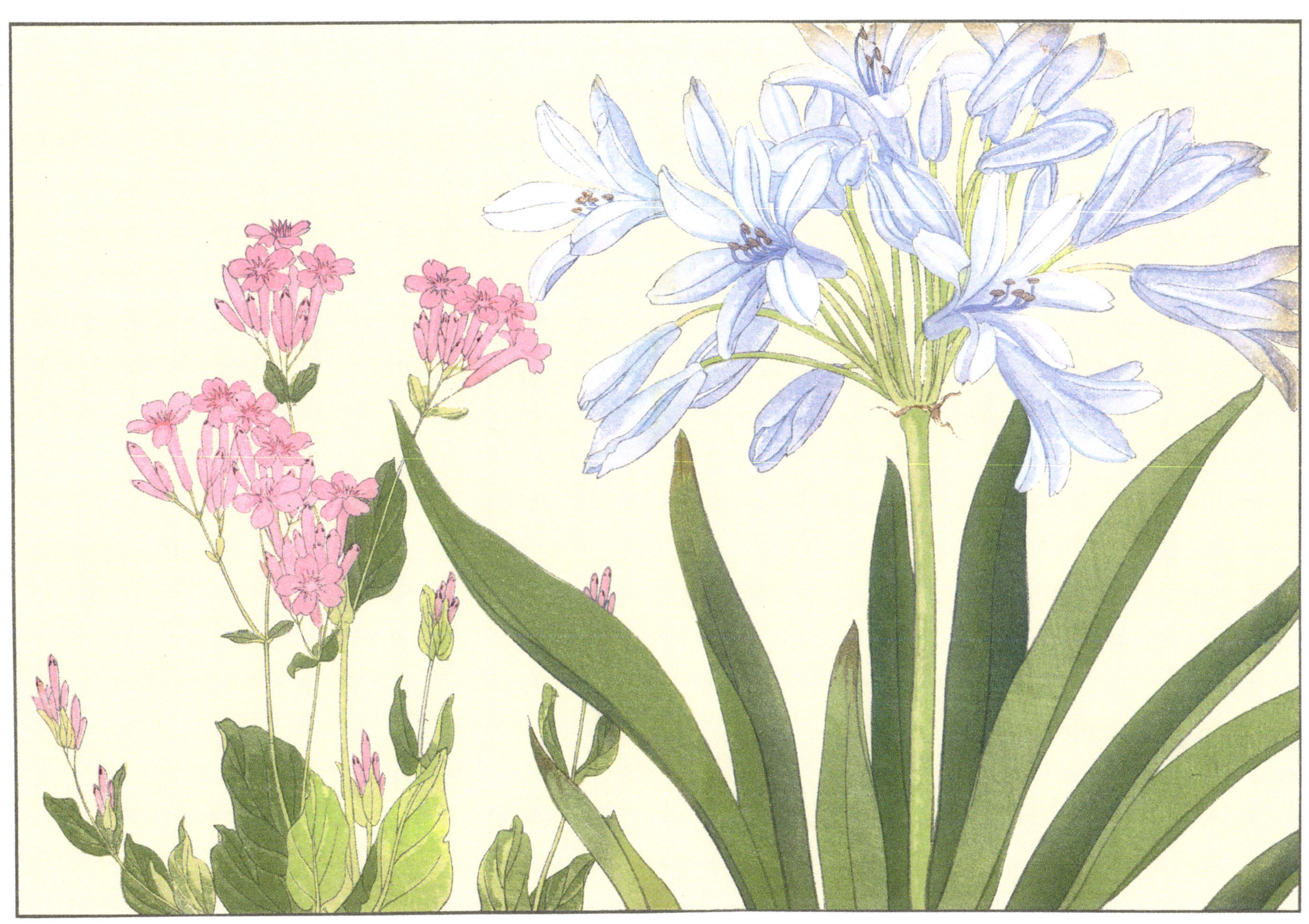

Agaranthus and Catchfly

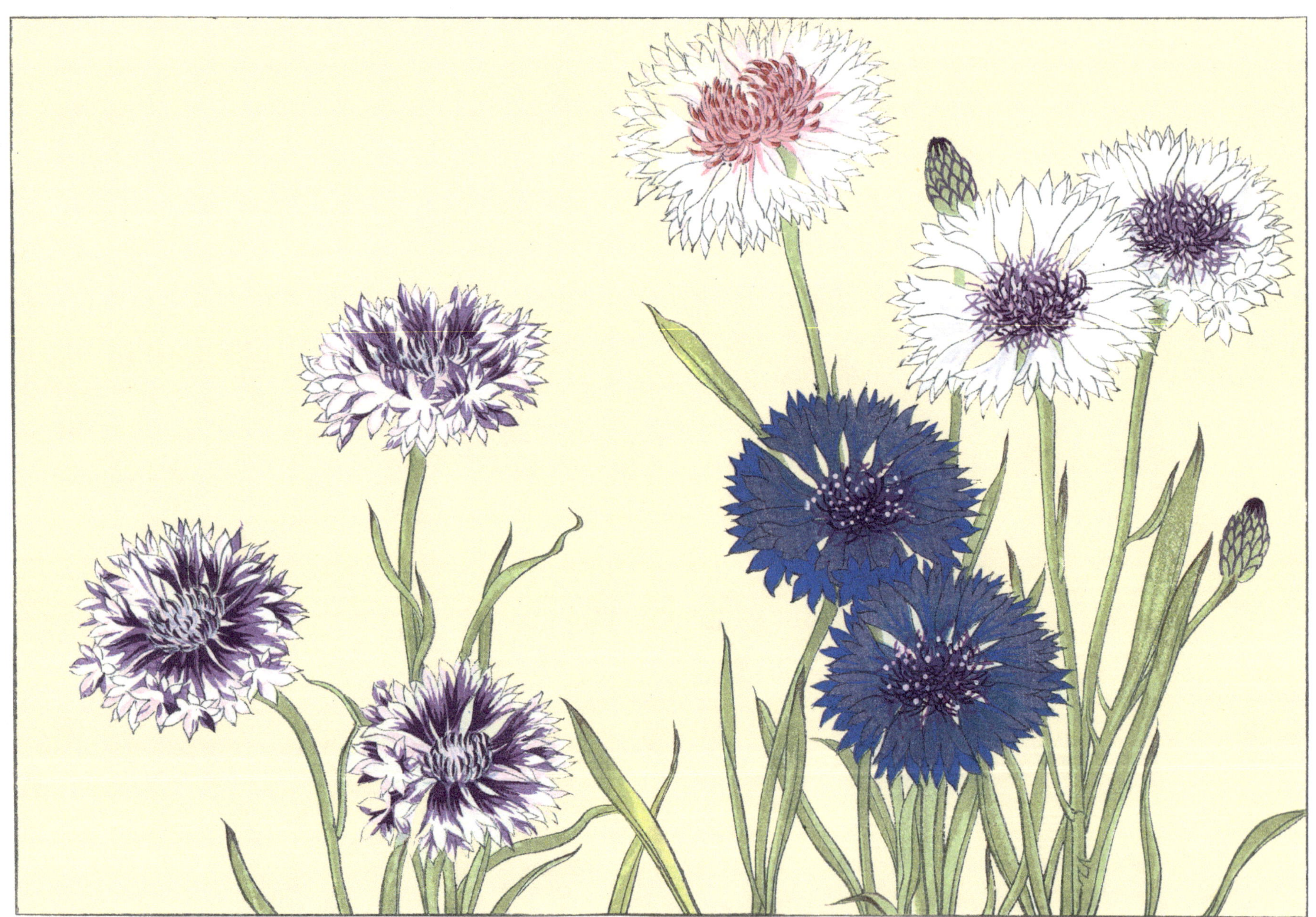

Centaurea

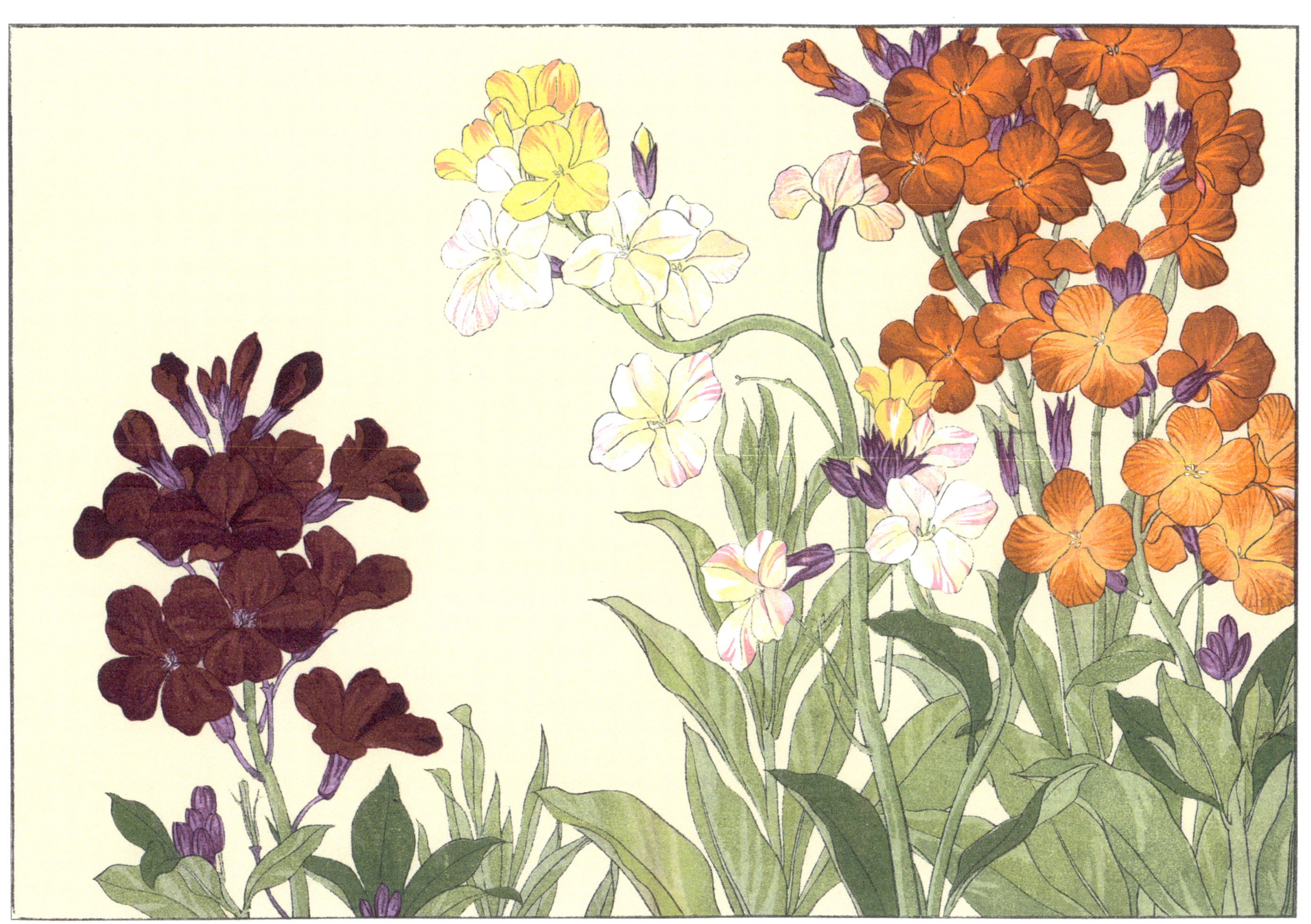

Wallflower

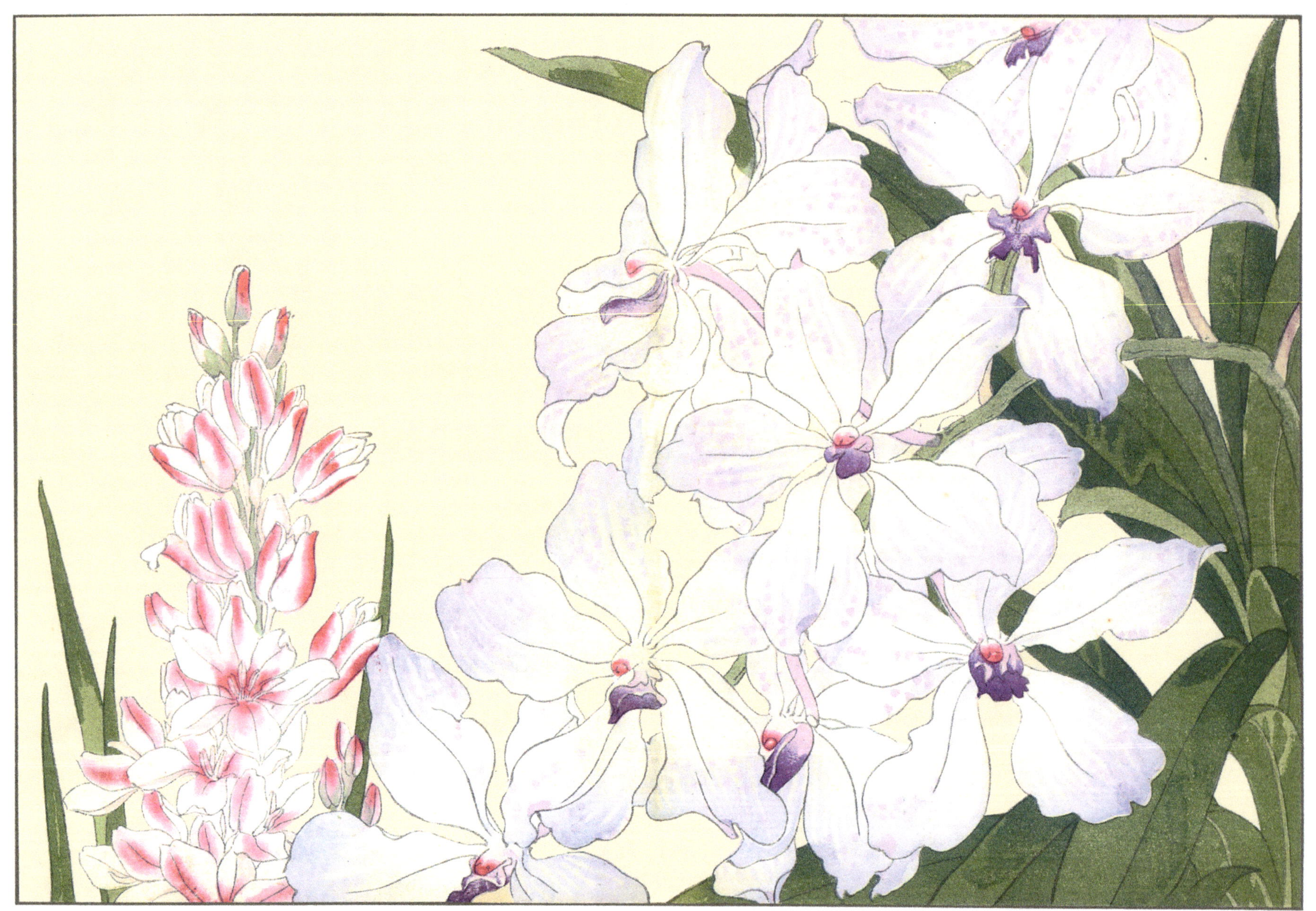

Vanda Caerulea and Ixia

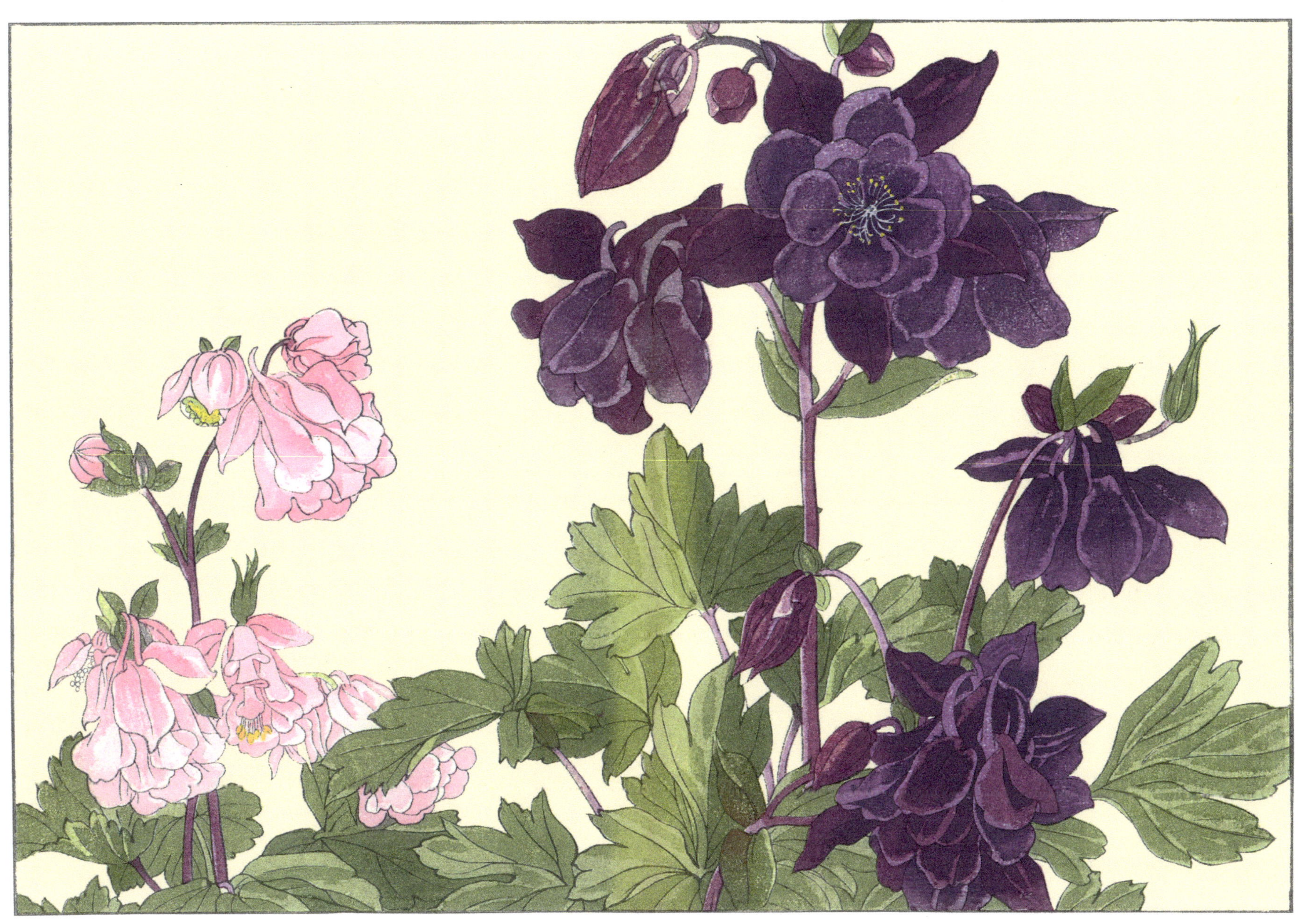

Aquilegia (or Columbine)

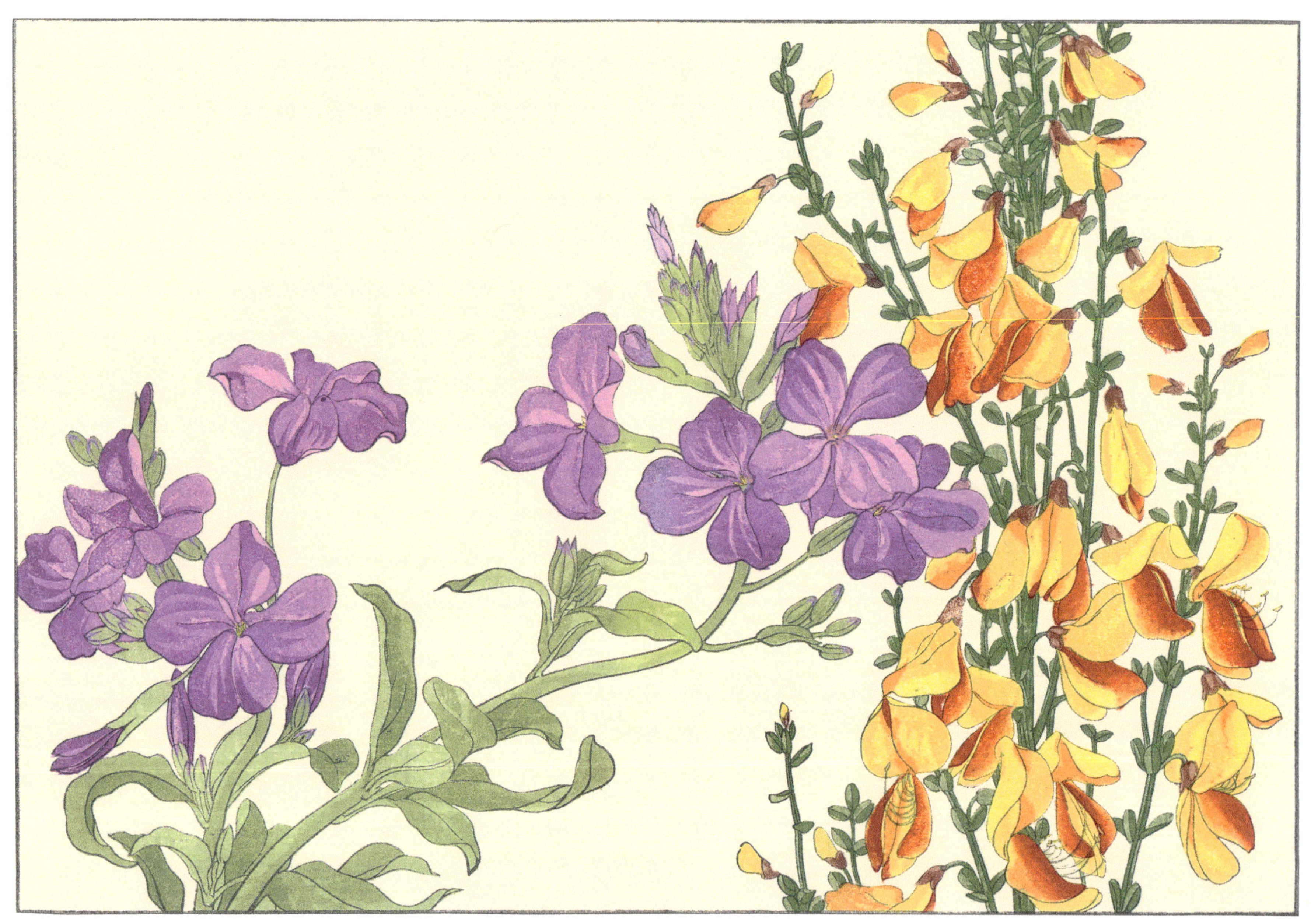

Cytisus (or Common Broom) and Cychinis

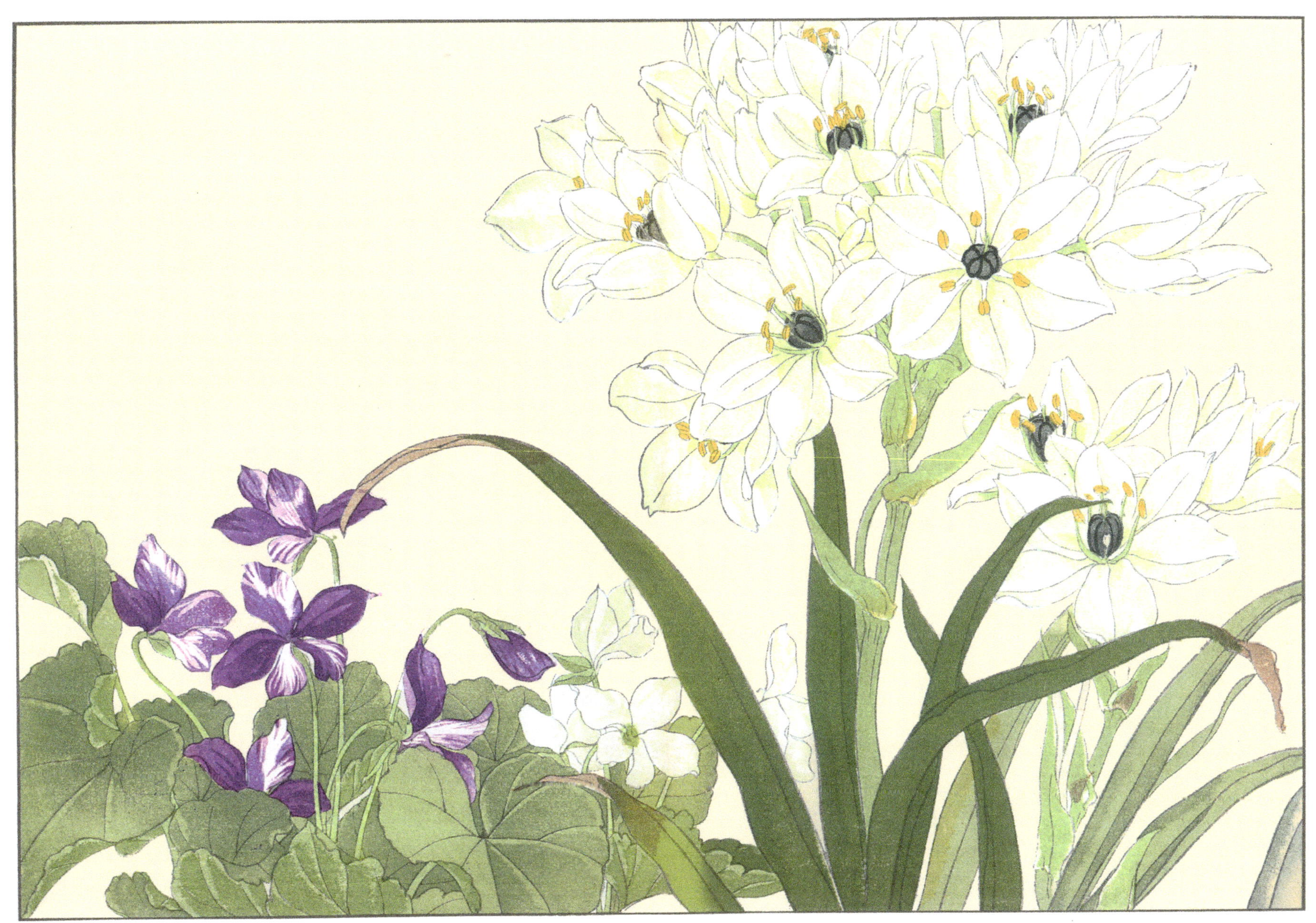

Scilla and Violet

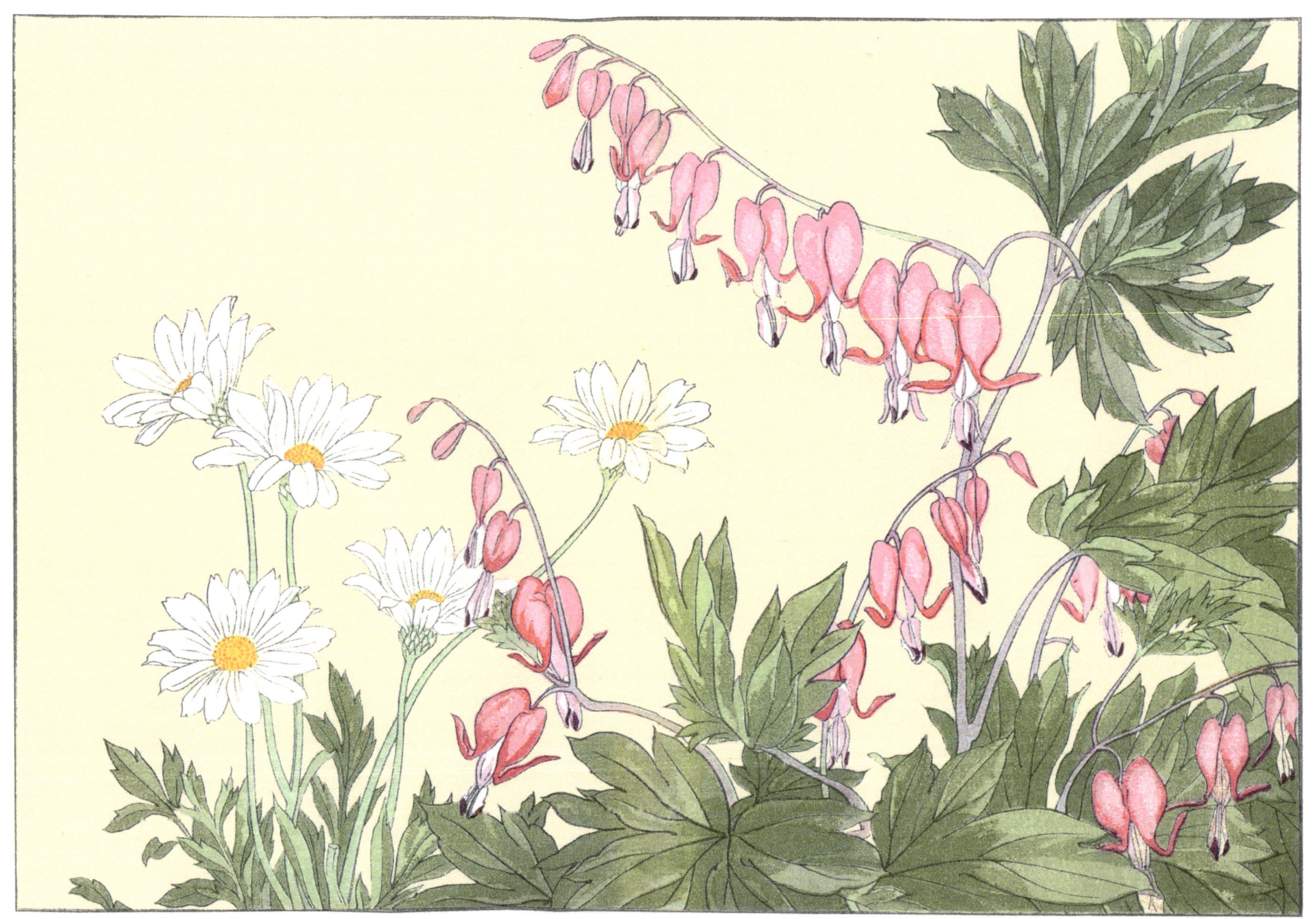

Bleeding Heart and Marguerite (or Daisy)

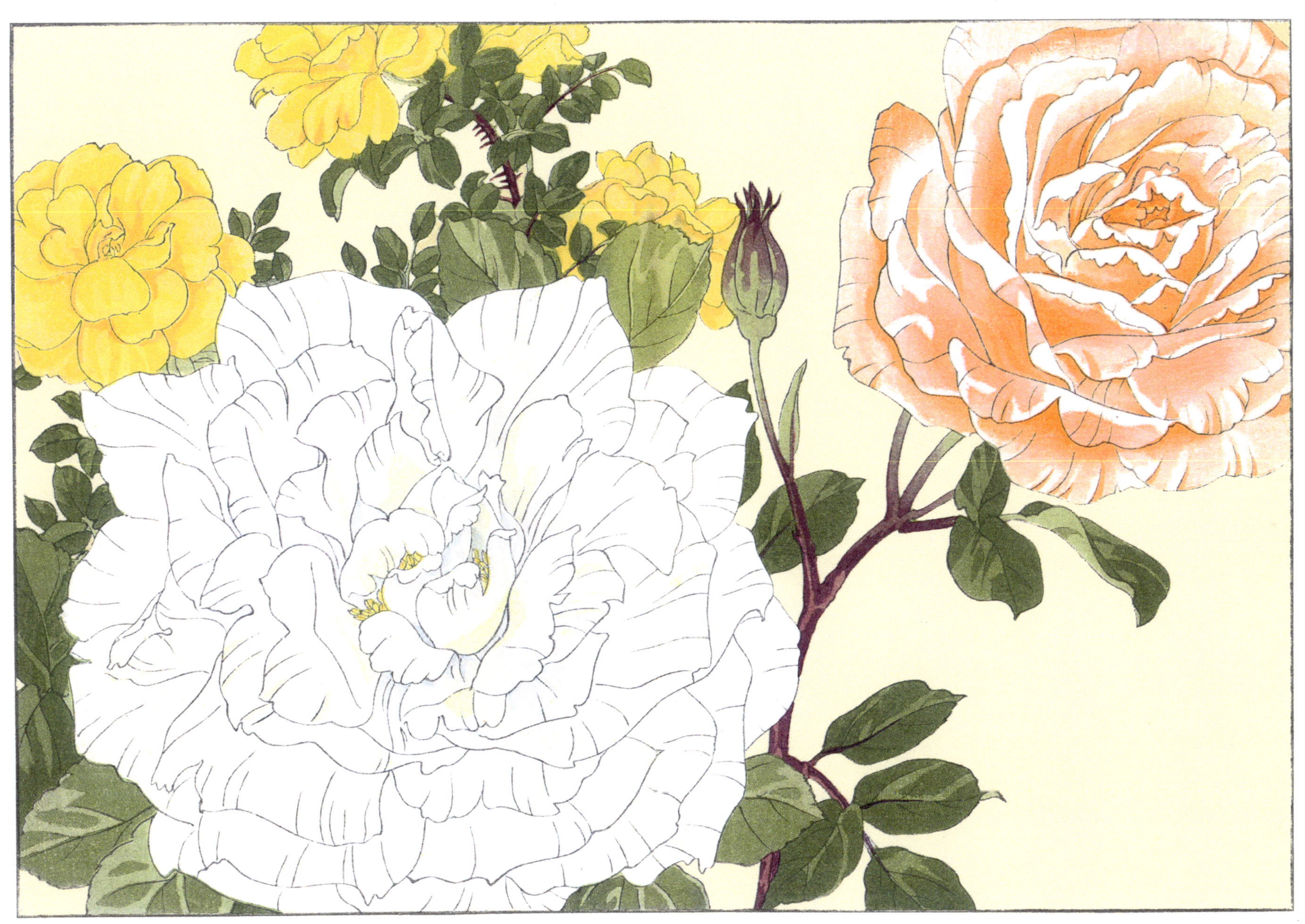

Rose

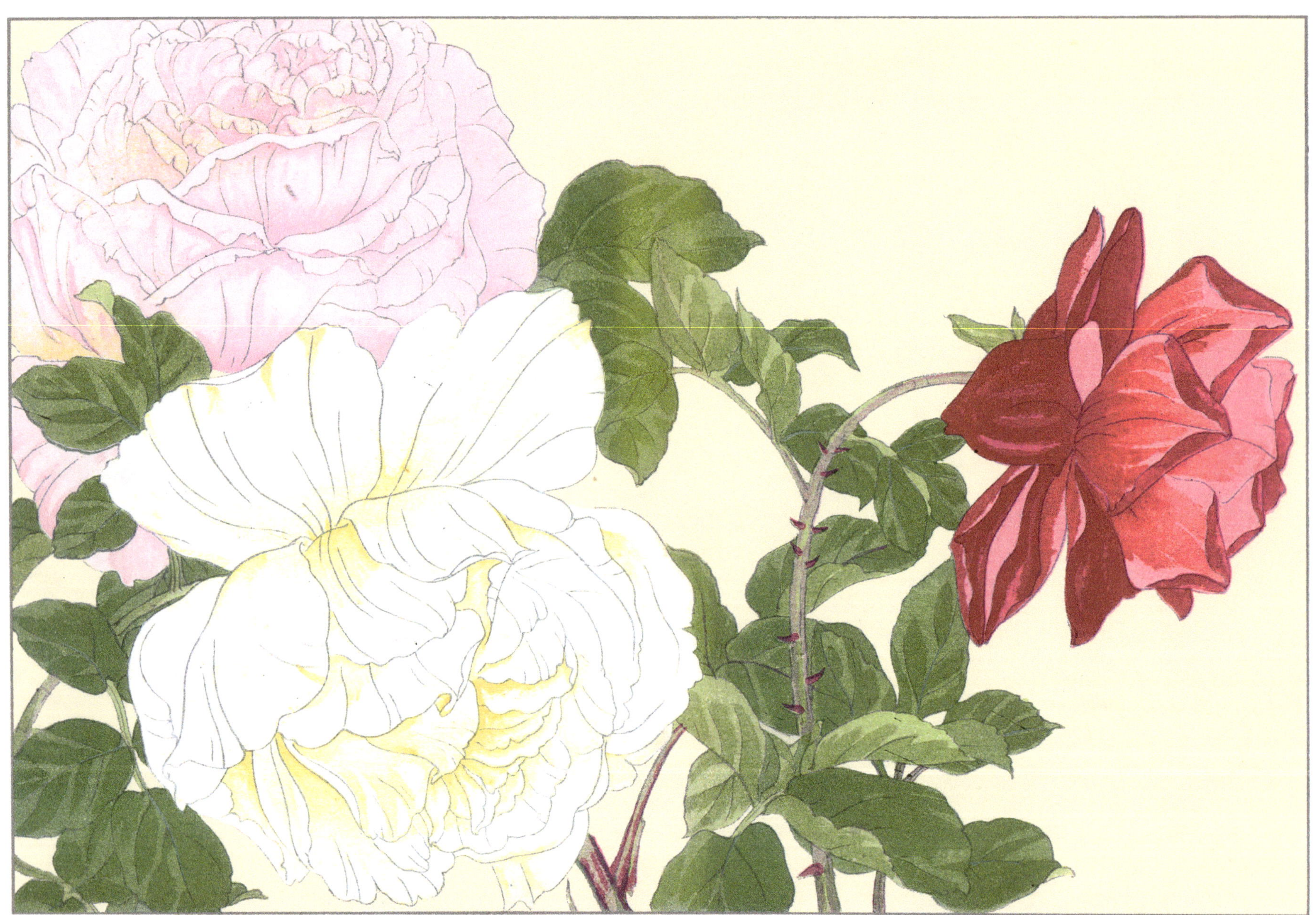

Rose

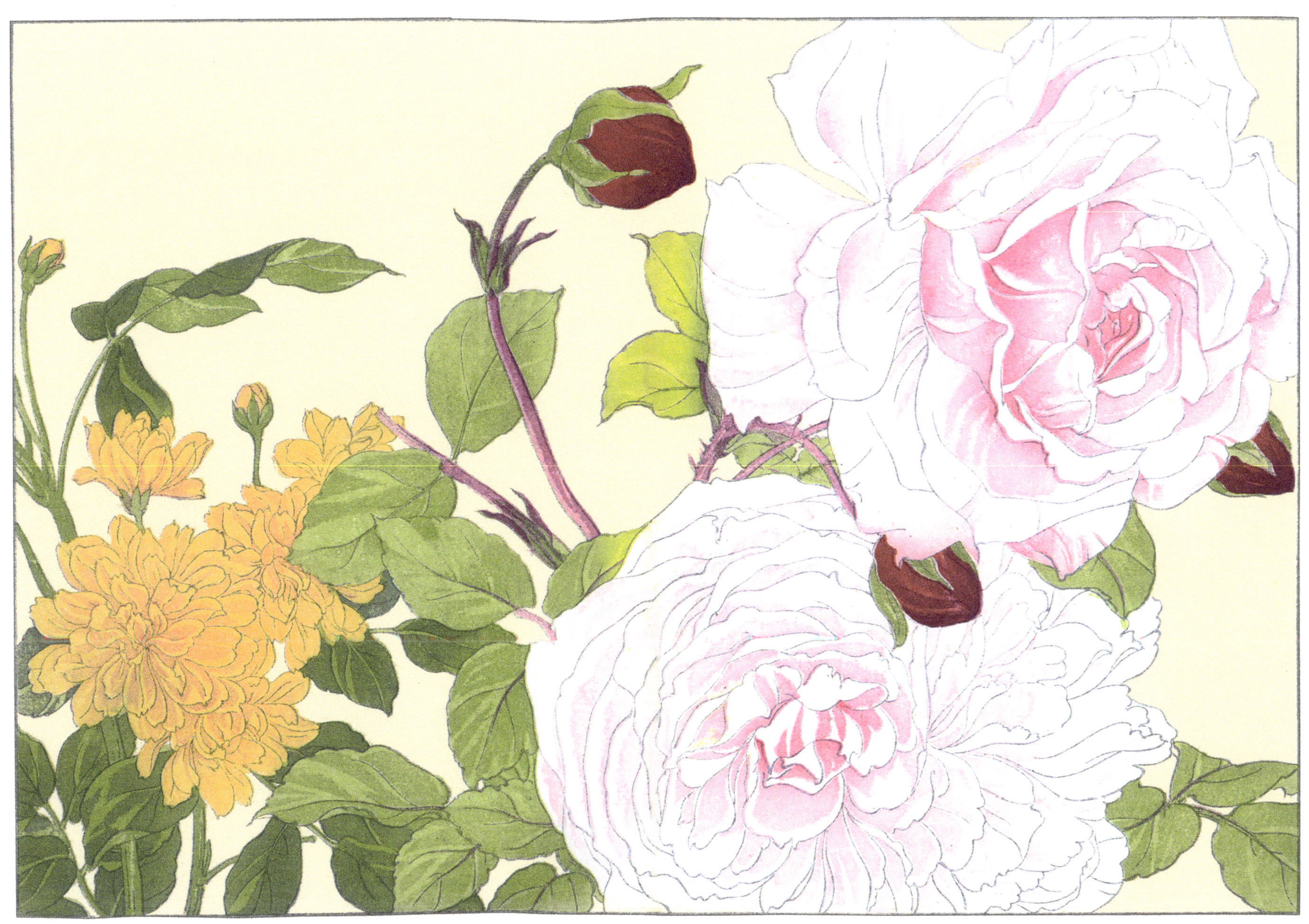

Rose

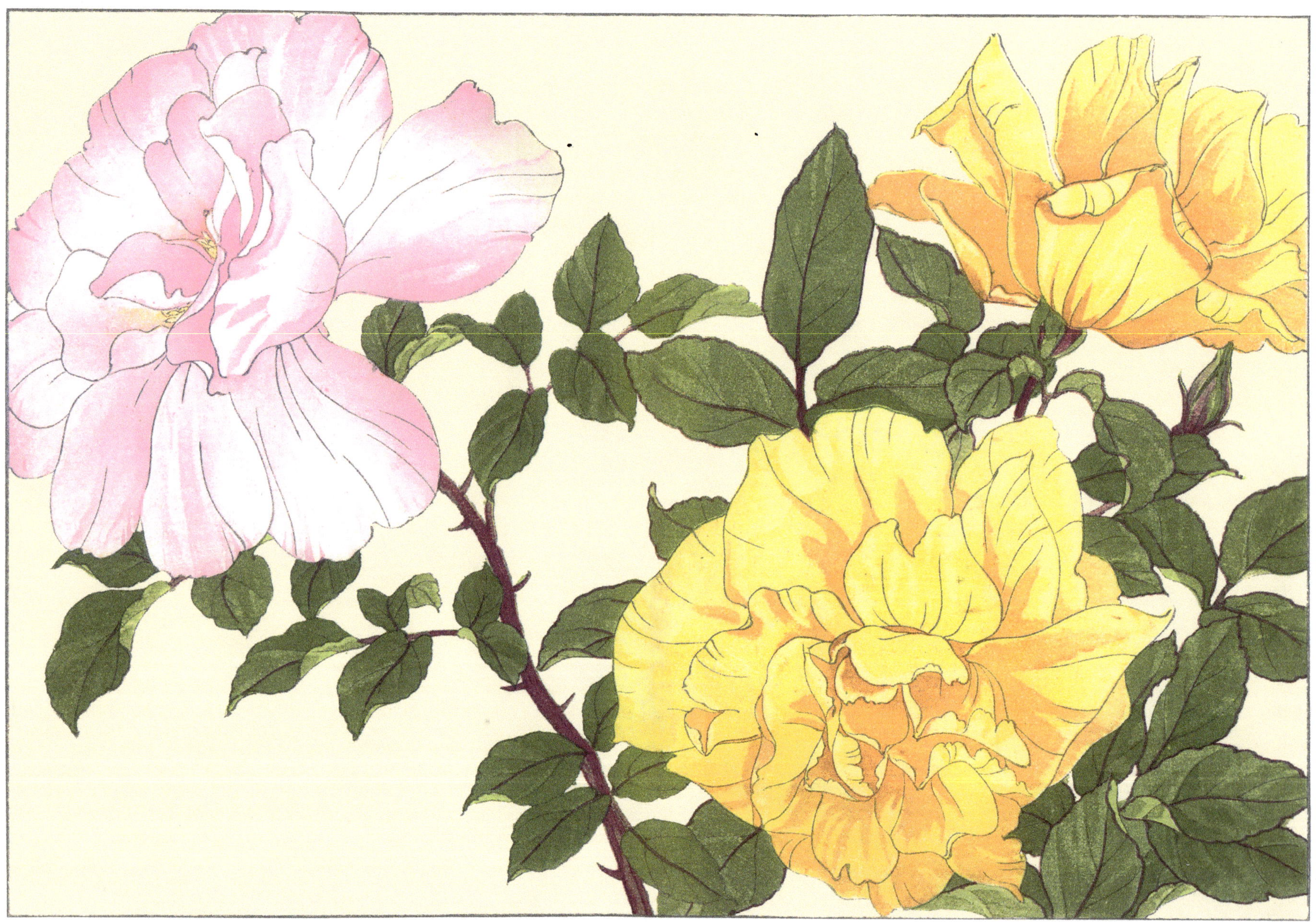

Rose

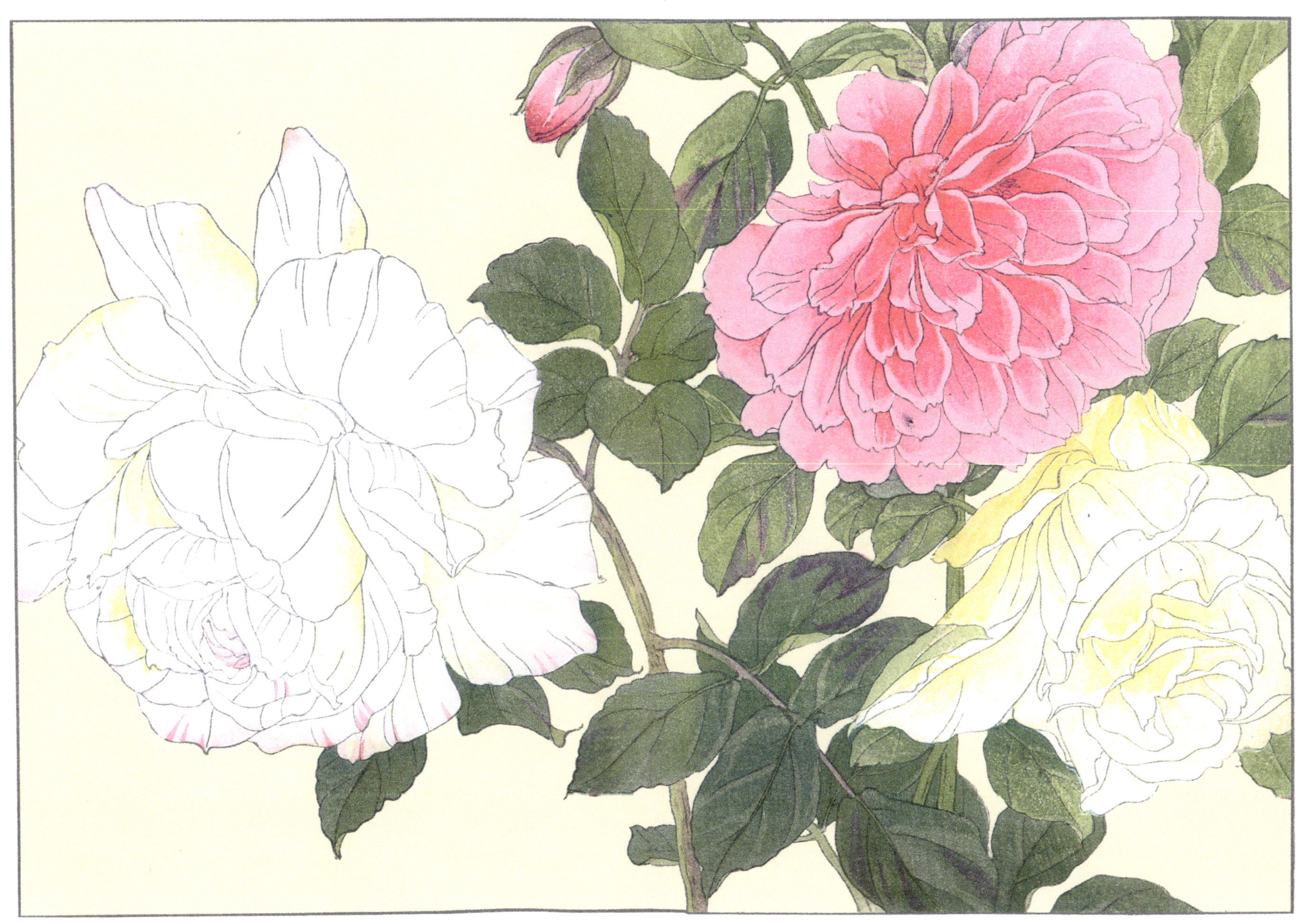

Rose

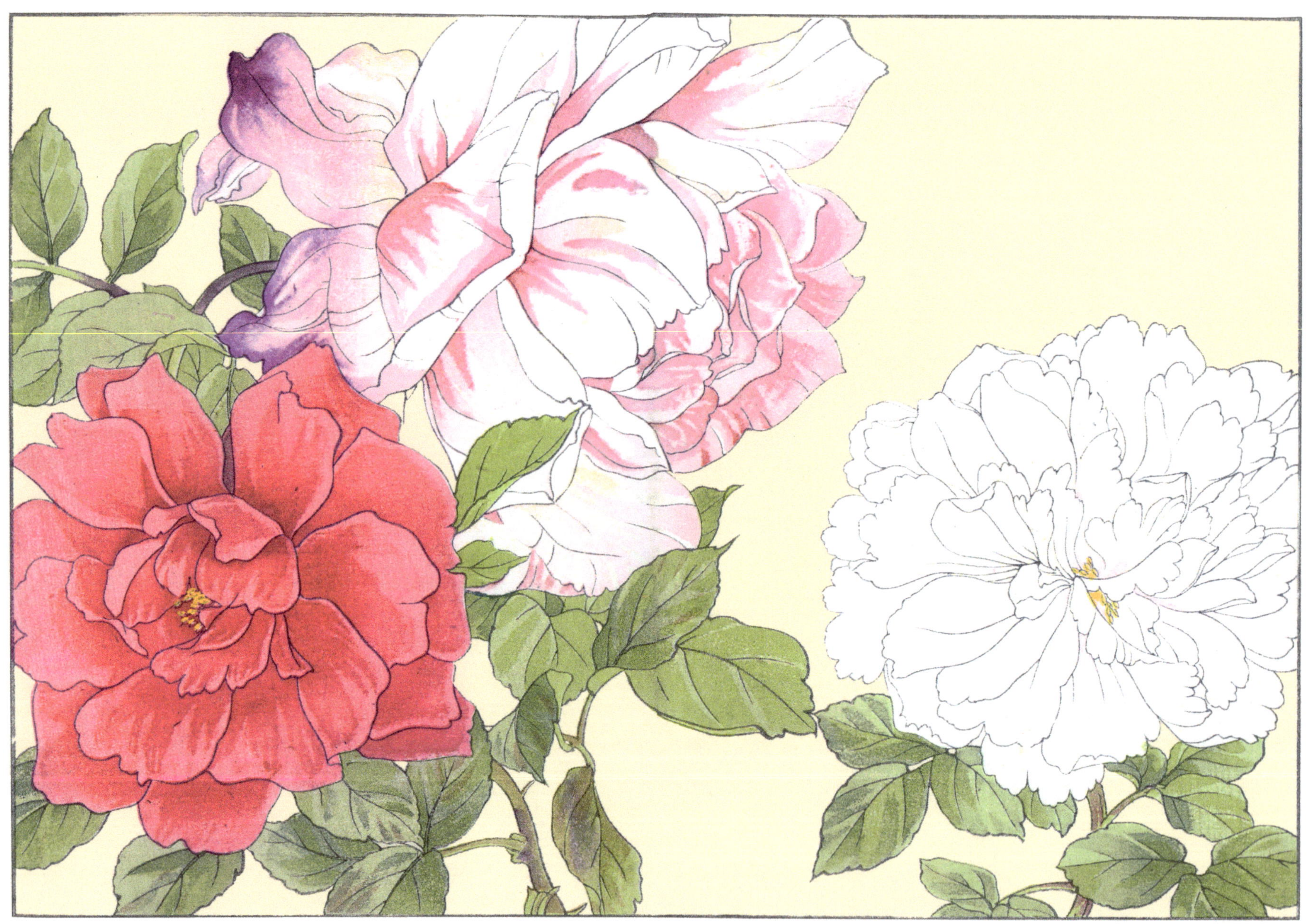

Rose

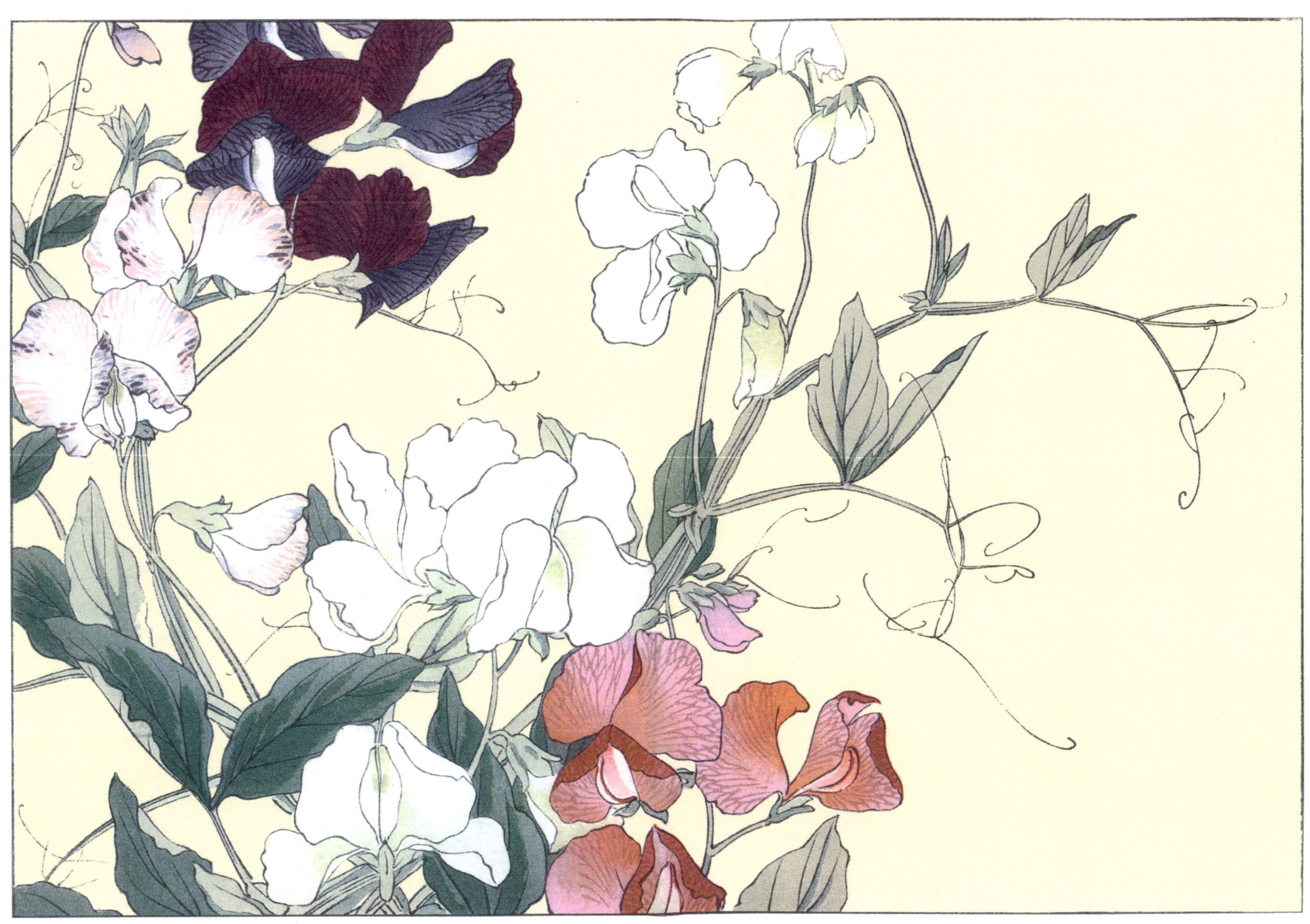

Sweet Pea

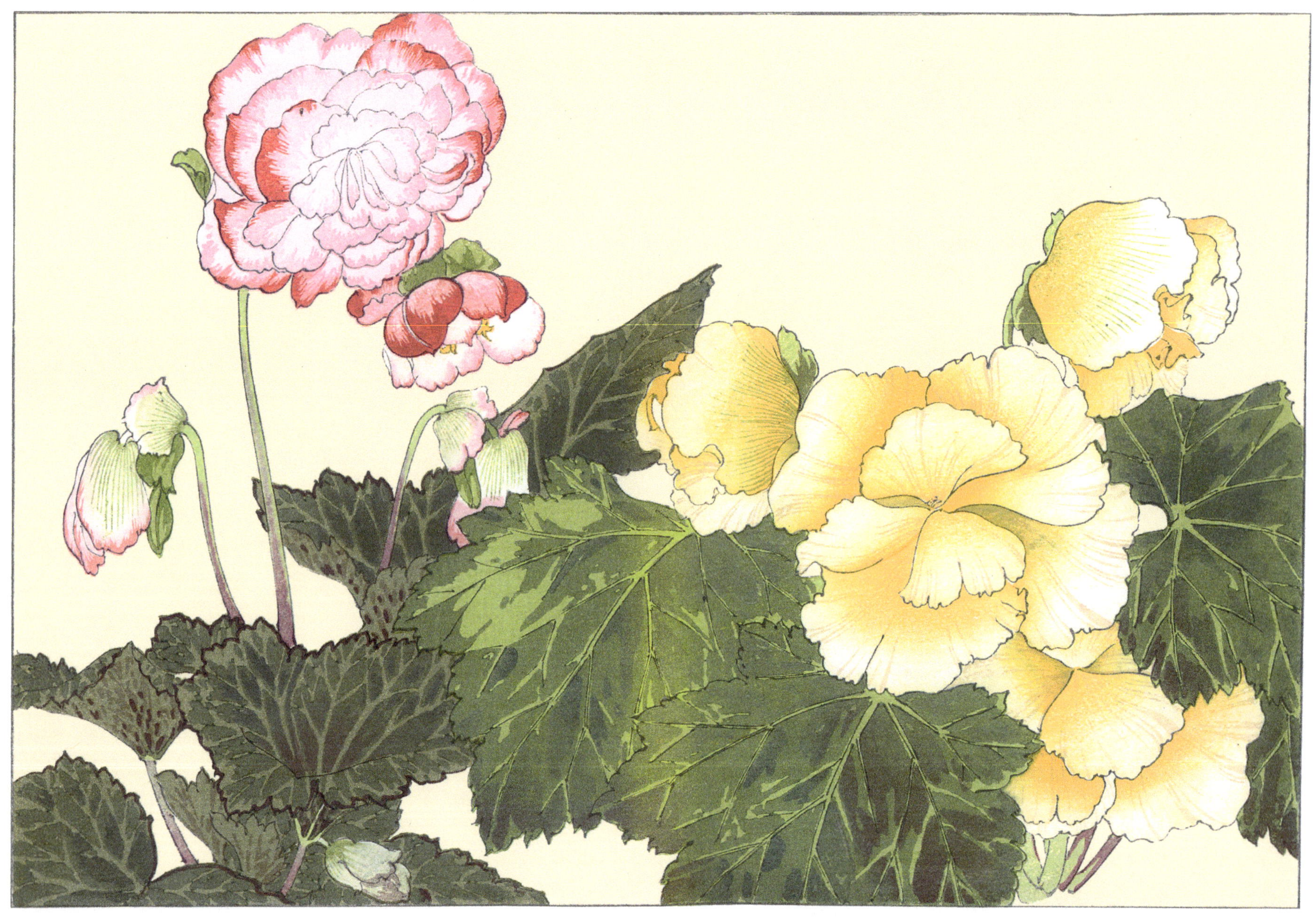

Begonia

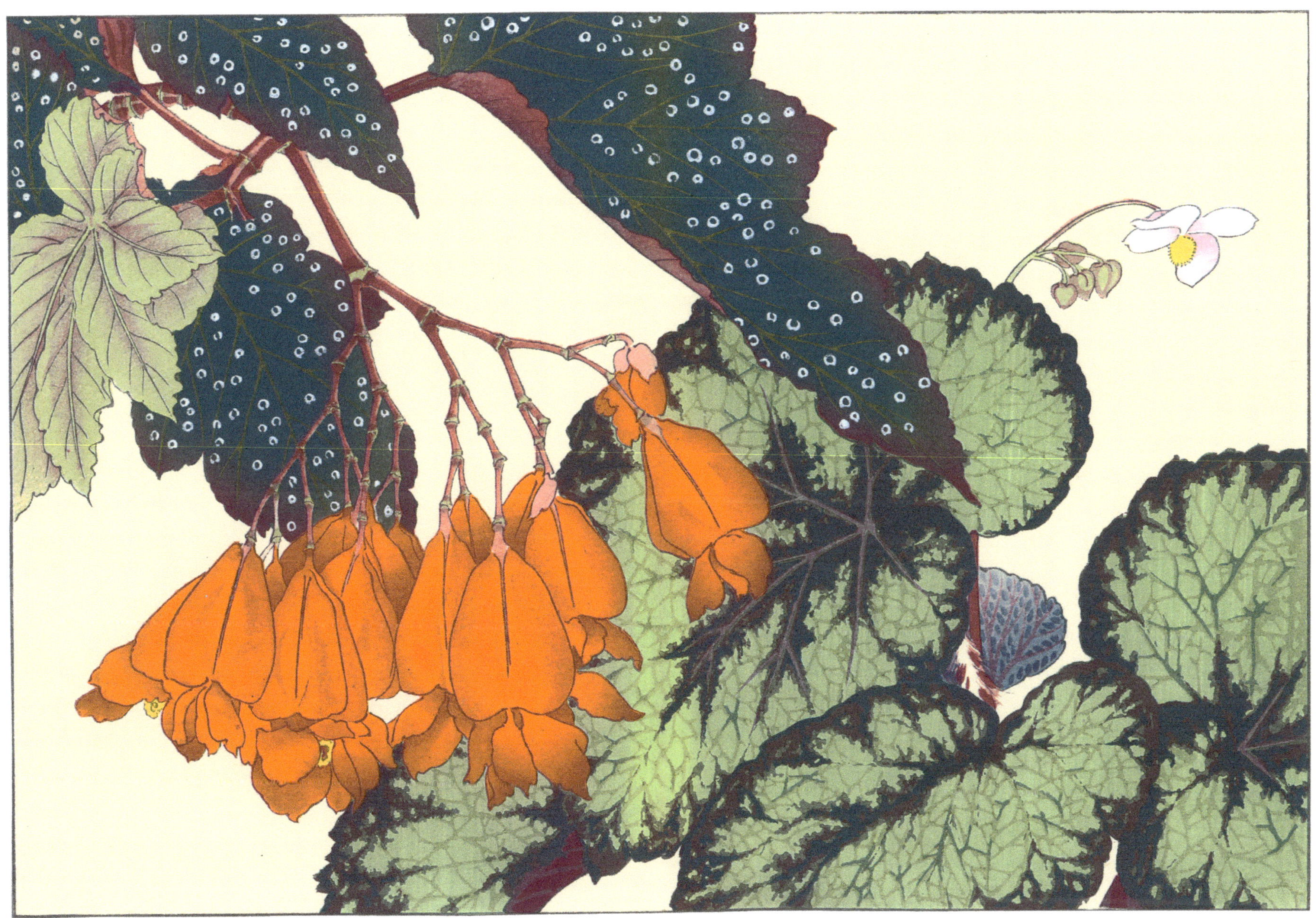

Begonia

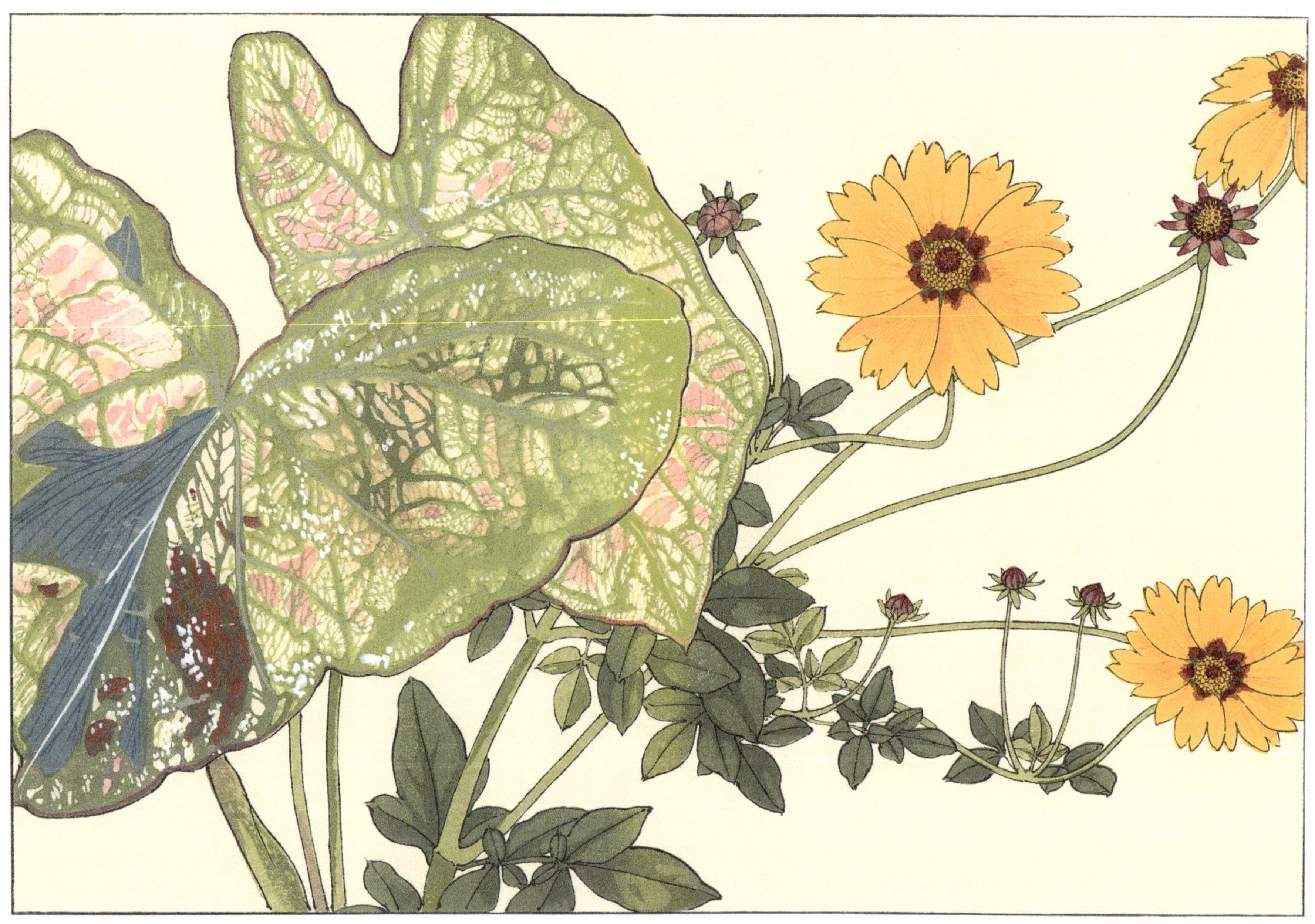

Coreopsis and Caladium

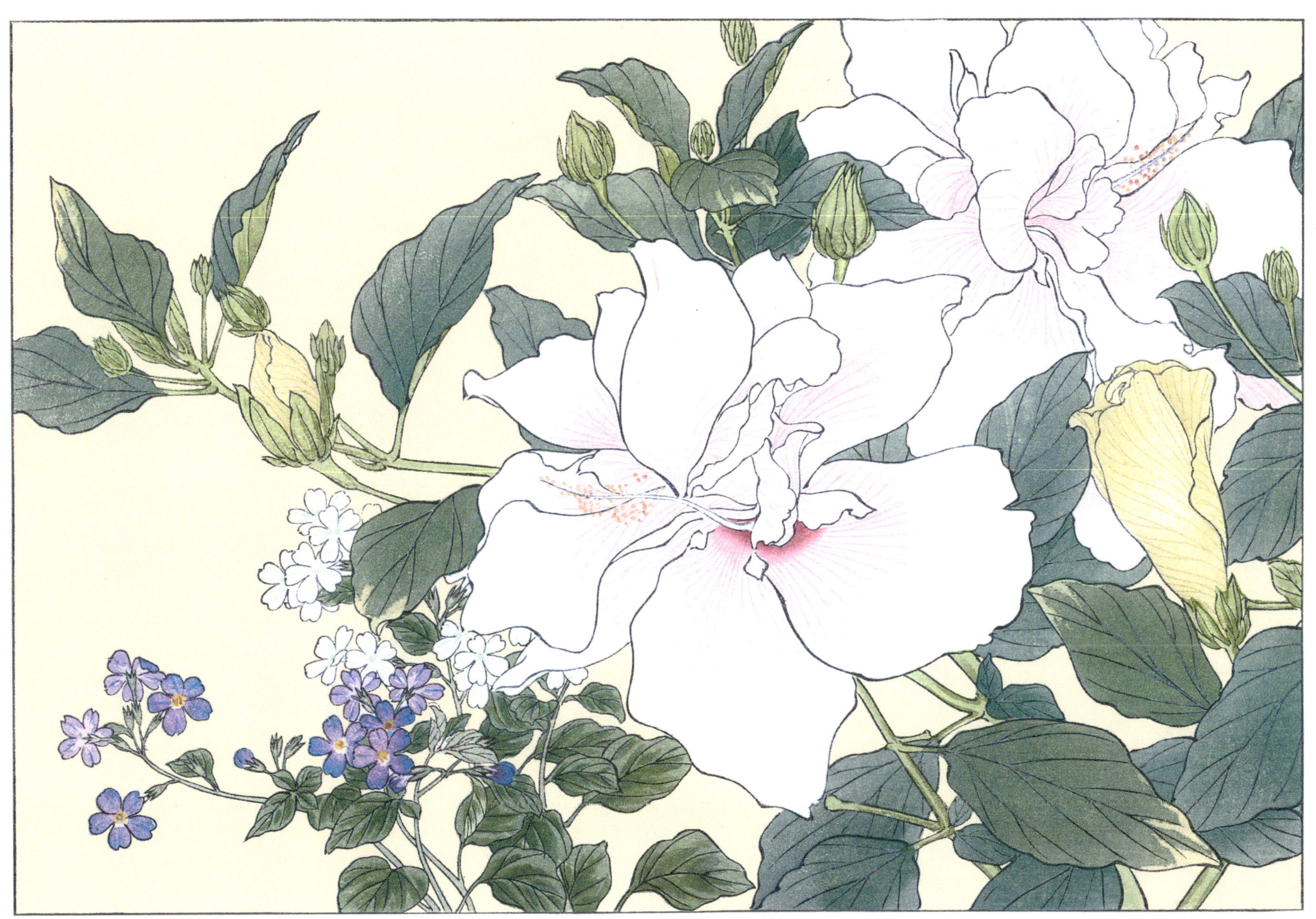

Hibiscus and Browallia

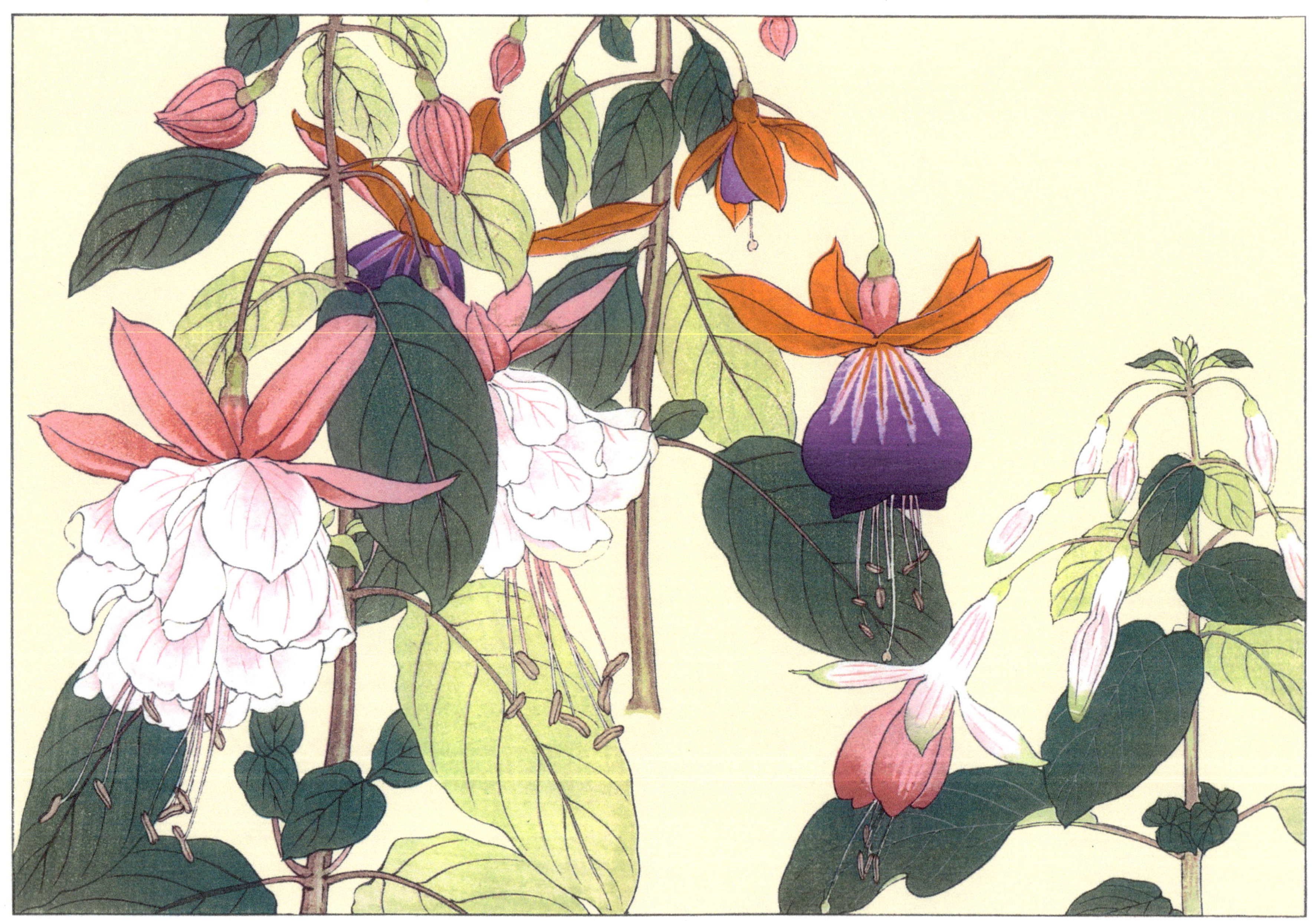

Fuchsia

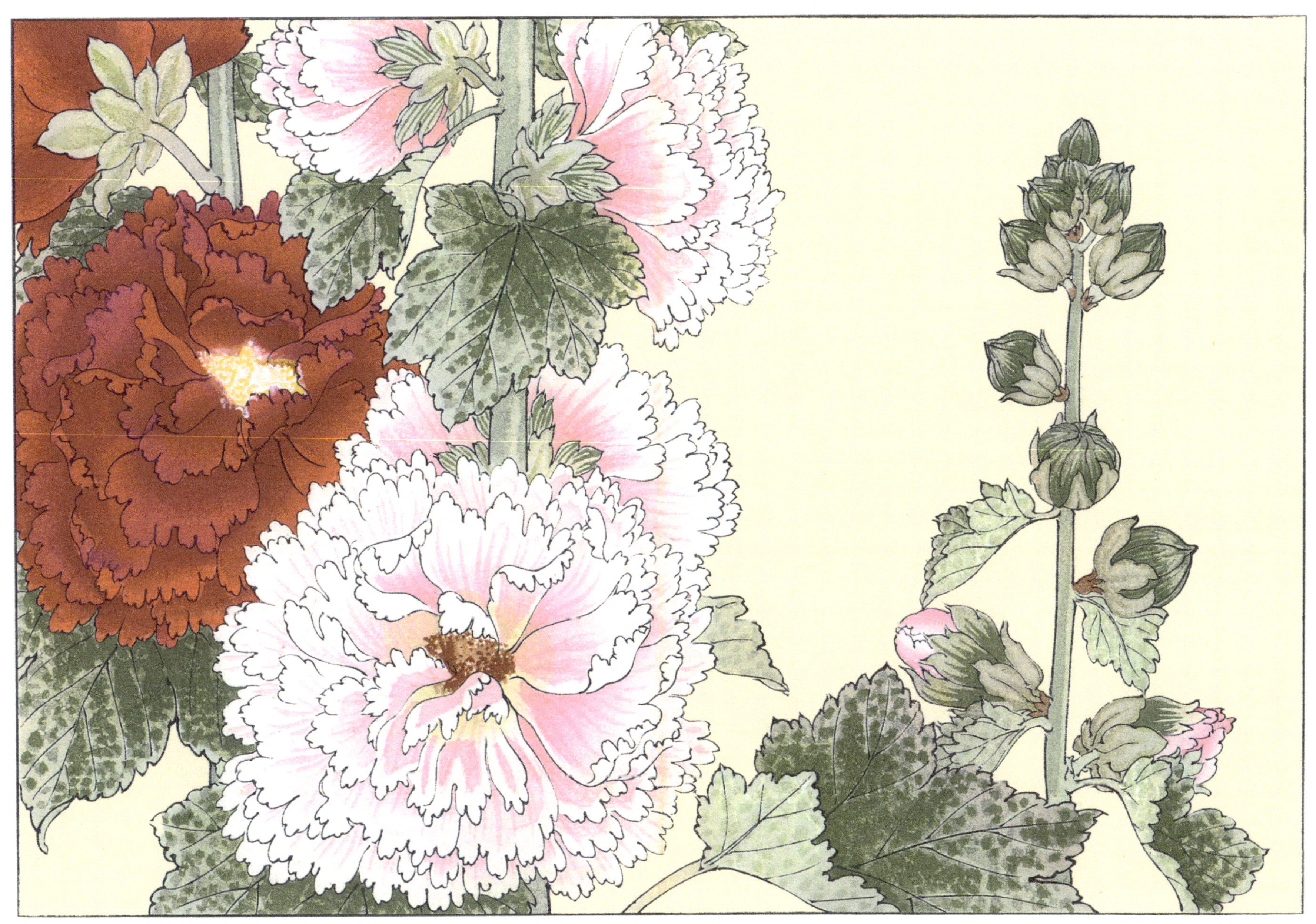

Hollyhock

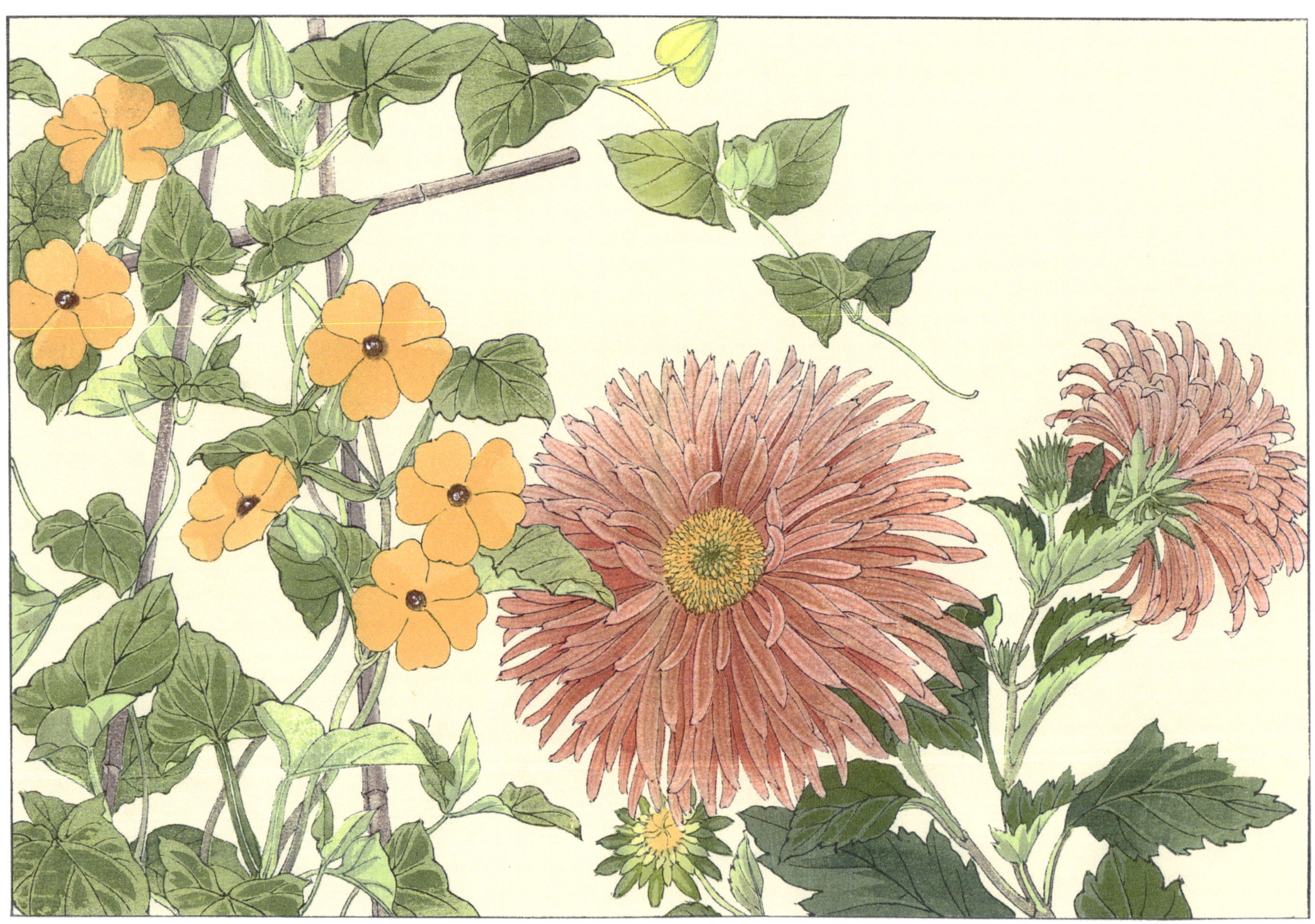

Aster and Thunbergia

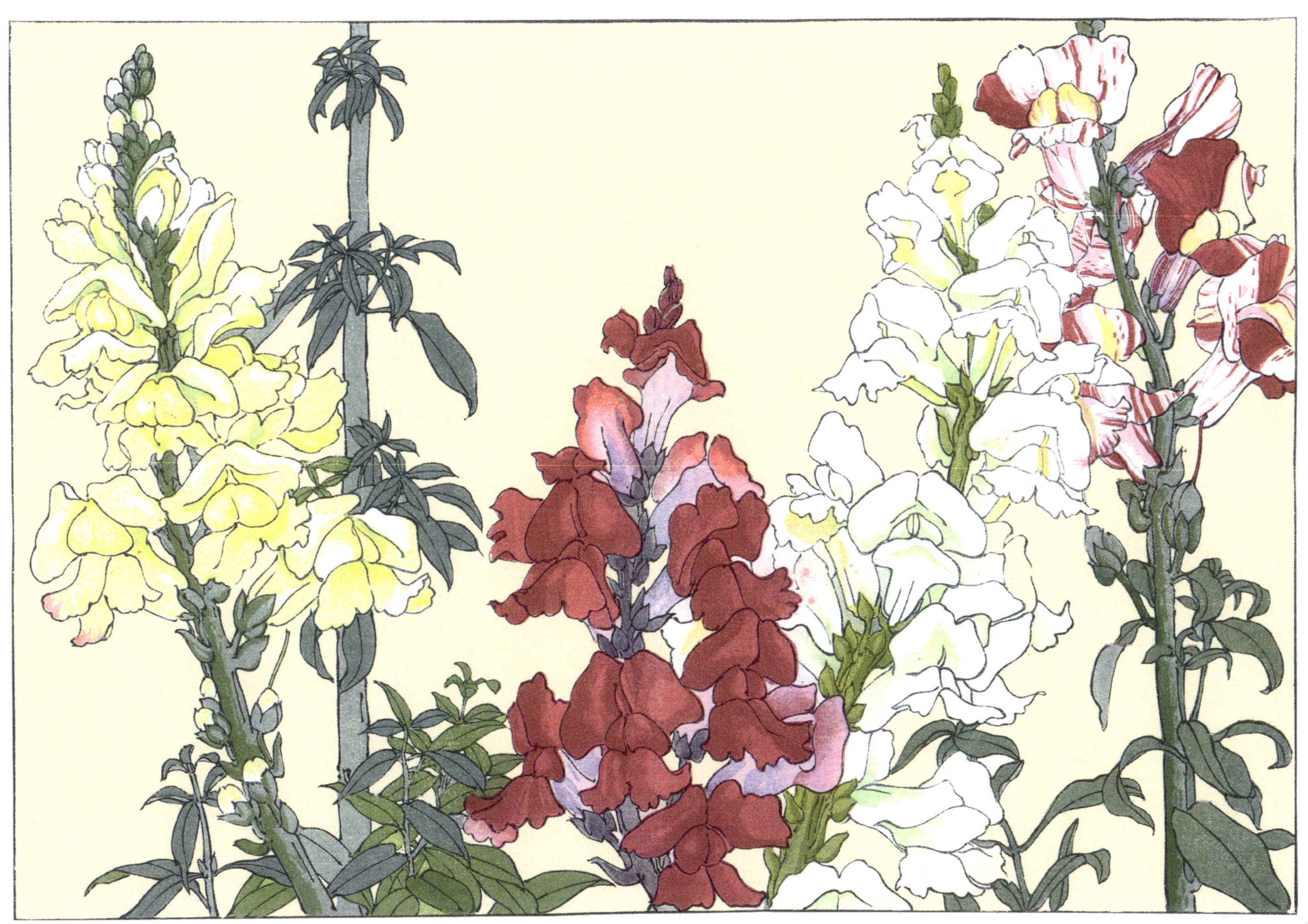

Antirrhinum (or Snapdragon)

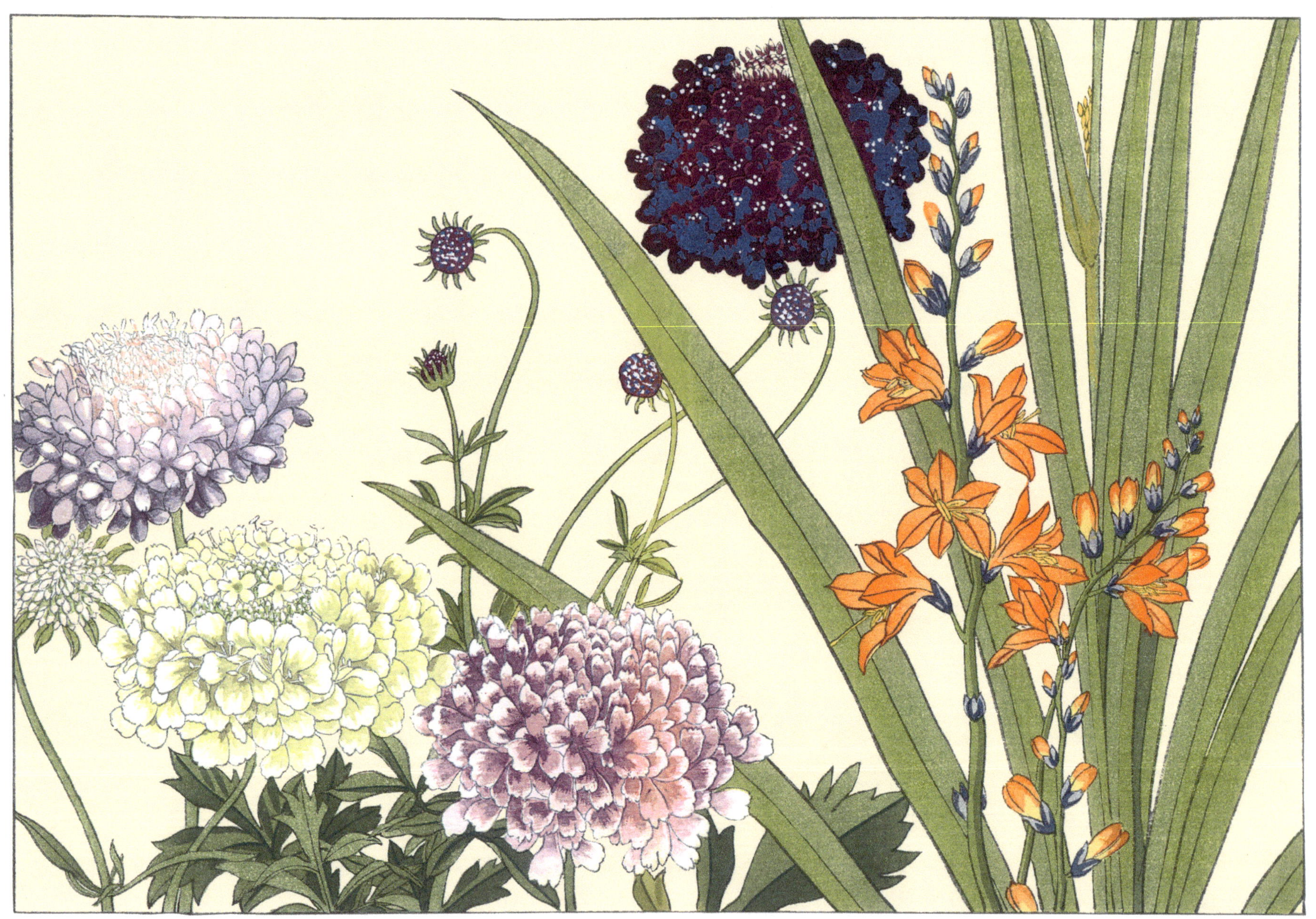

Montbretia and Scabiosa

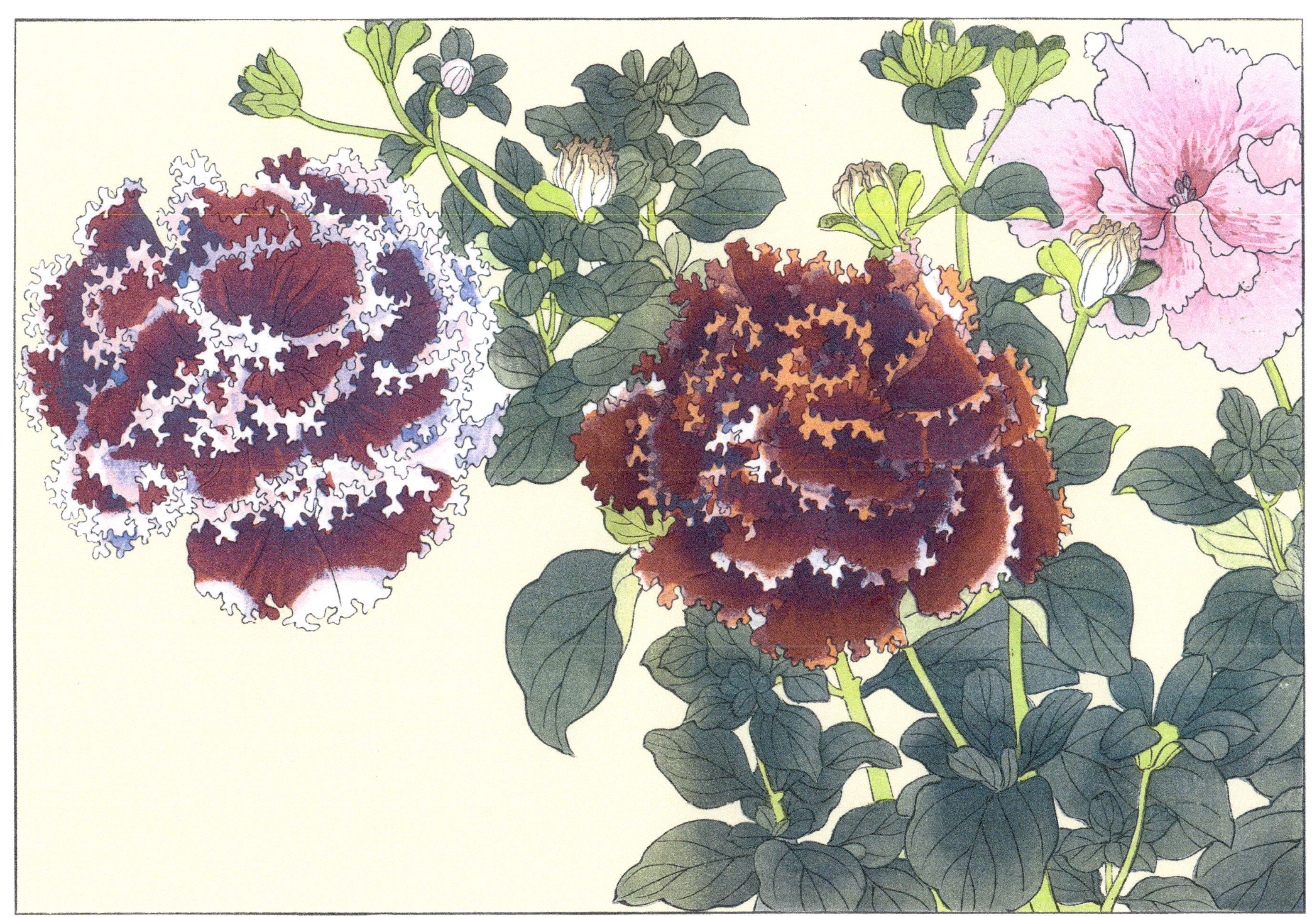

Petunia

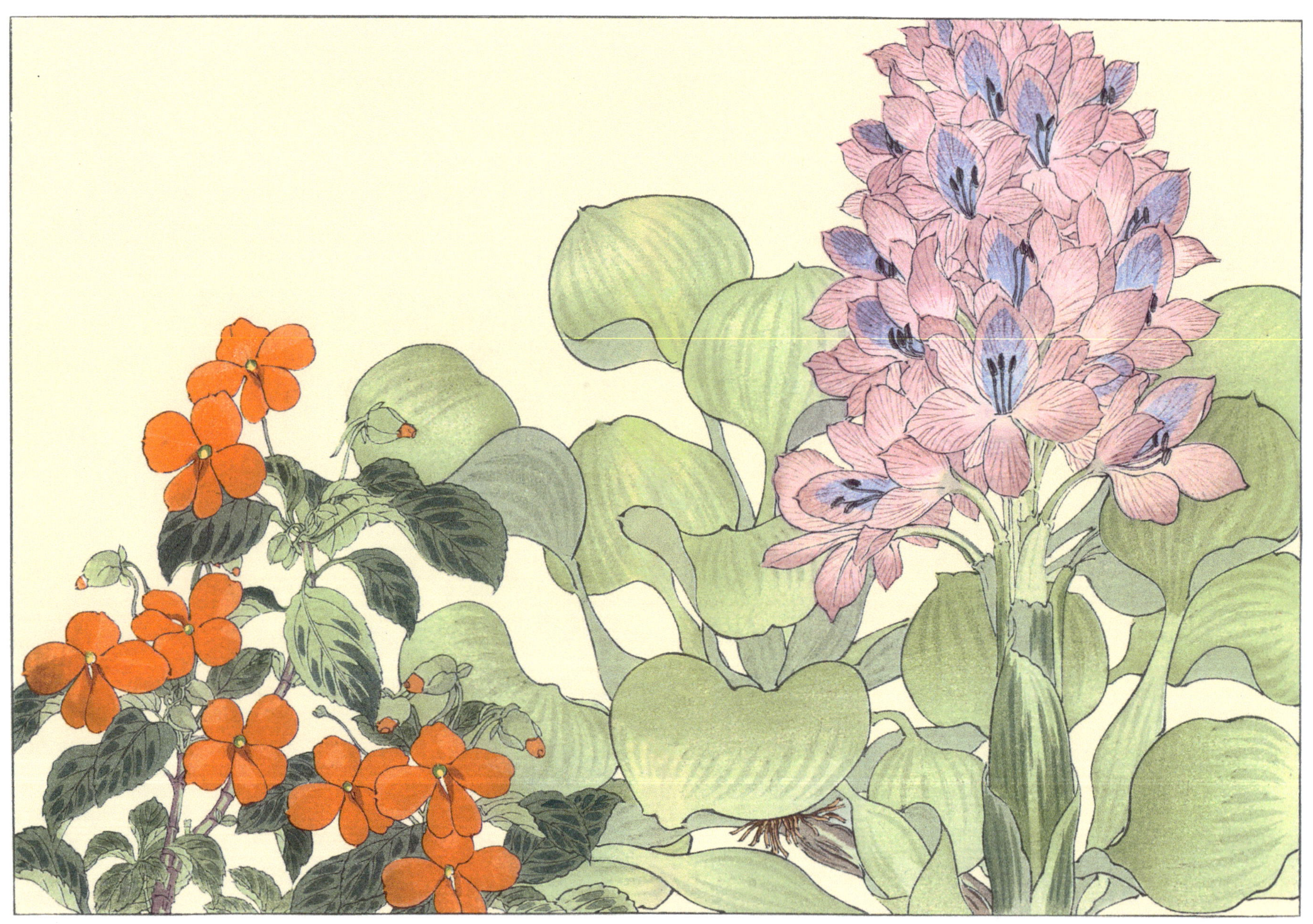

Water Hyacinth and Impatiens

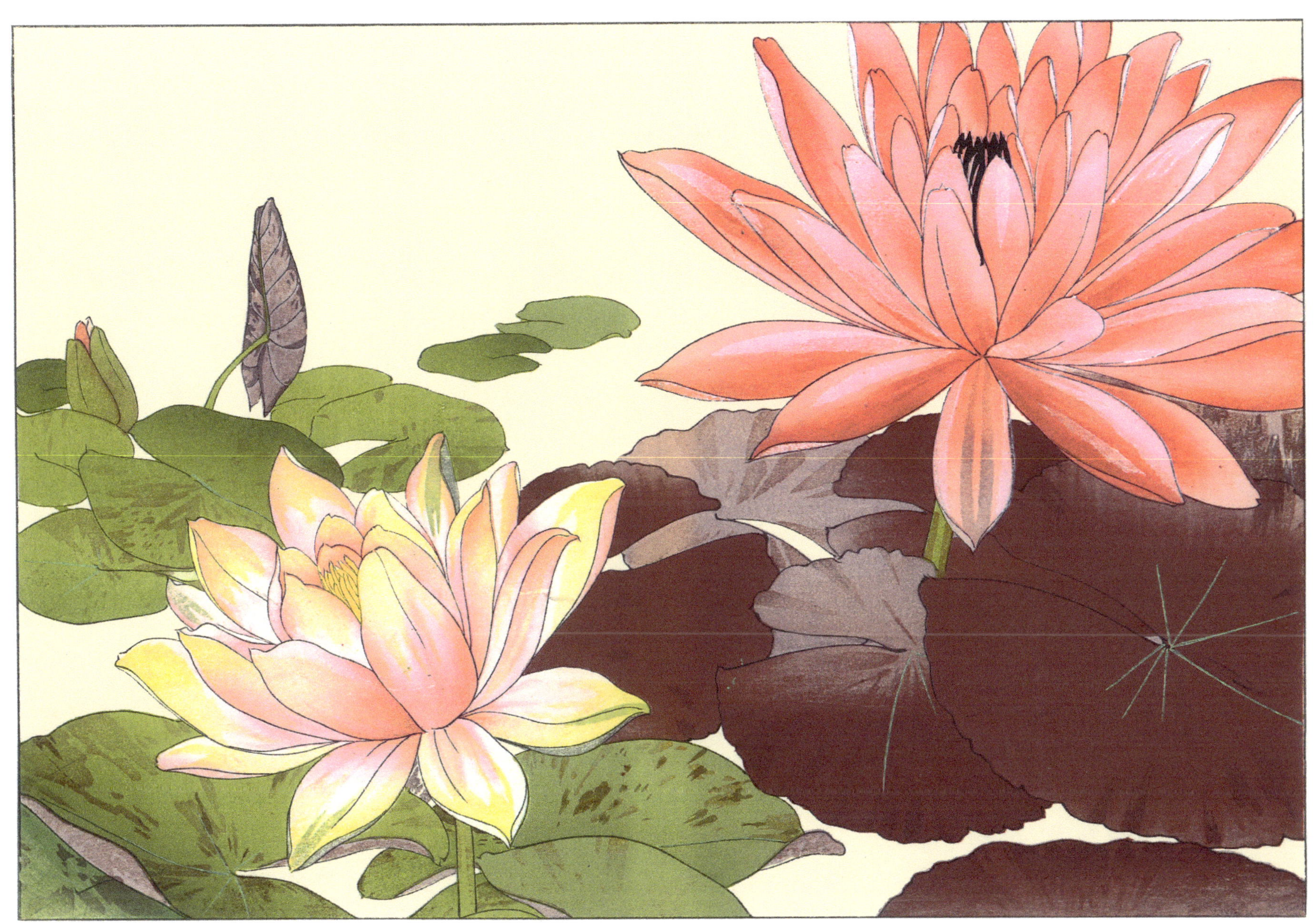

Water Lily

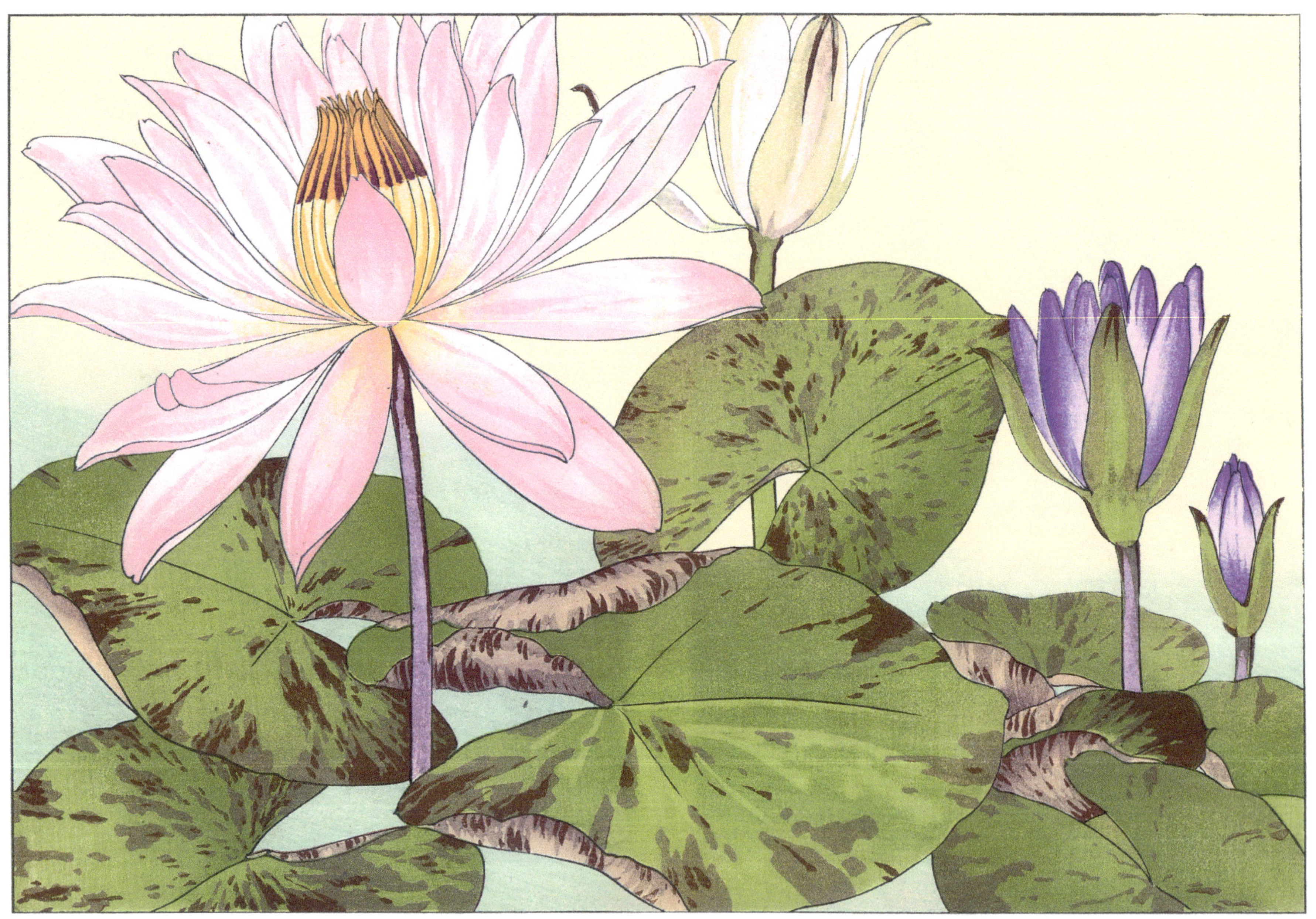

Water Lily

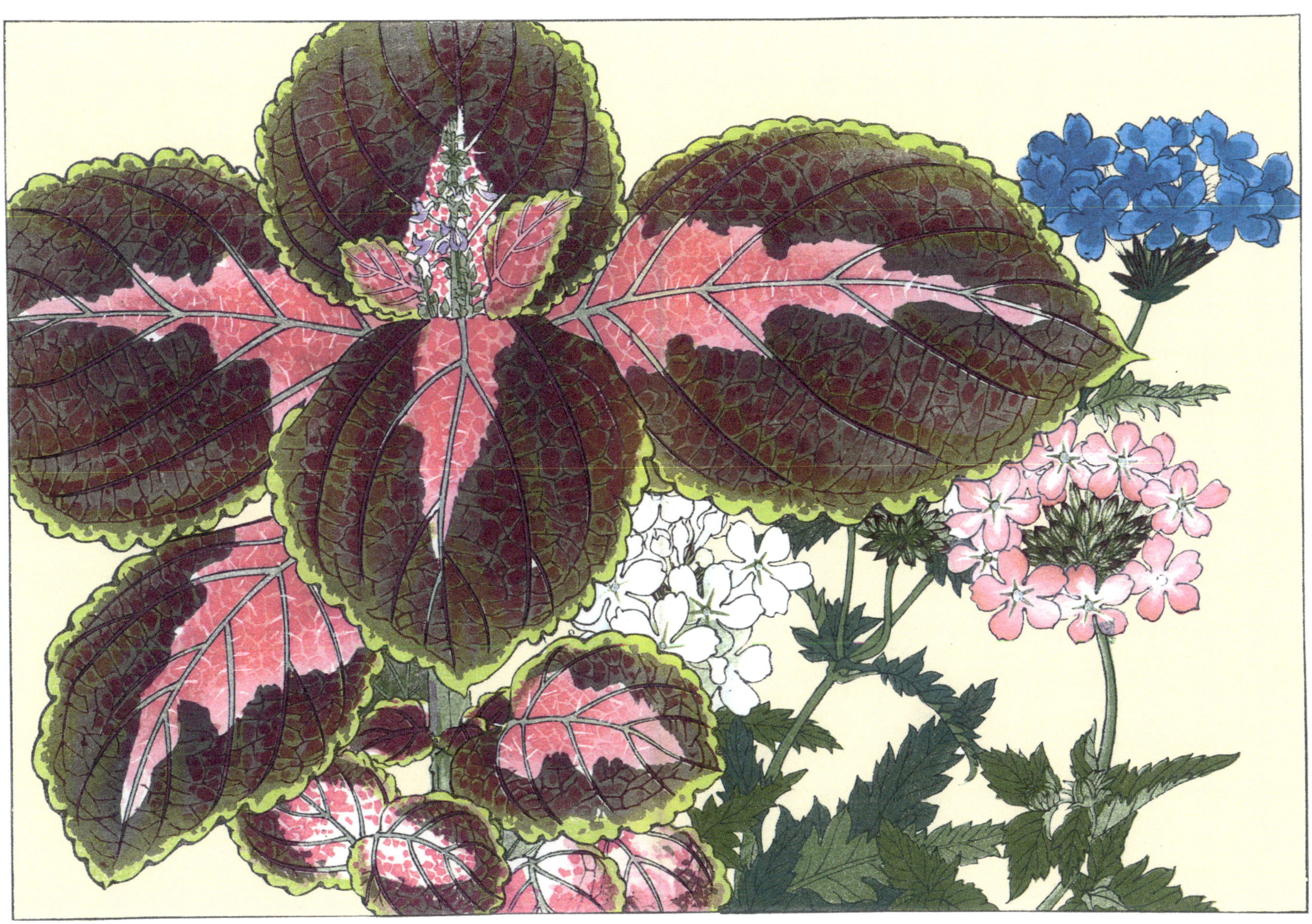

Verbena and Coleus

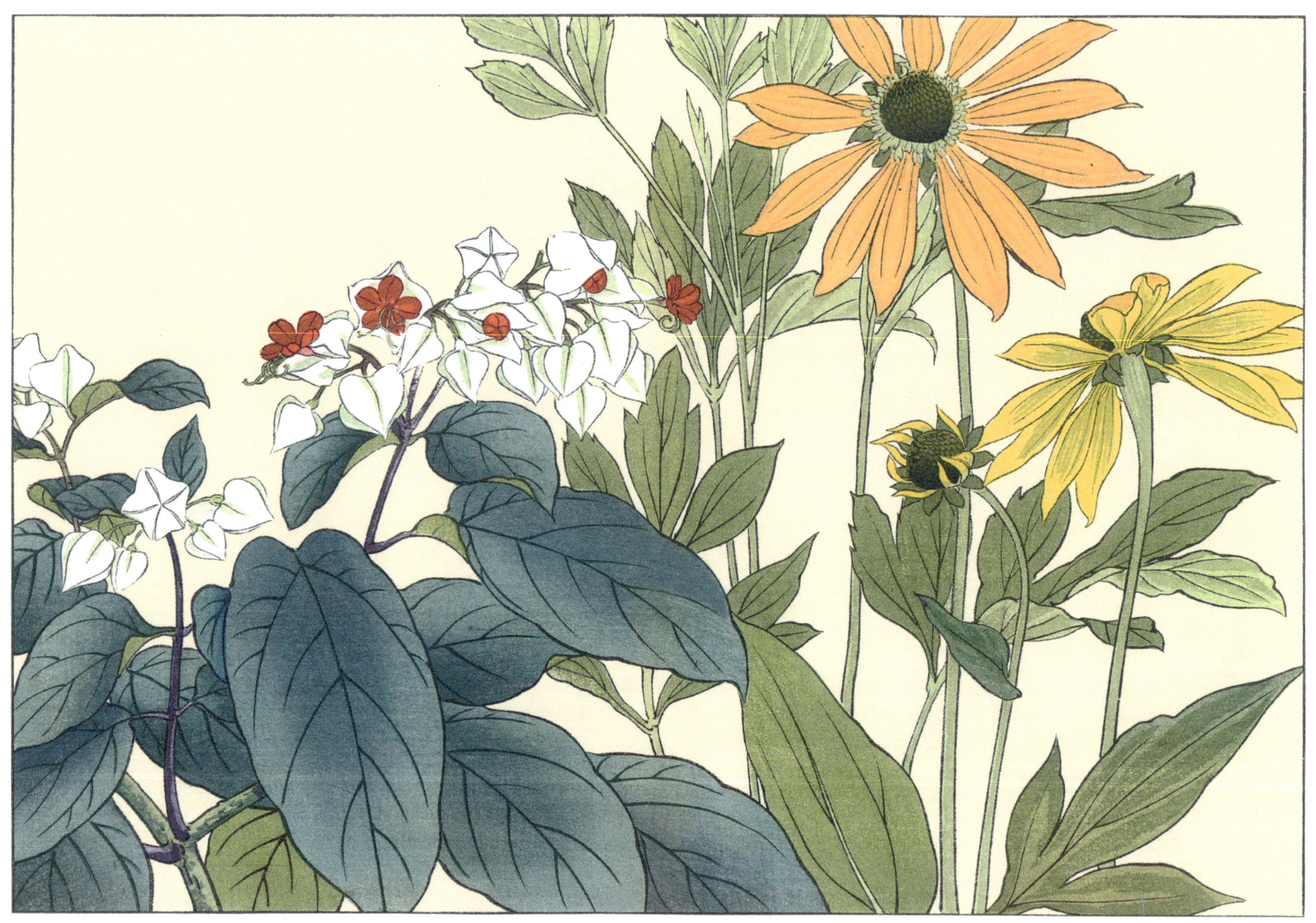

Rudbeckia (or Cone Flower) and Clerodendron

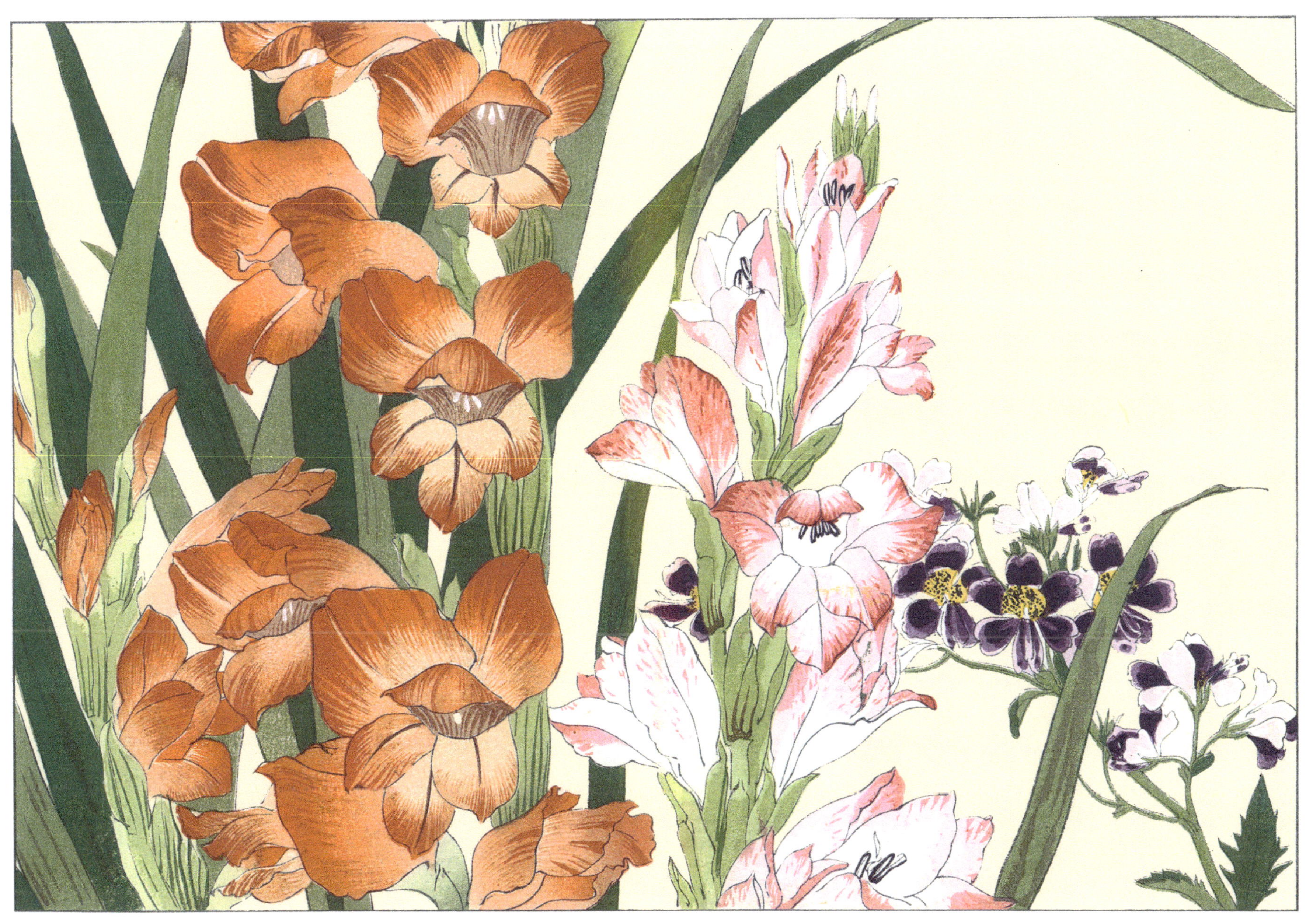

Schizanthus and Gladiolus

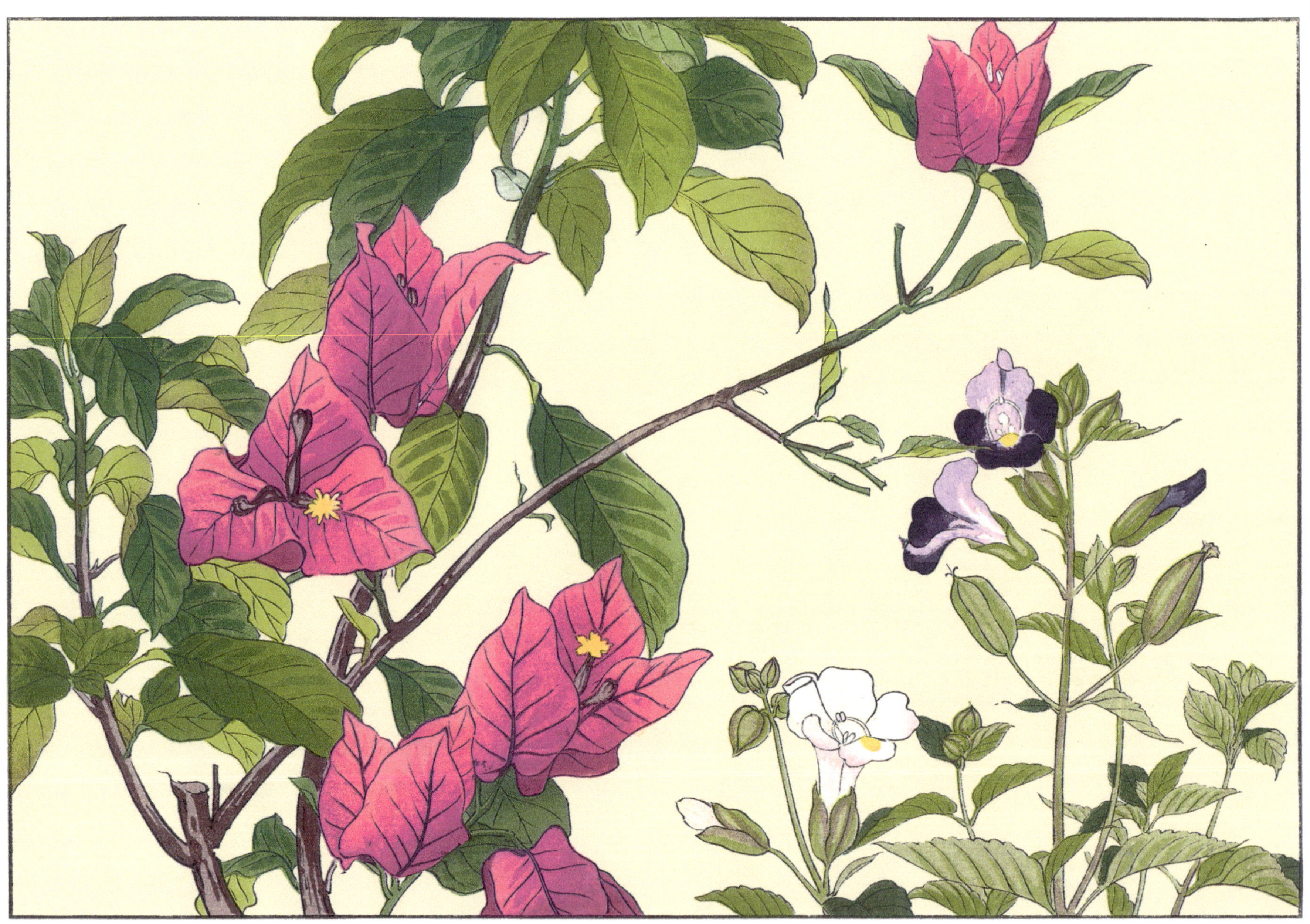

Torenia and Bougainvillea

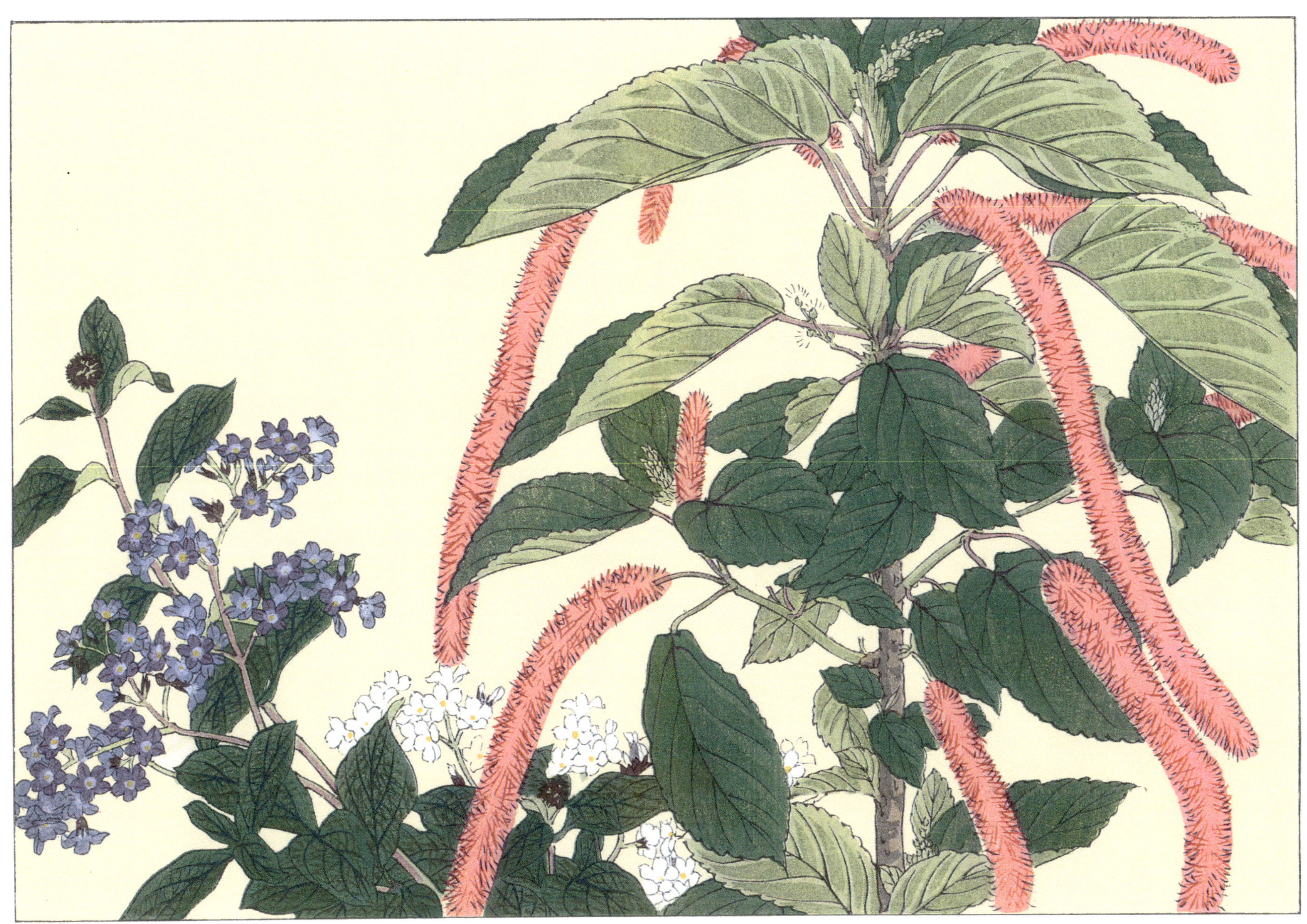

Acalypha (or Chenille Plant) and Heliotrope

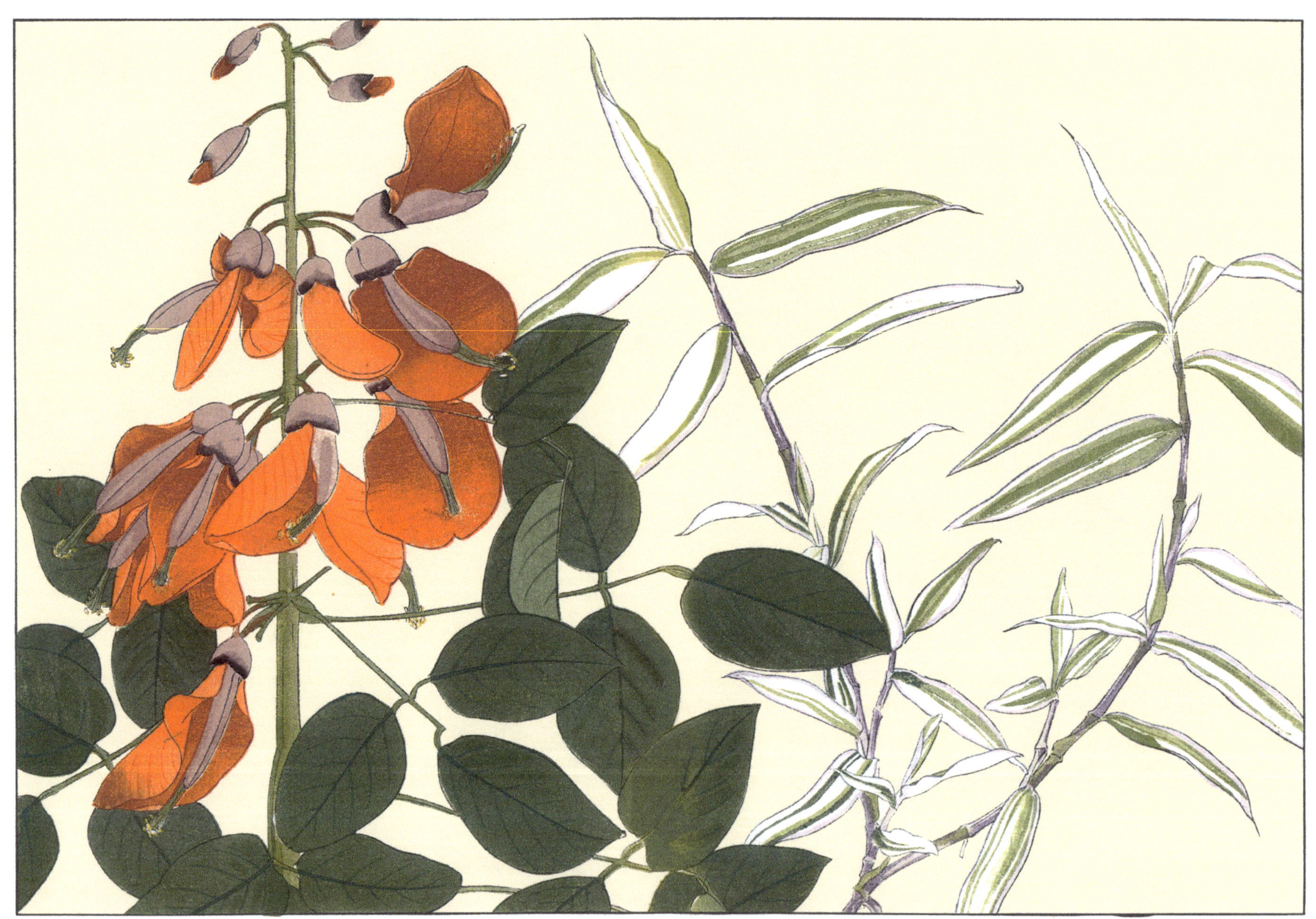

Panicum and Erythrina

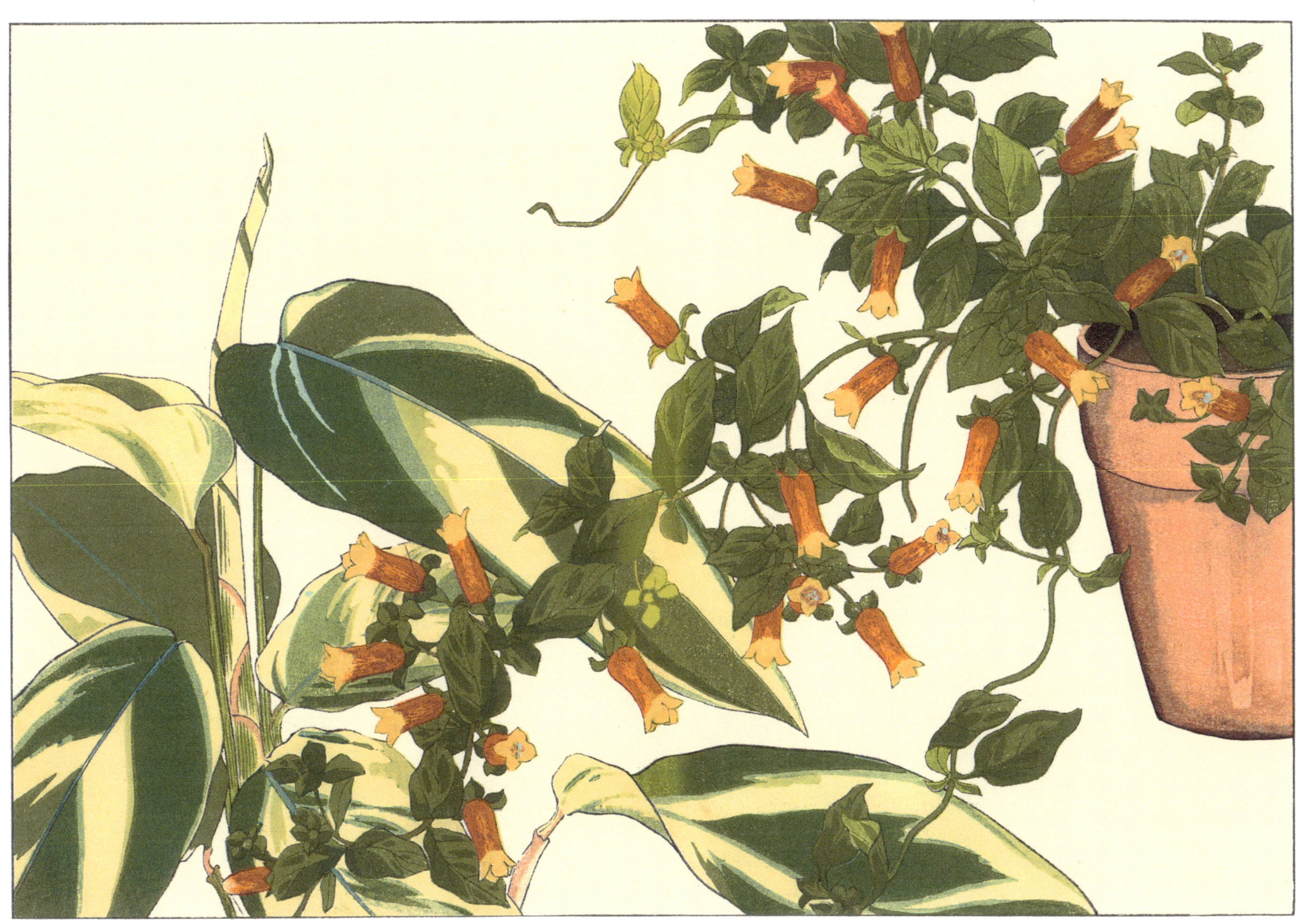

Manettia (or Firecracker Vine) and Maranta

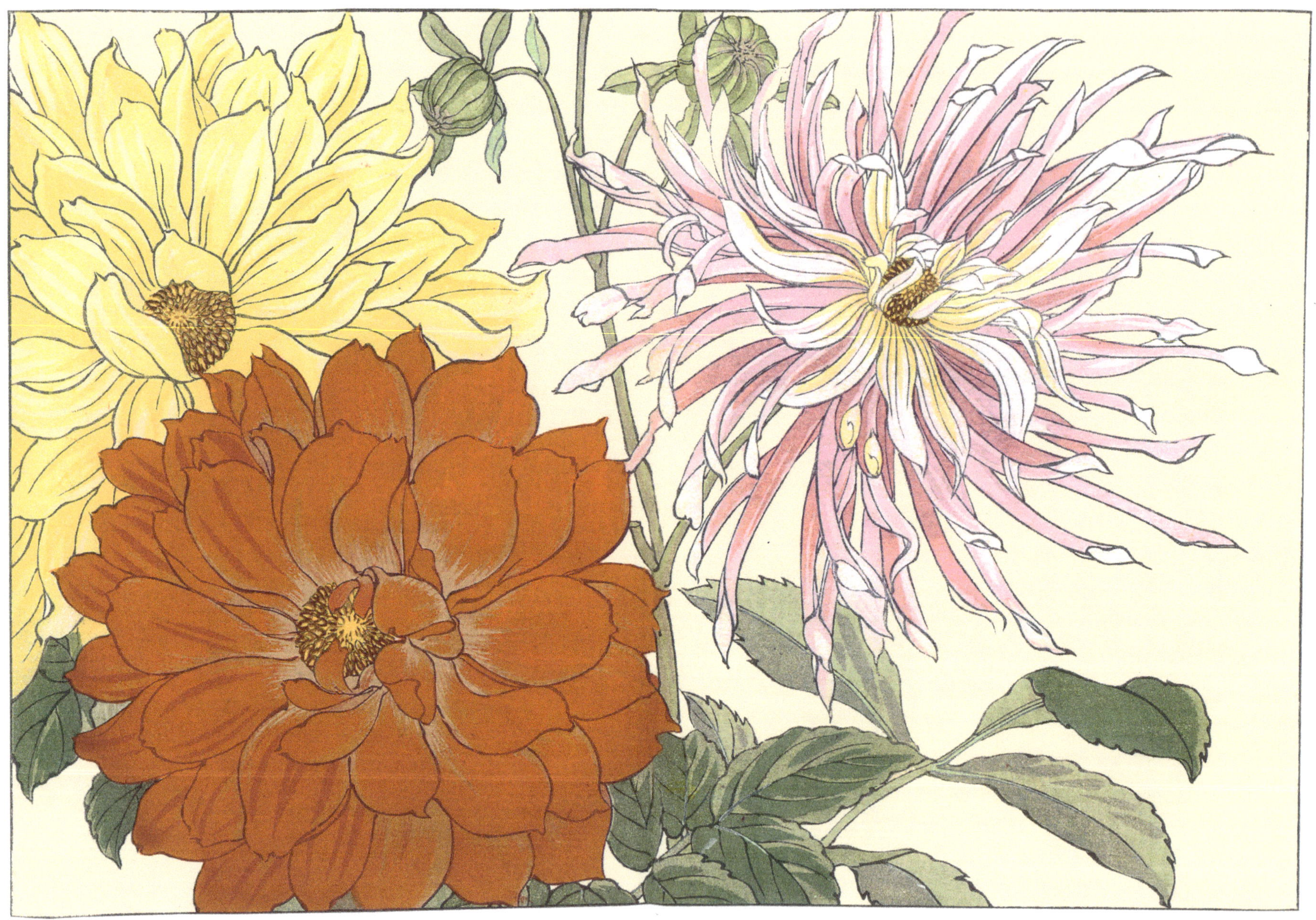

Dahlia

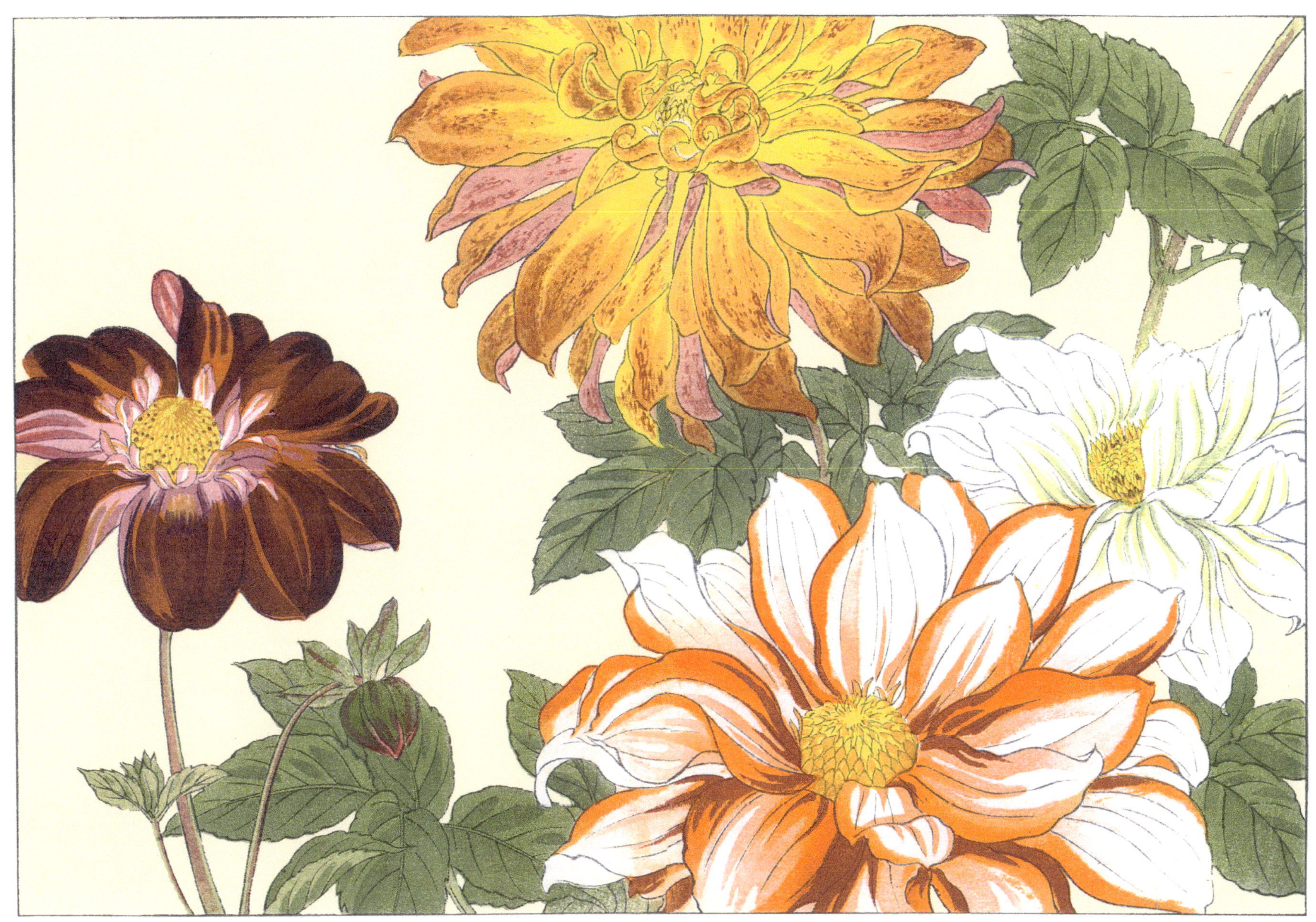

Dahlia

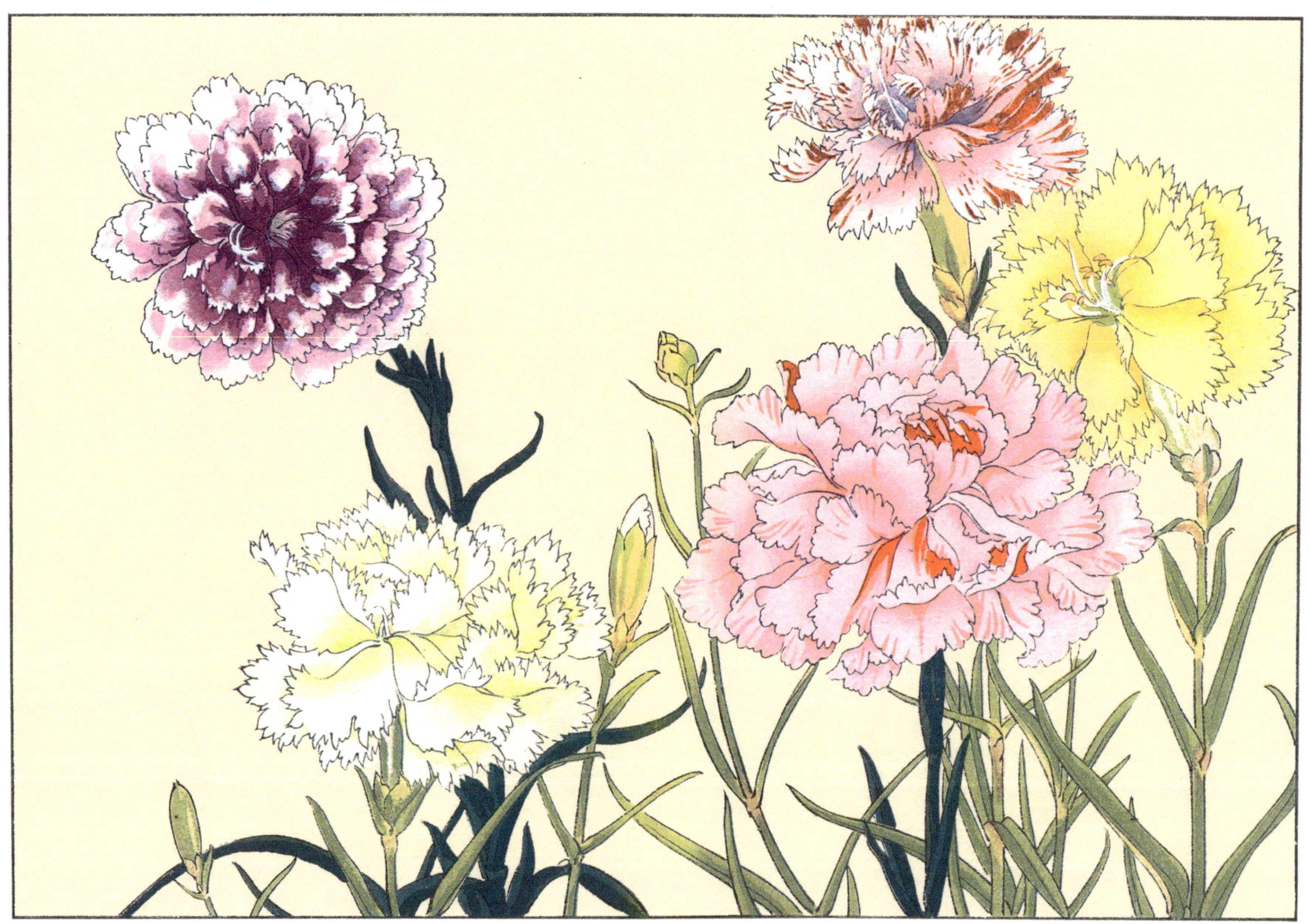

Carnation

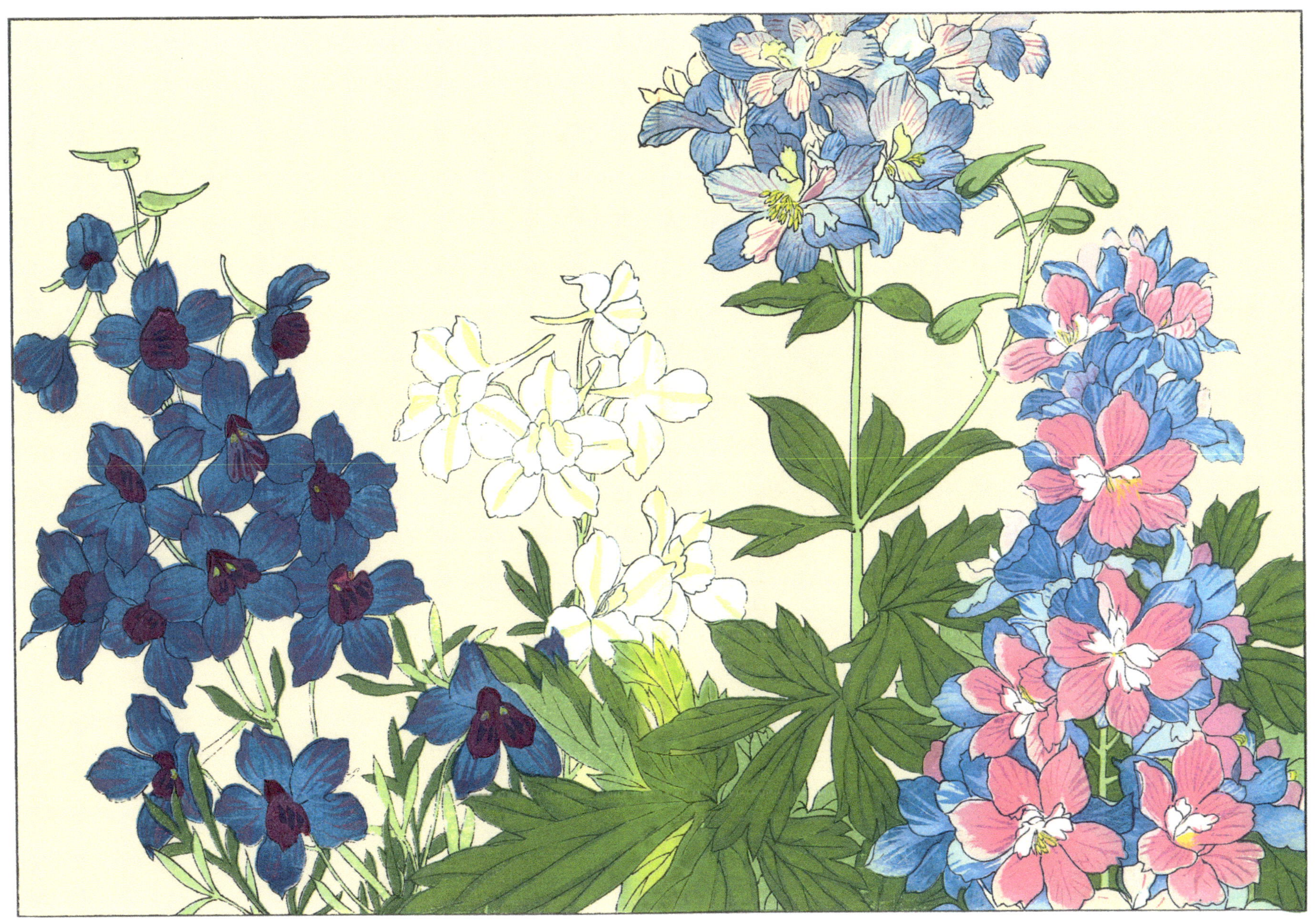

Delphinium

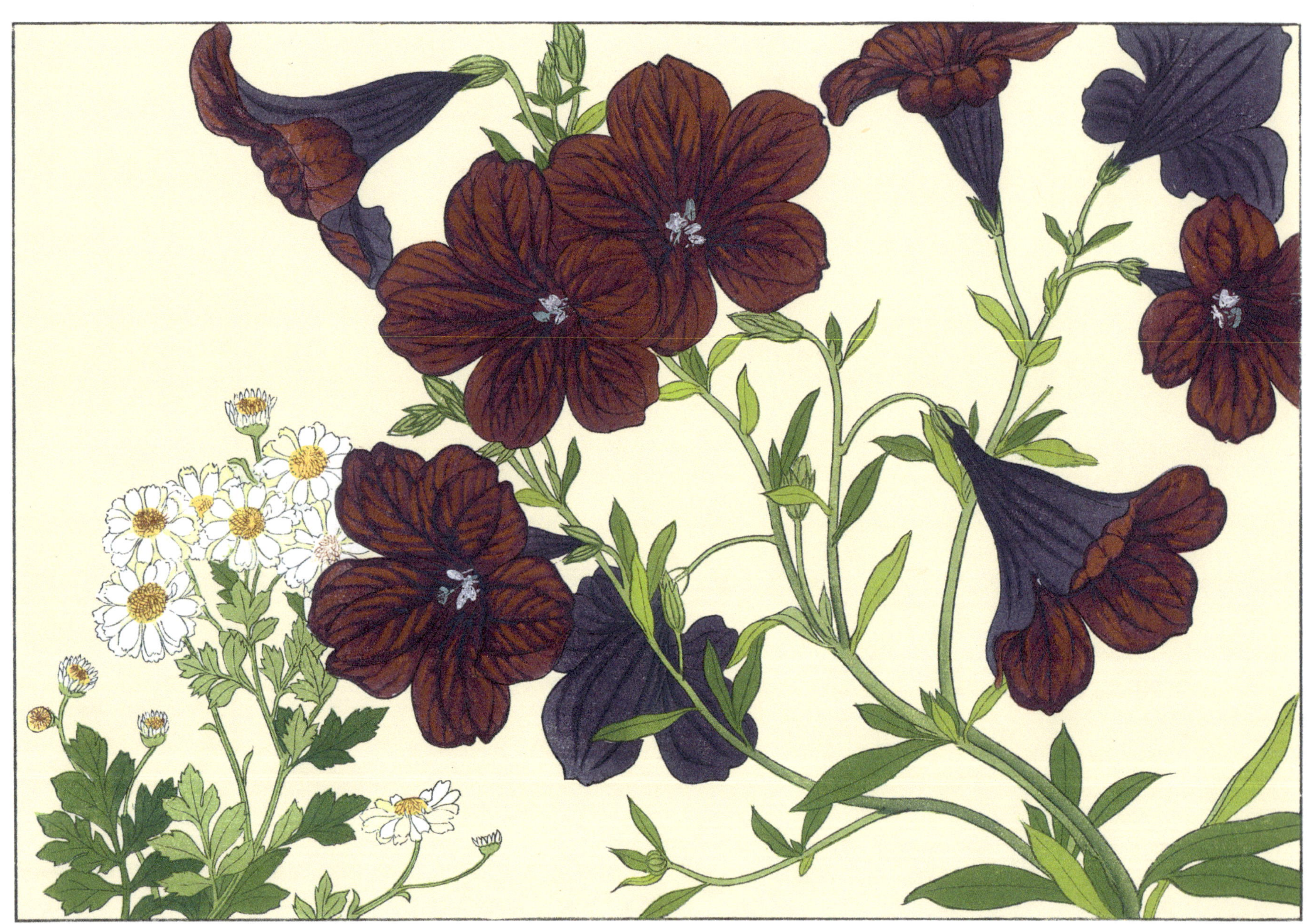

Salpiglossis and Matricaria

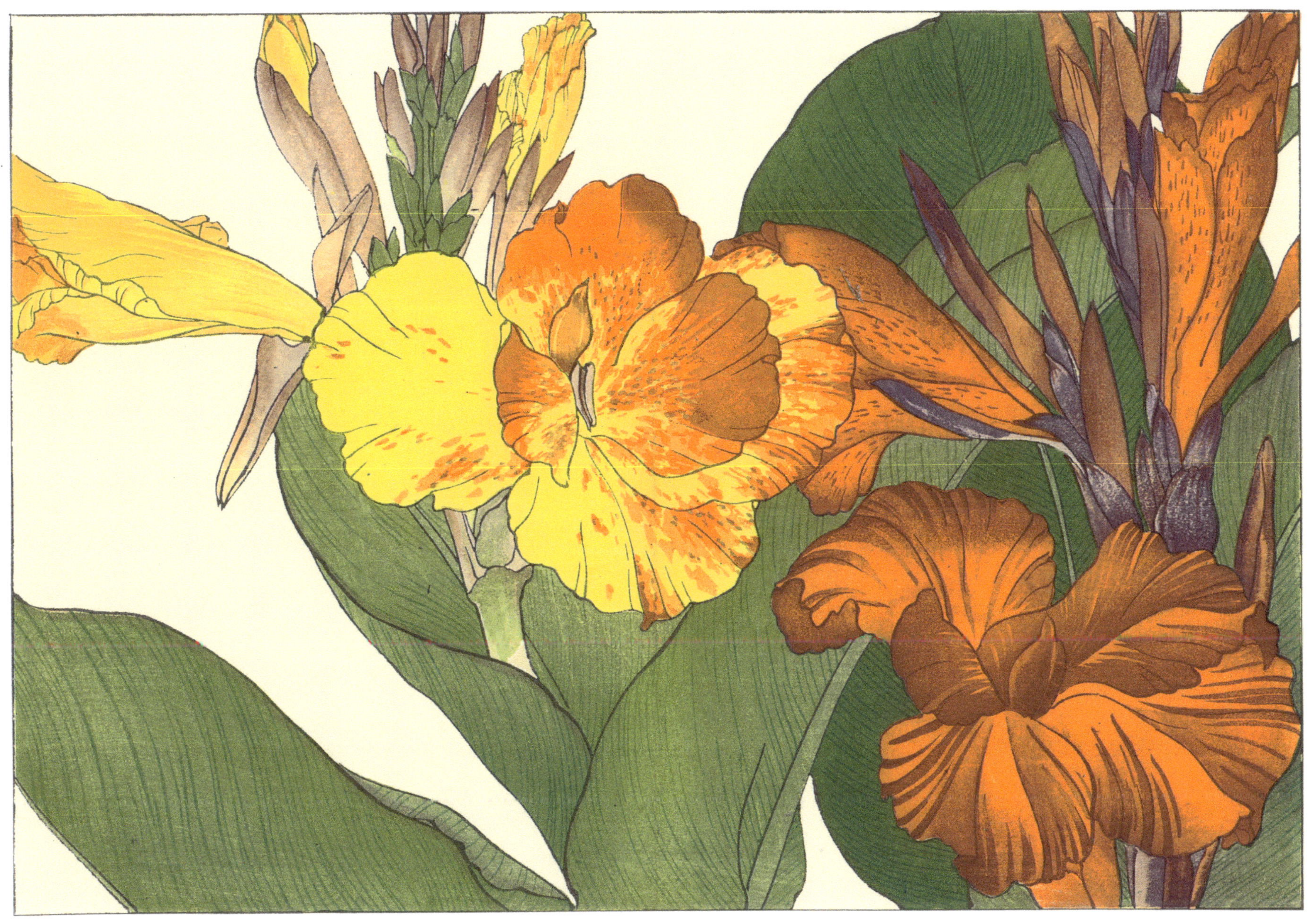

Canna

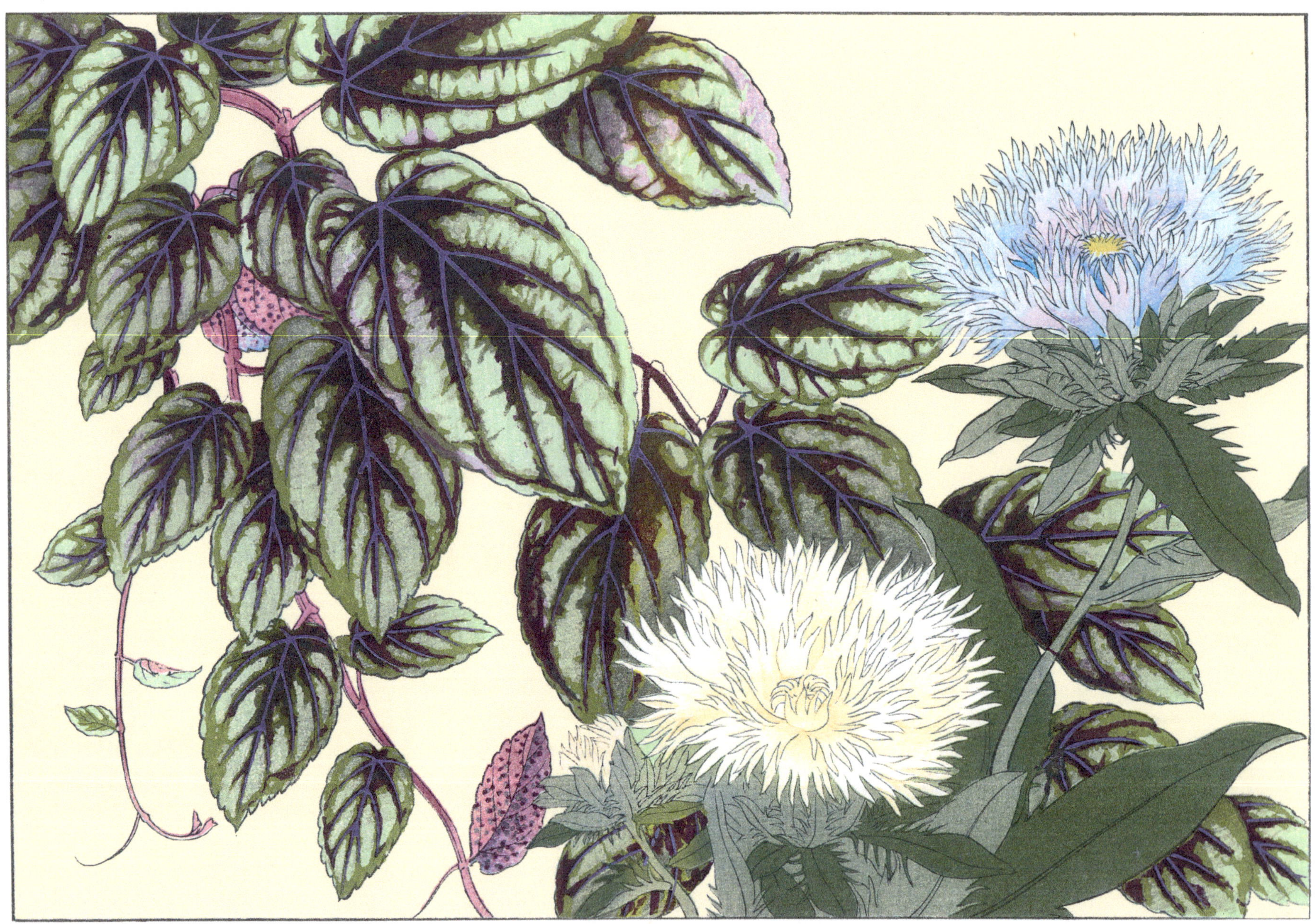

Stokesia and Vitis (or Grape)

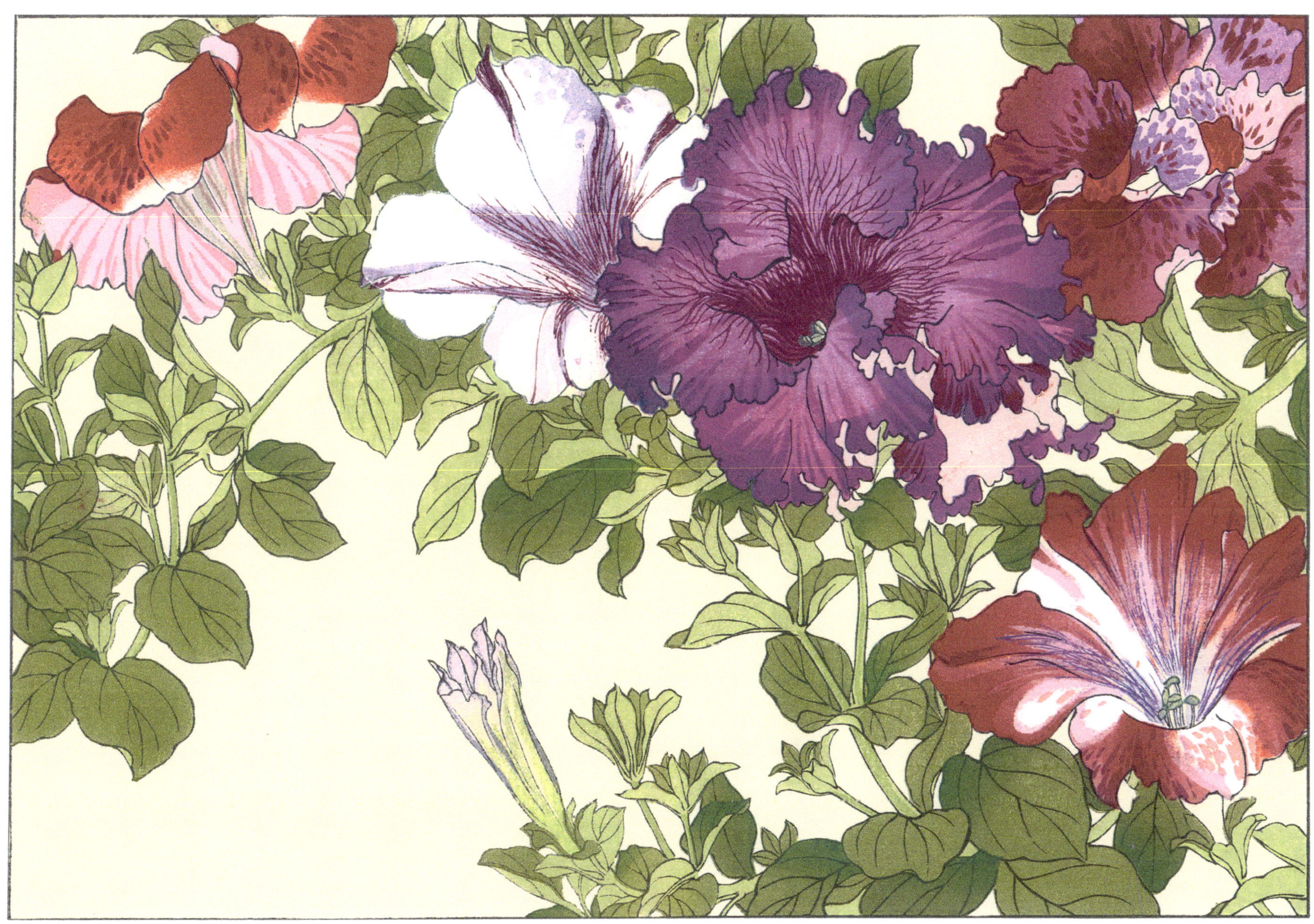

Petunia

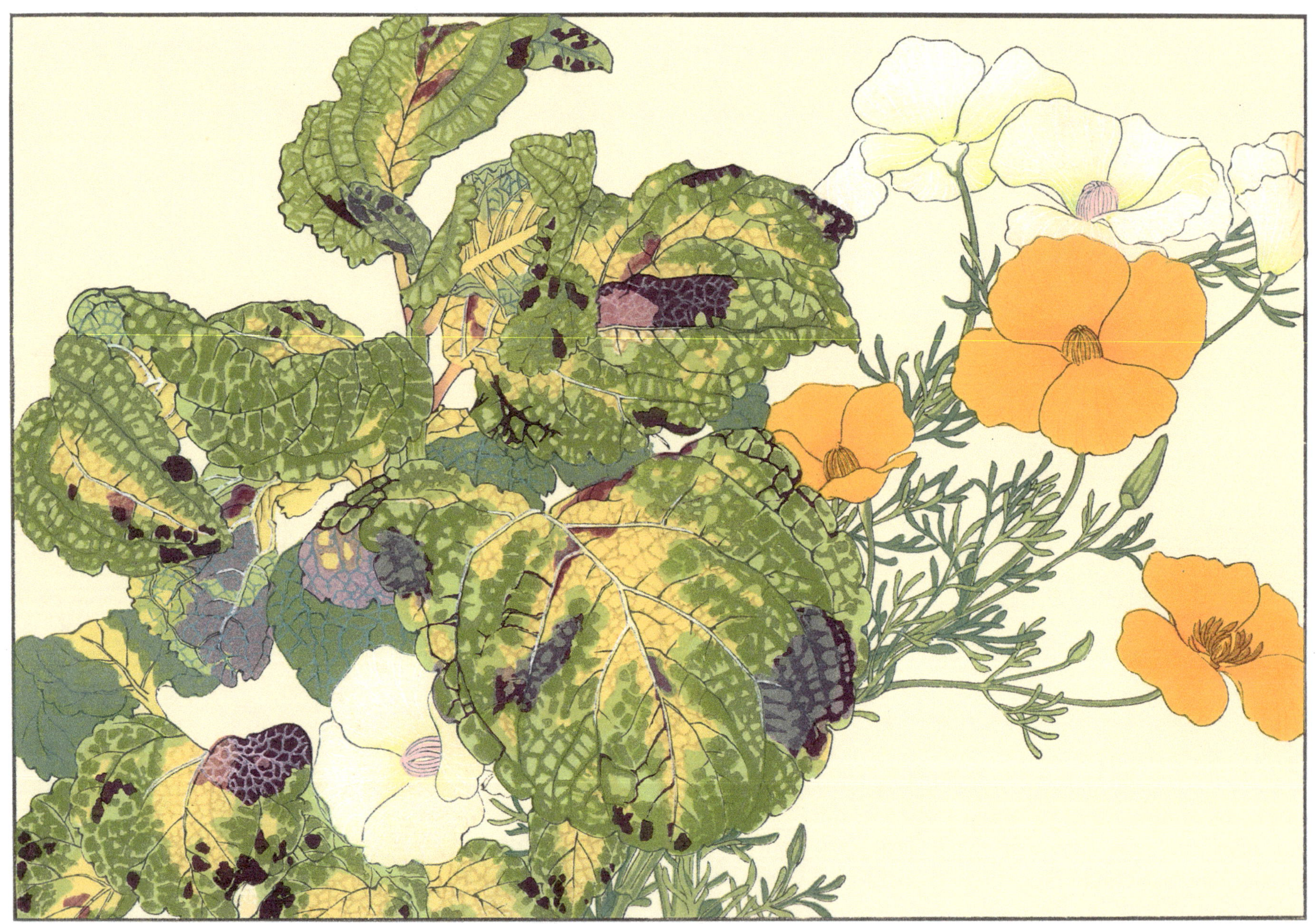

California Poppy and Coleus

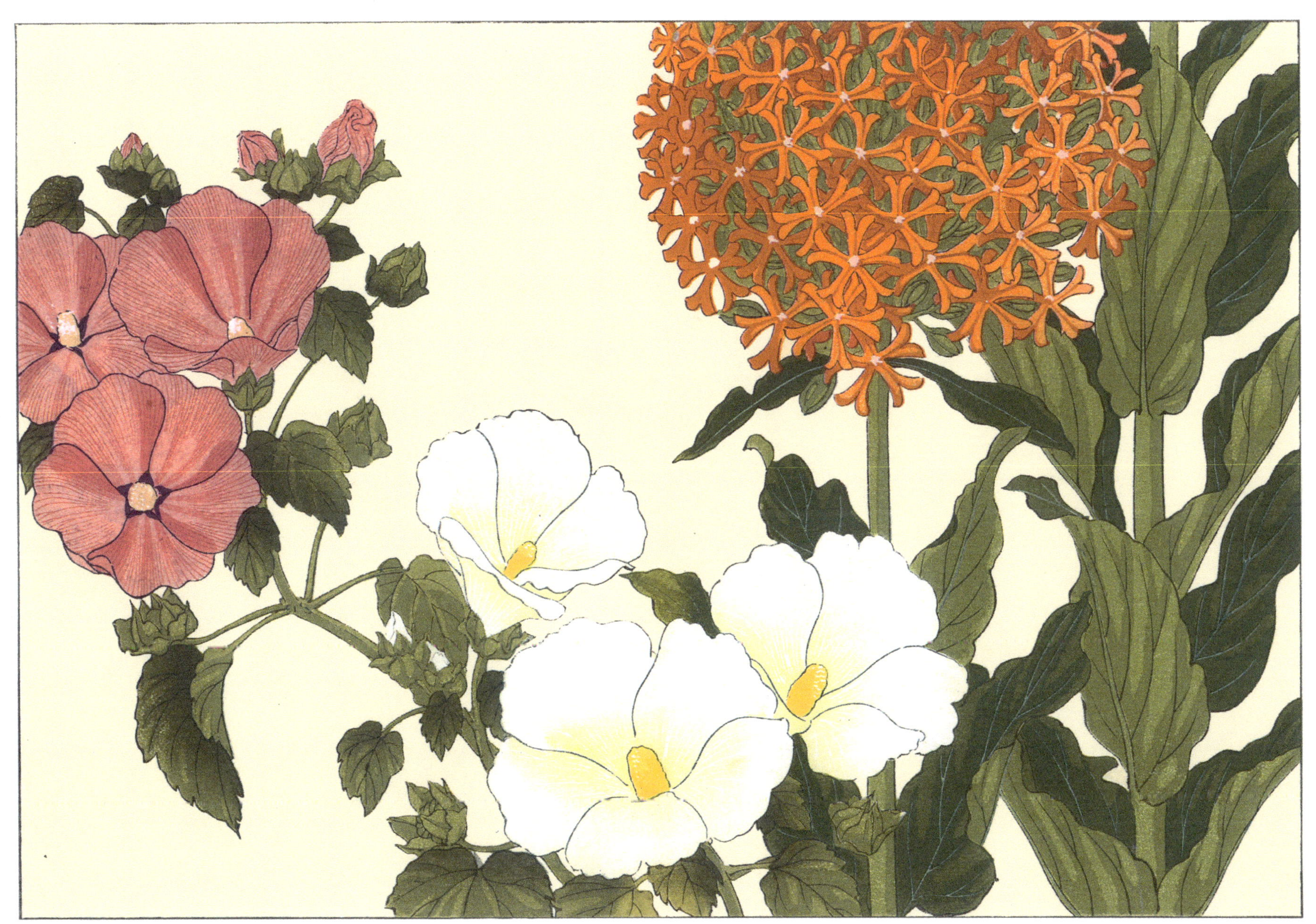

Lychnis and Mallow

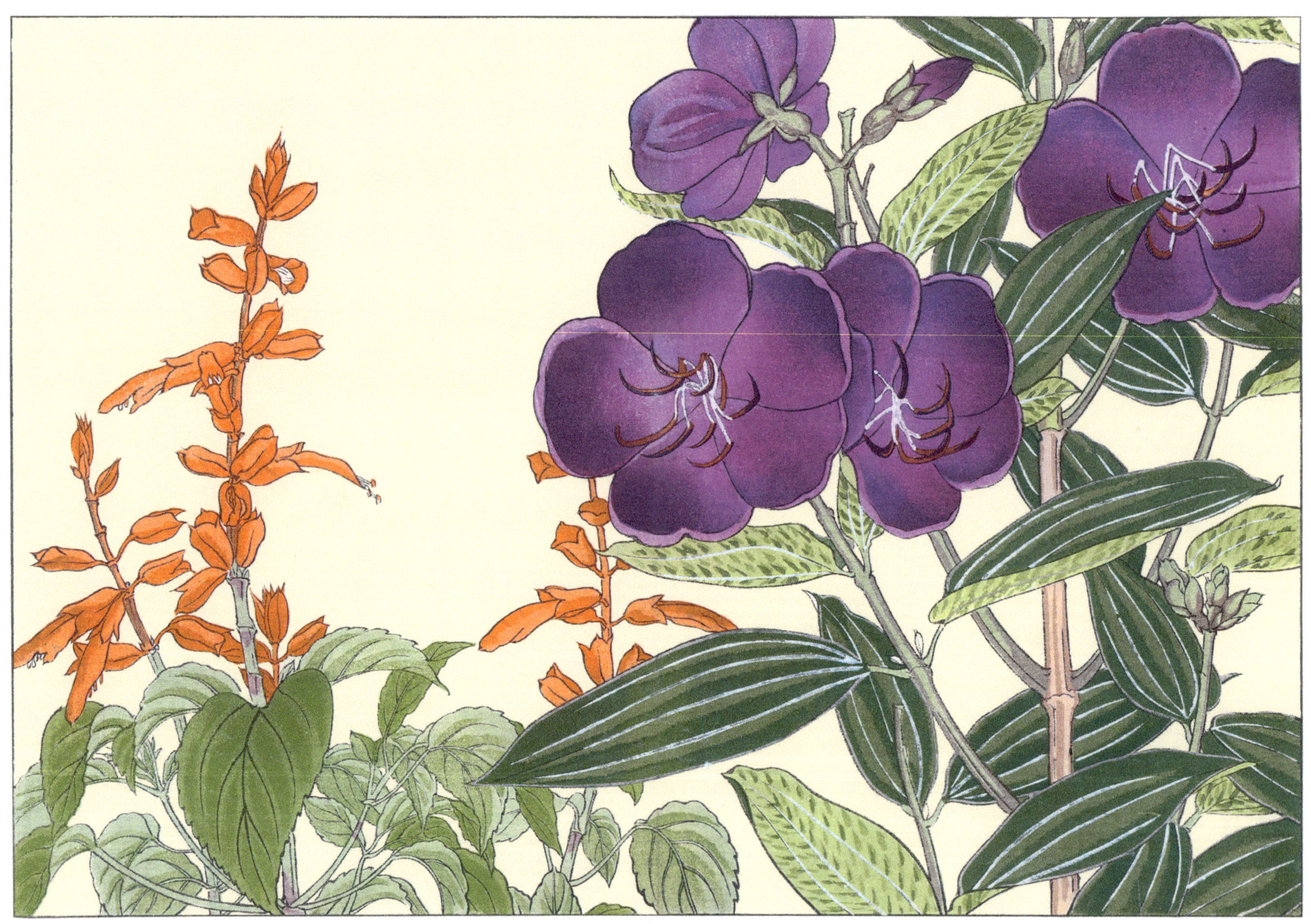

Melastoma and Salvia

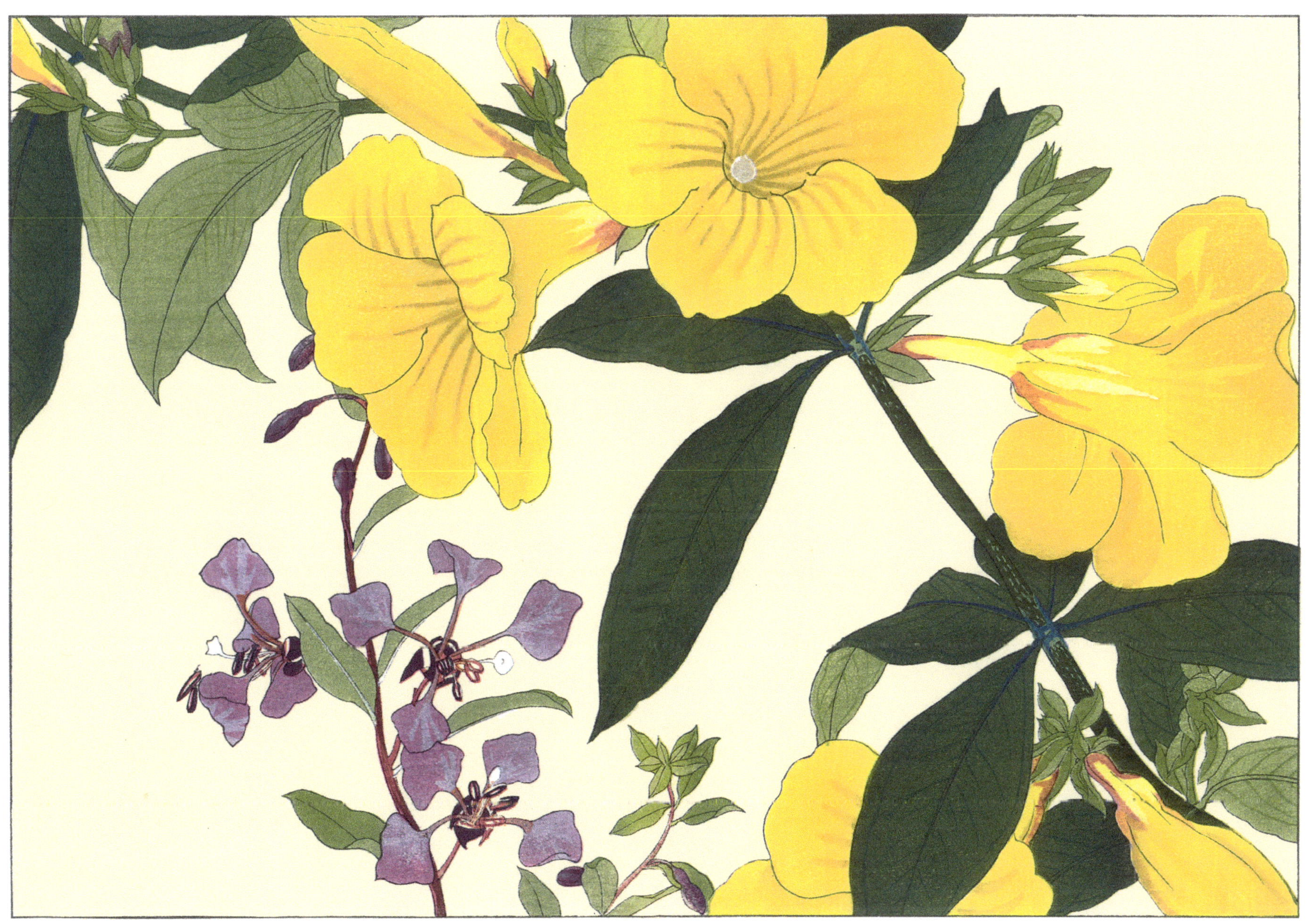

Allamanda and Clarkia

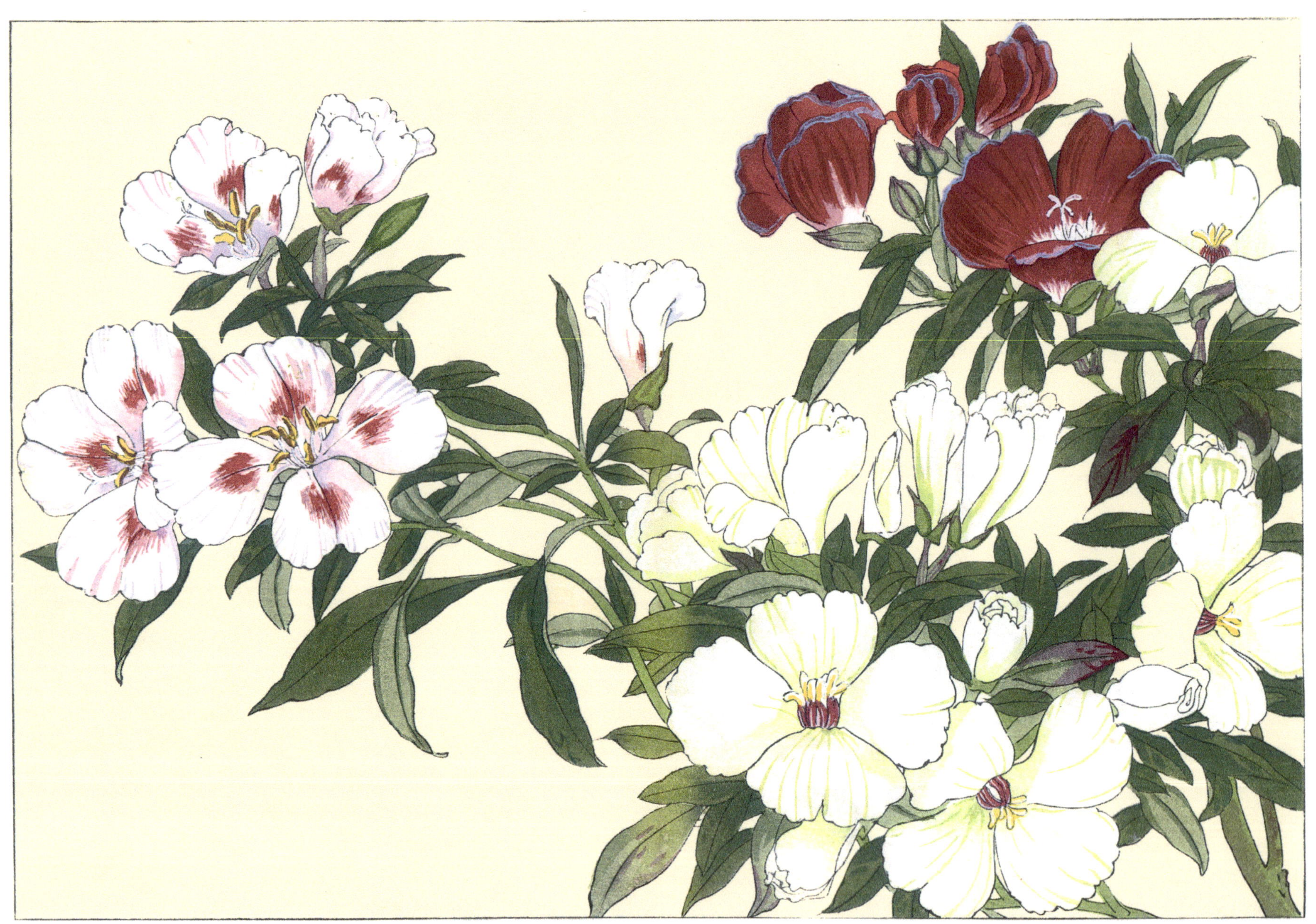

Godetia

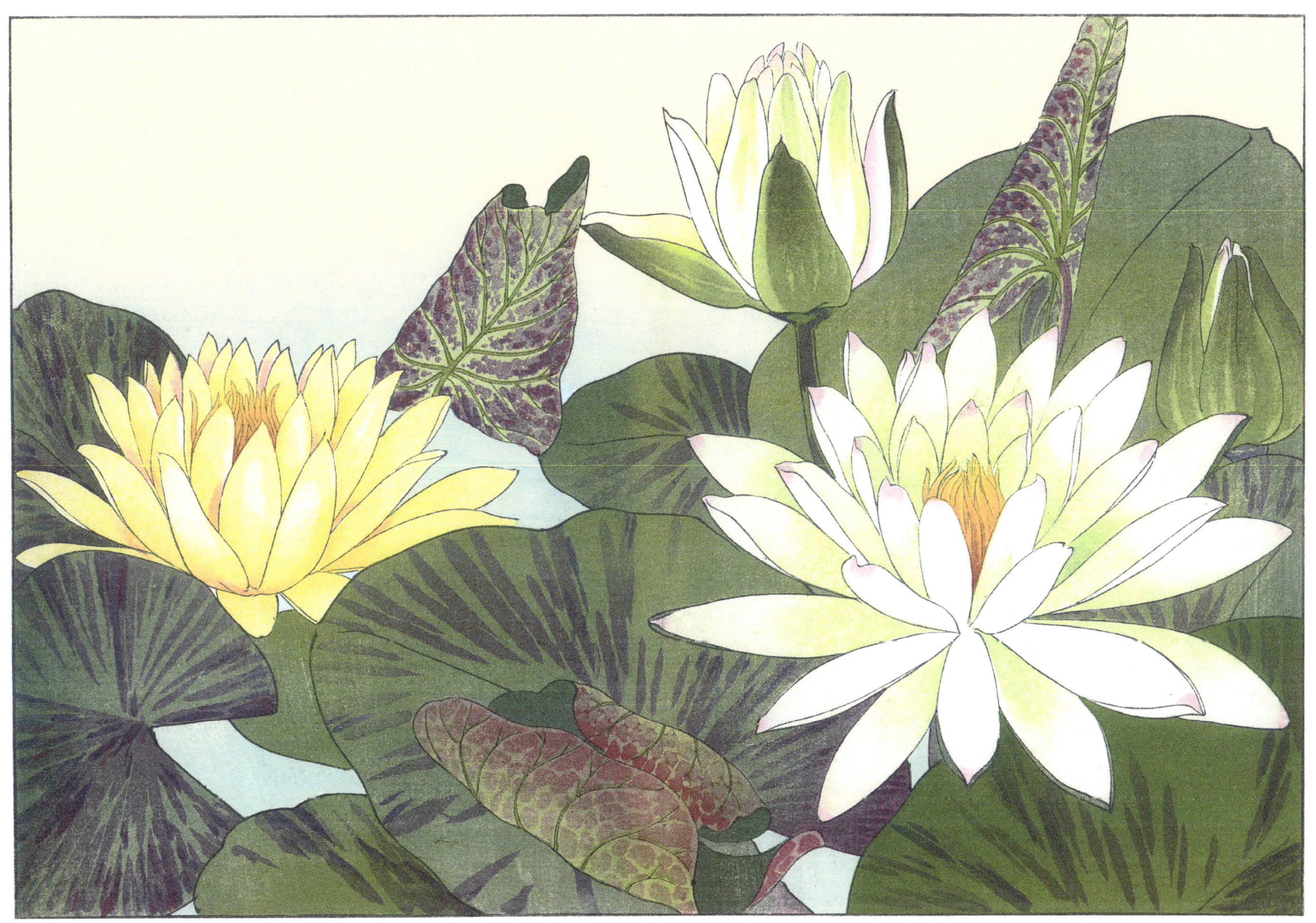

Water Lily

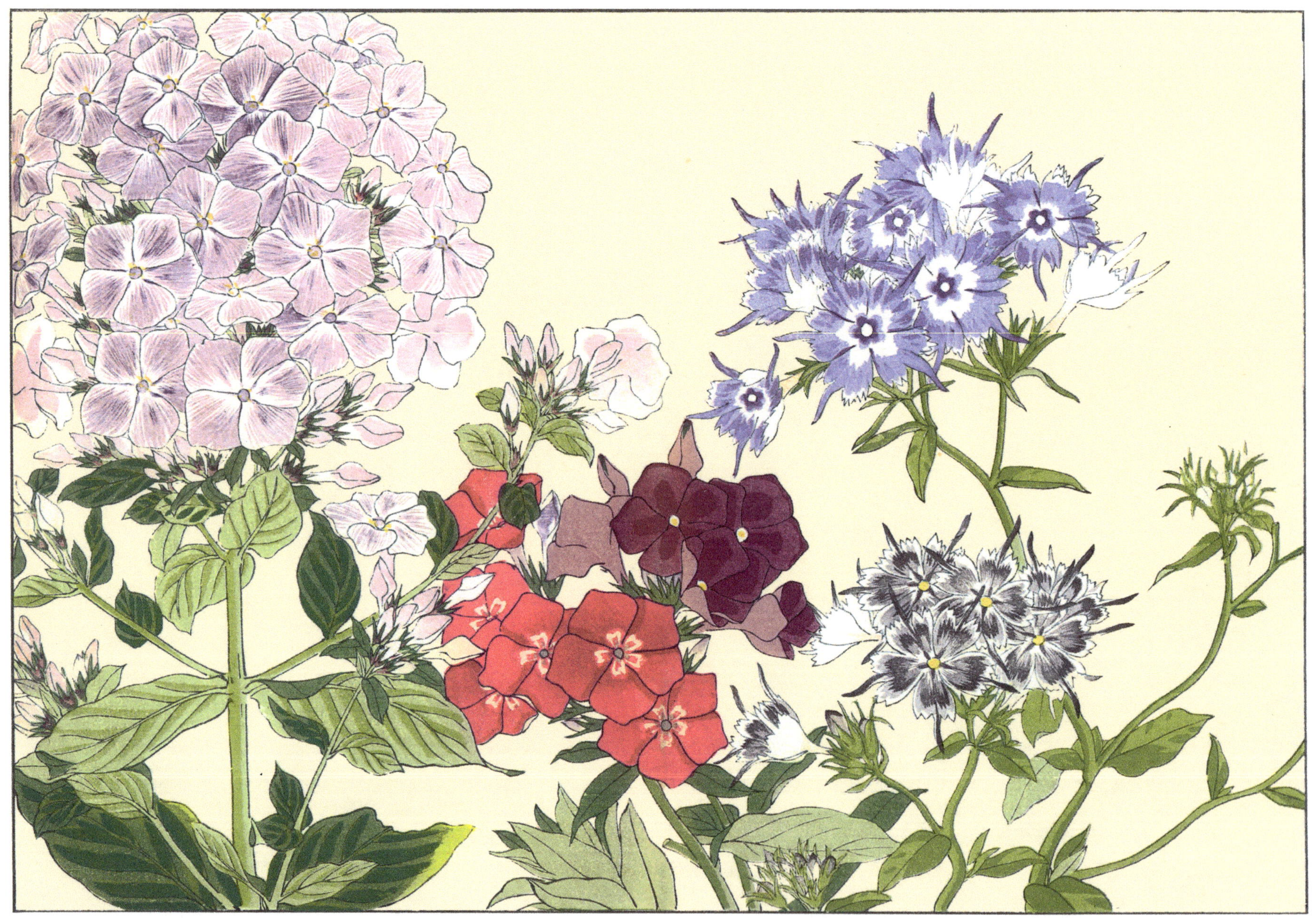

Phlox

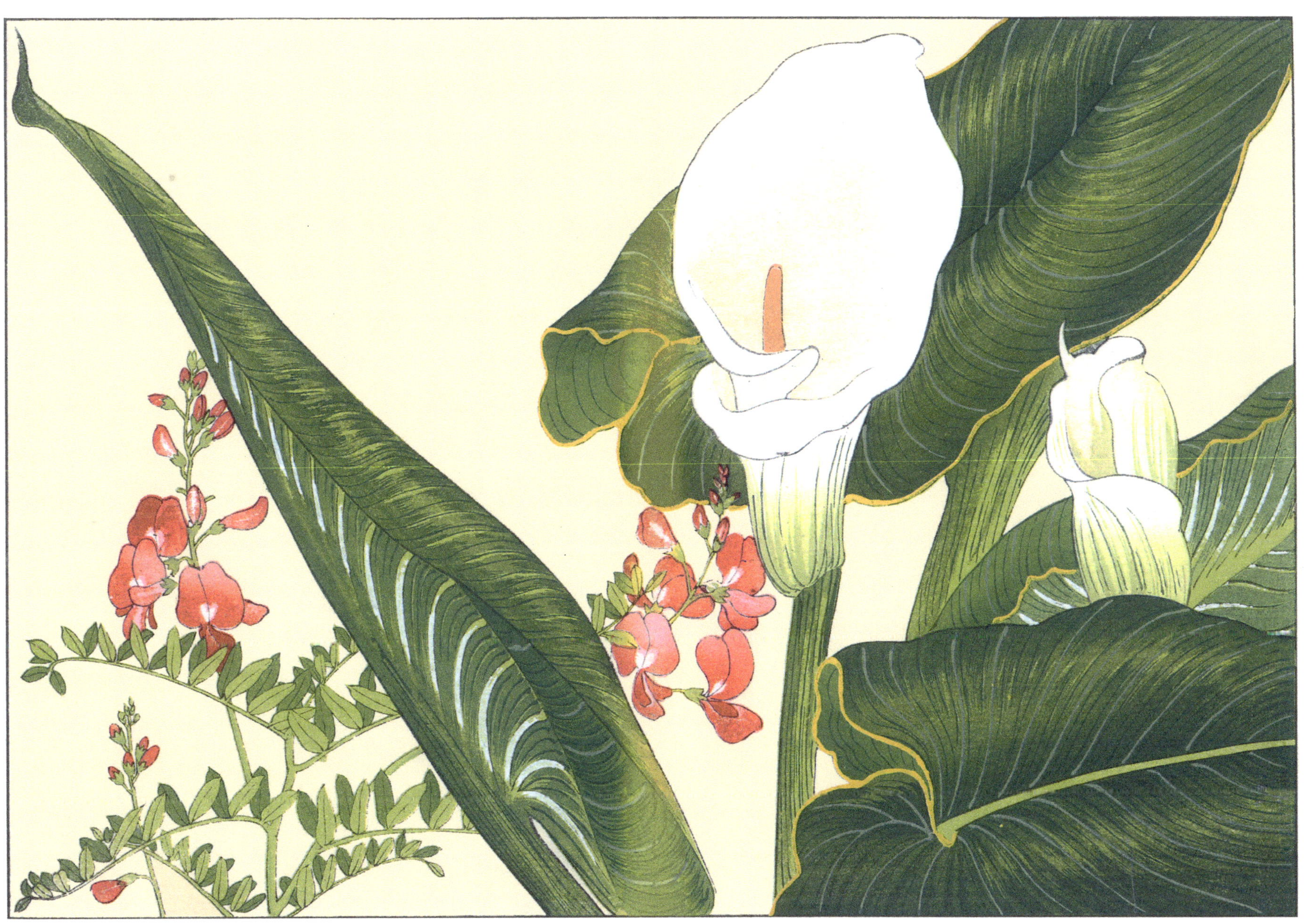

Calla and Lathyrus

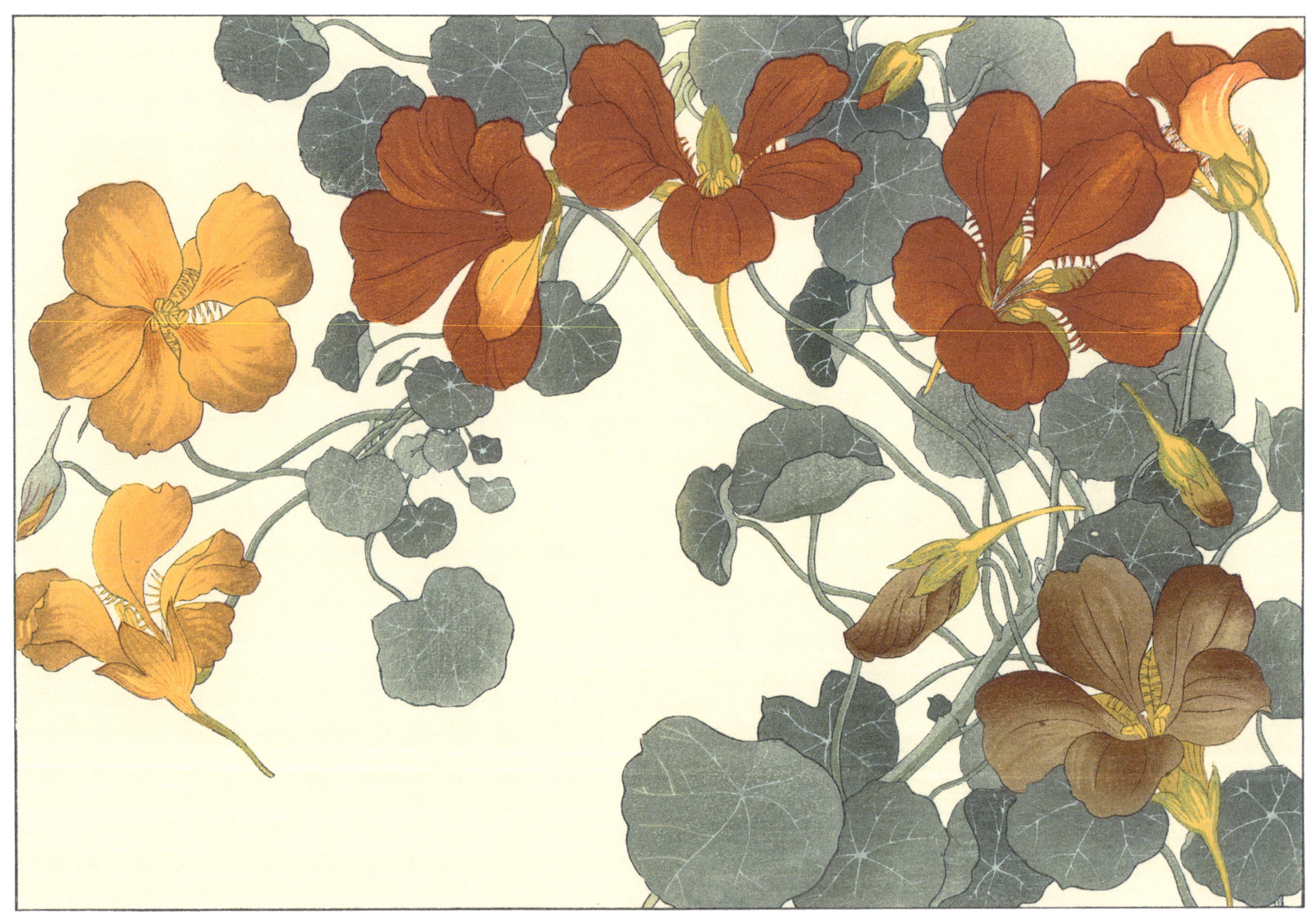

Nasturtium

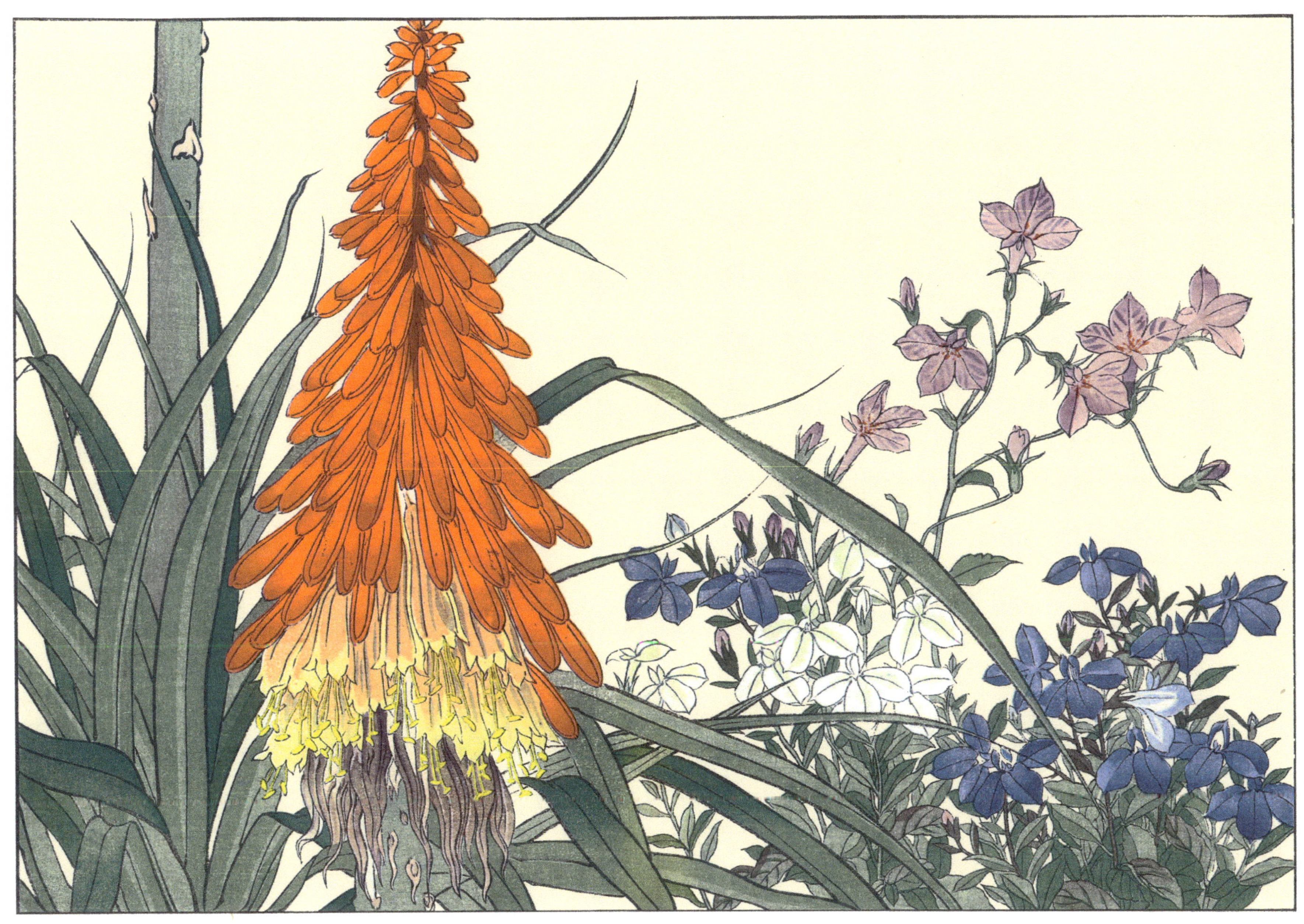

Lobelia and Tritoma (or Red-Hot Poker)

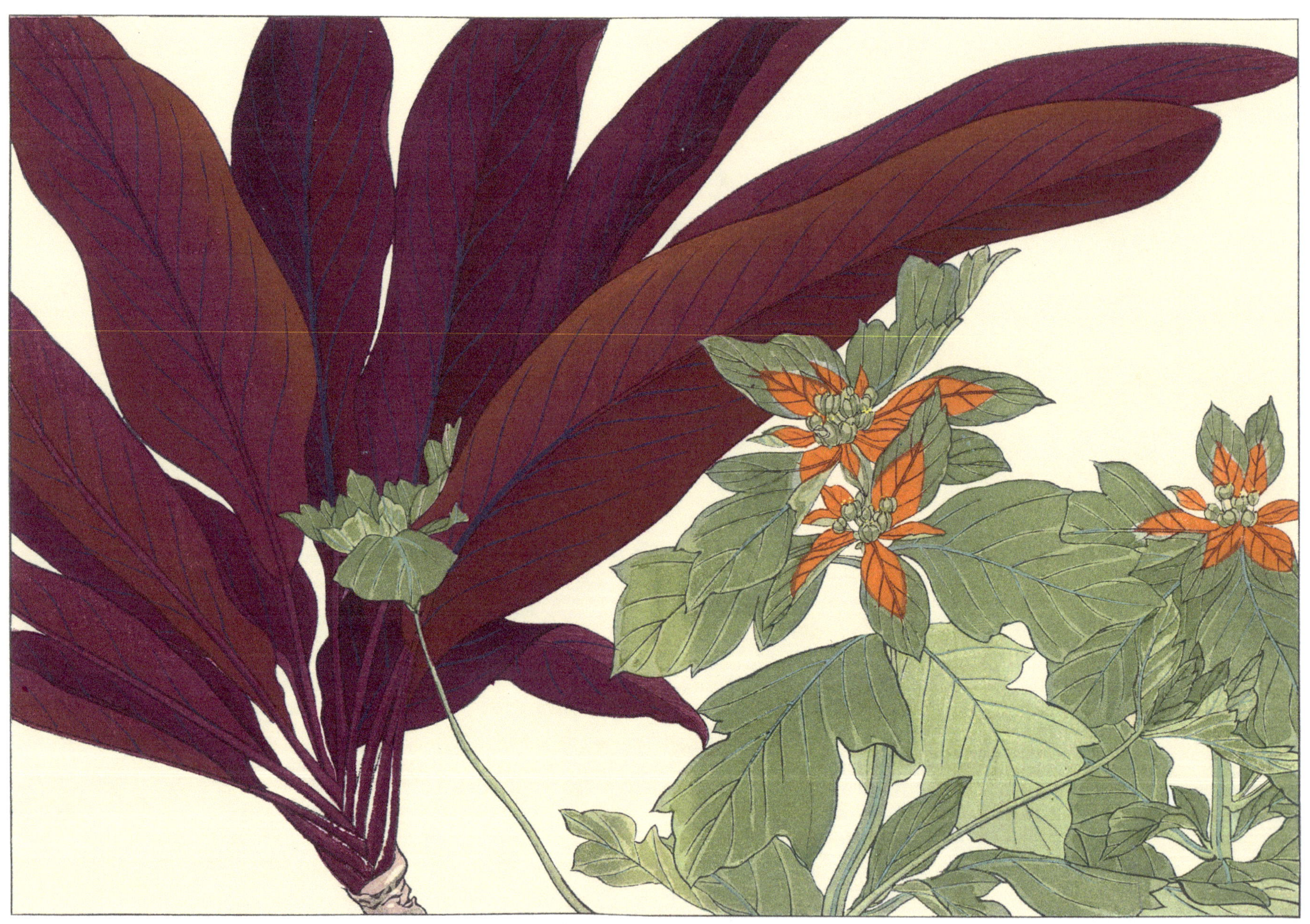

Poinsettia and Dracaena

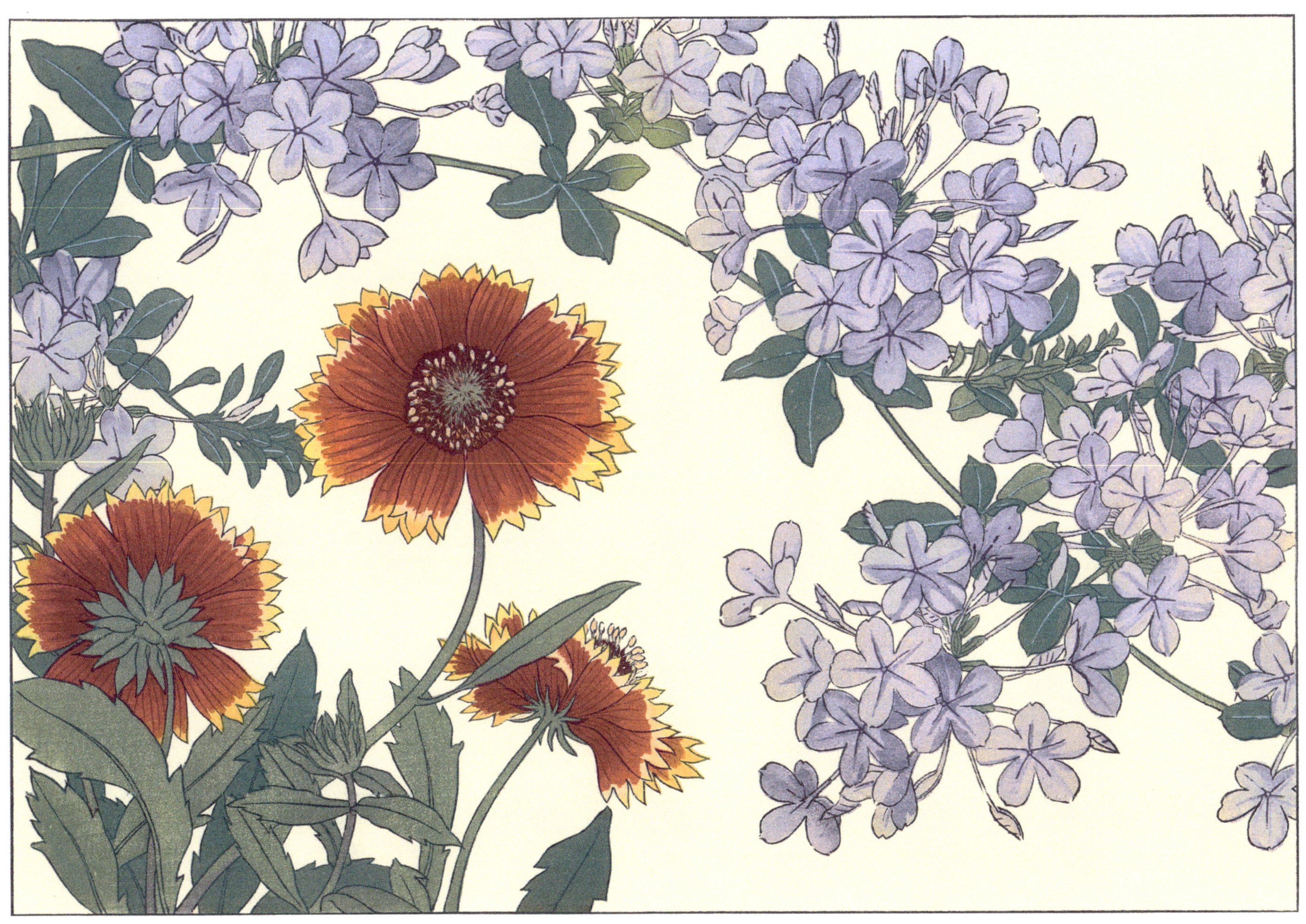

Plumbago and Gaillardia

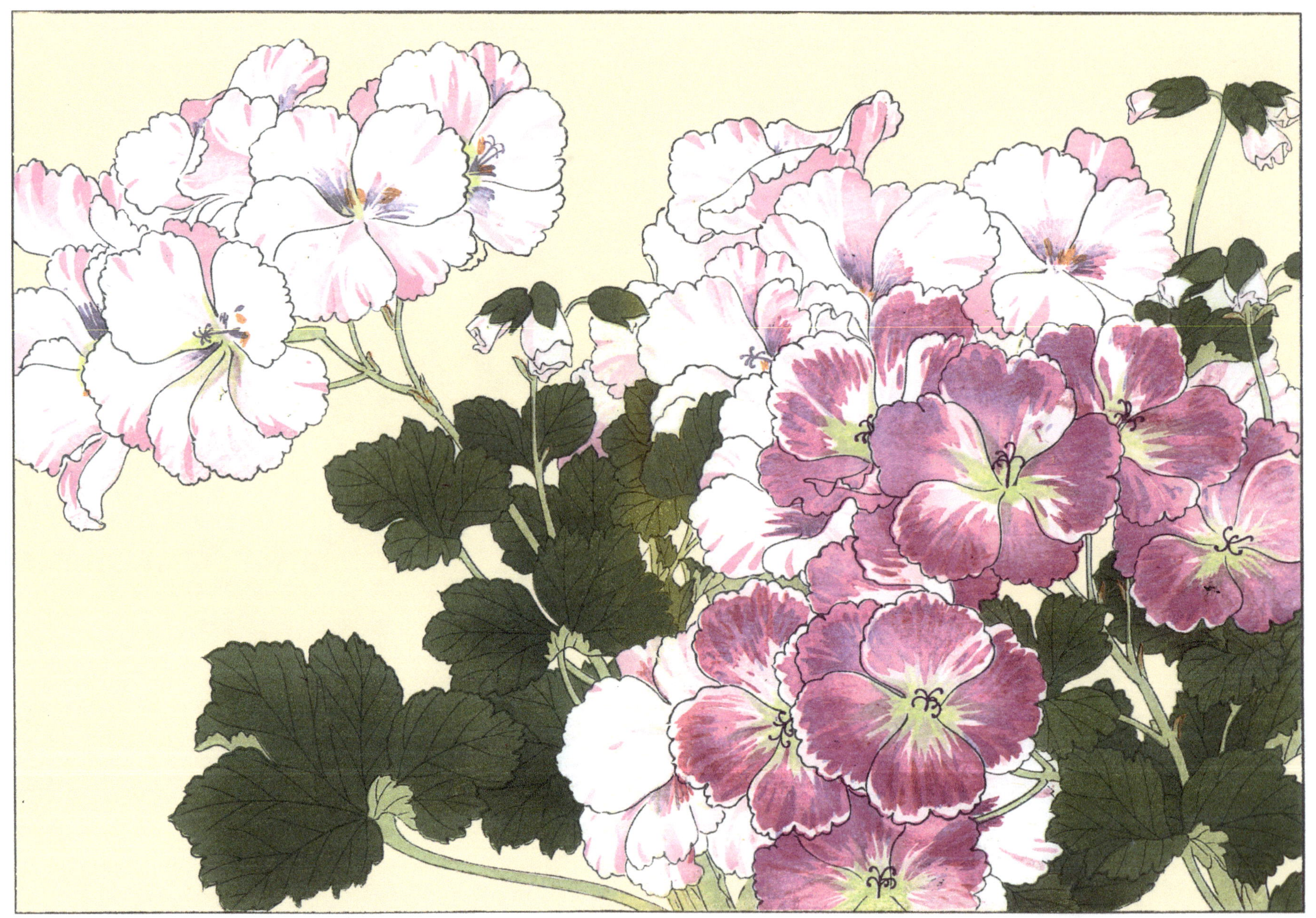

Pelargonium

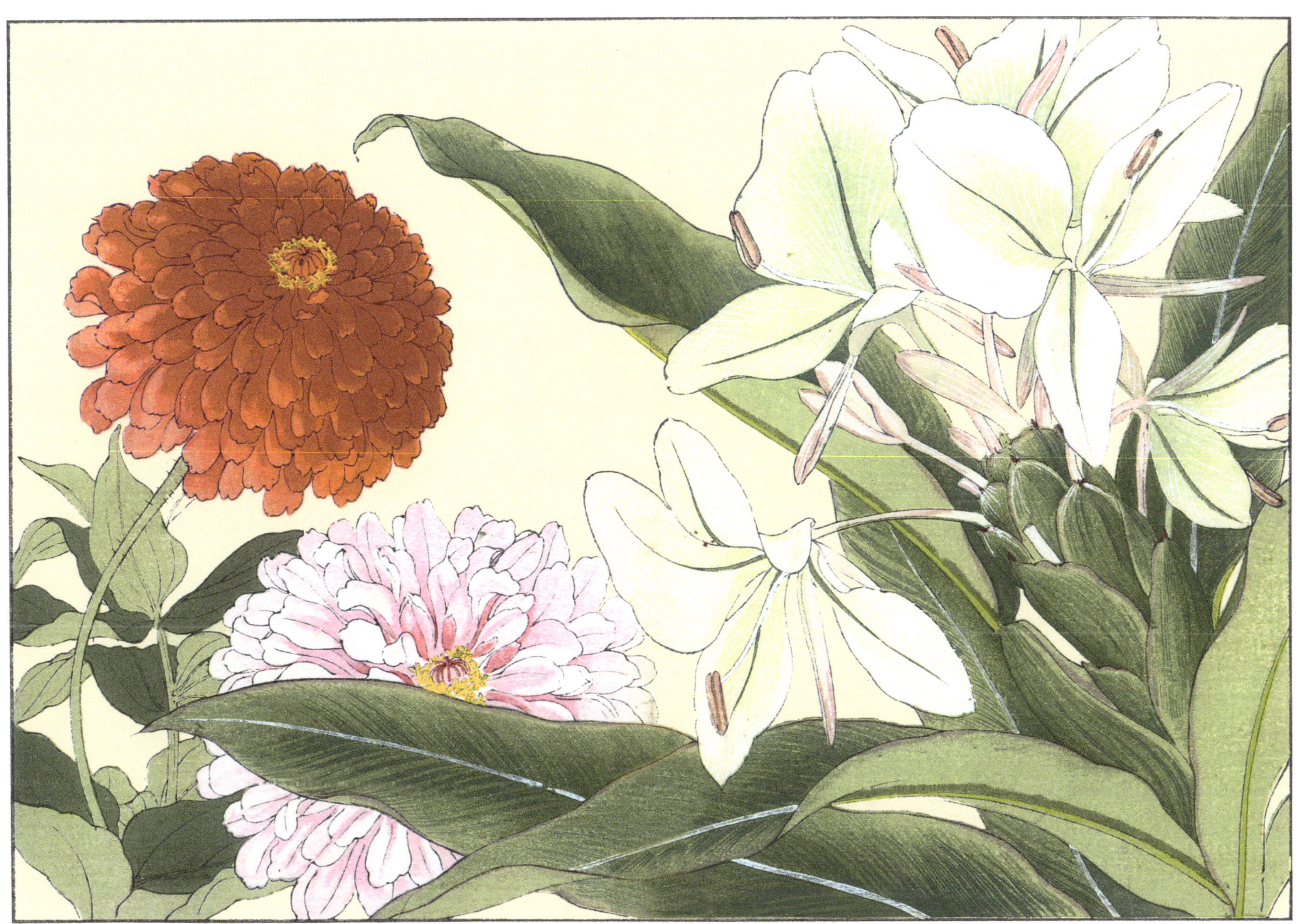

Ginger and Zinnia

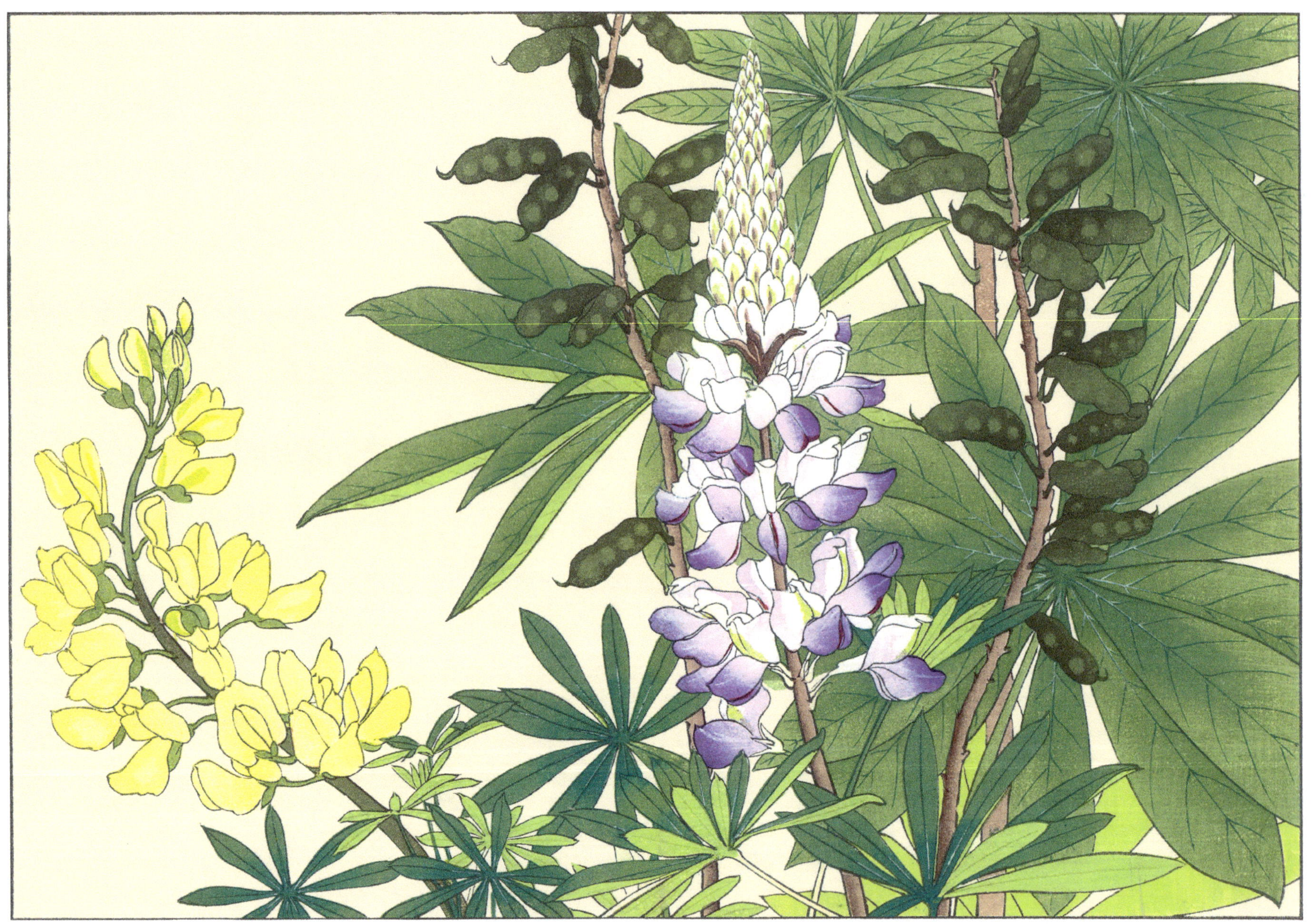

Lupine

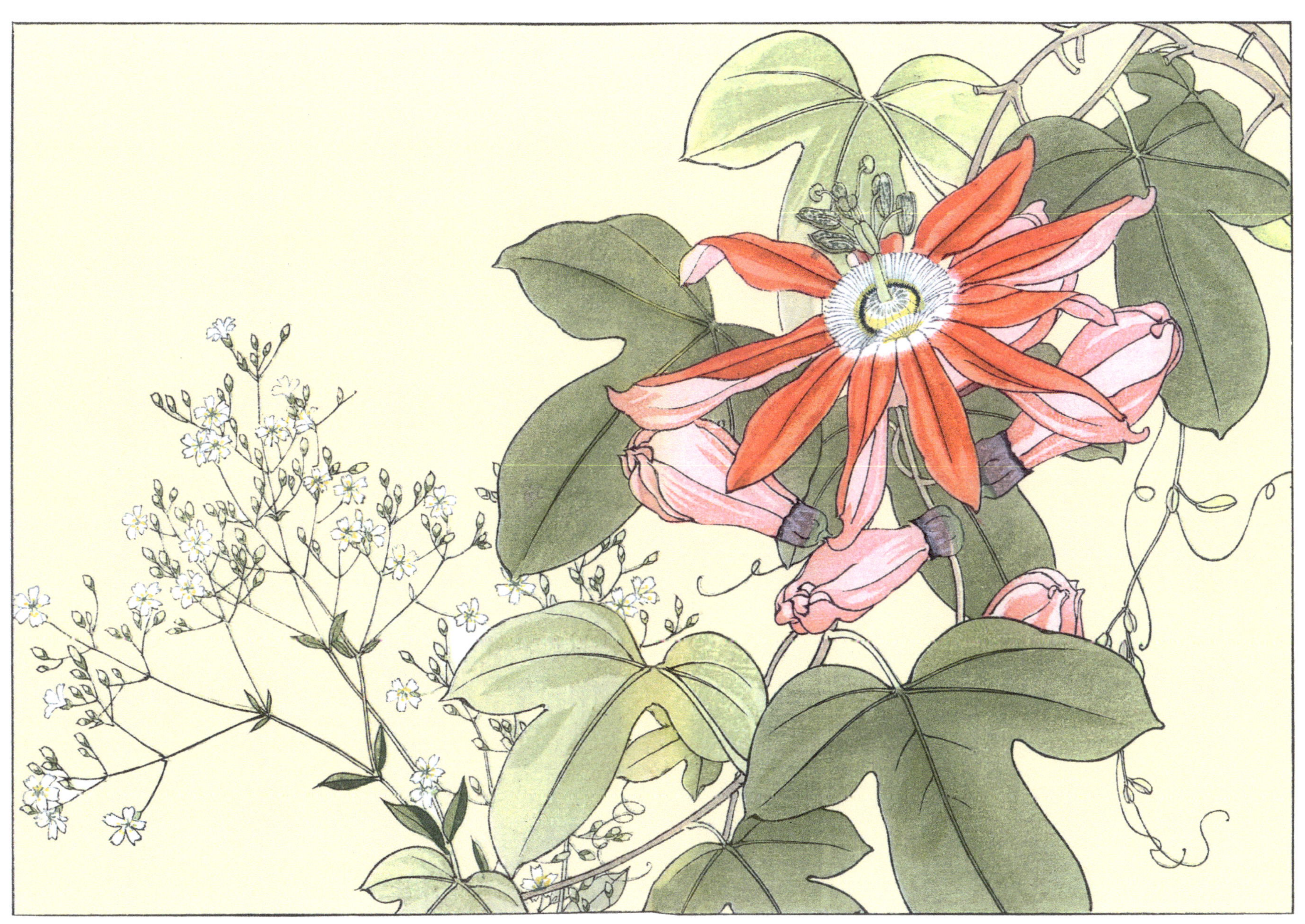

Passion Flower and Gypsophilia

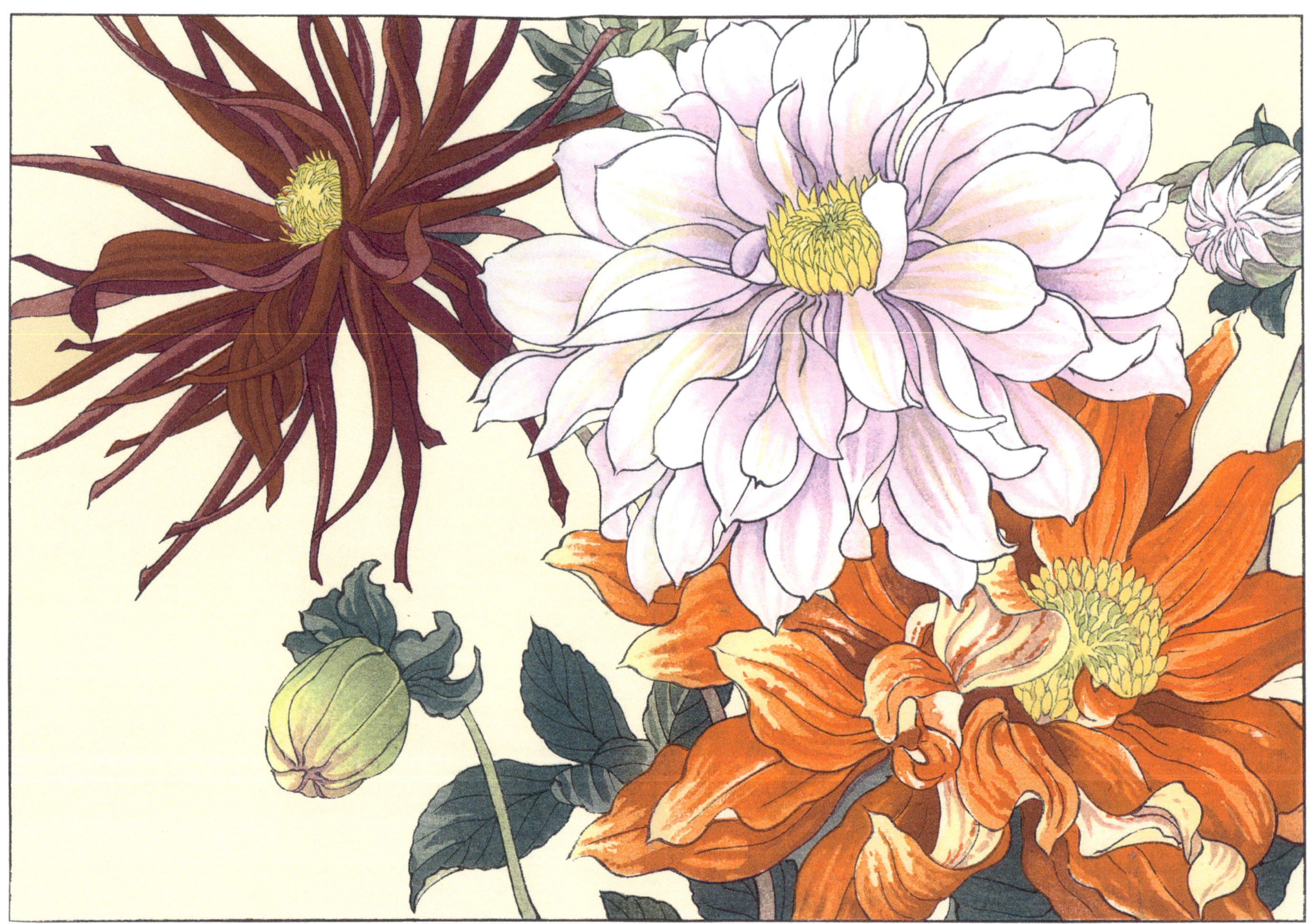

Dahlia

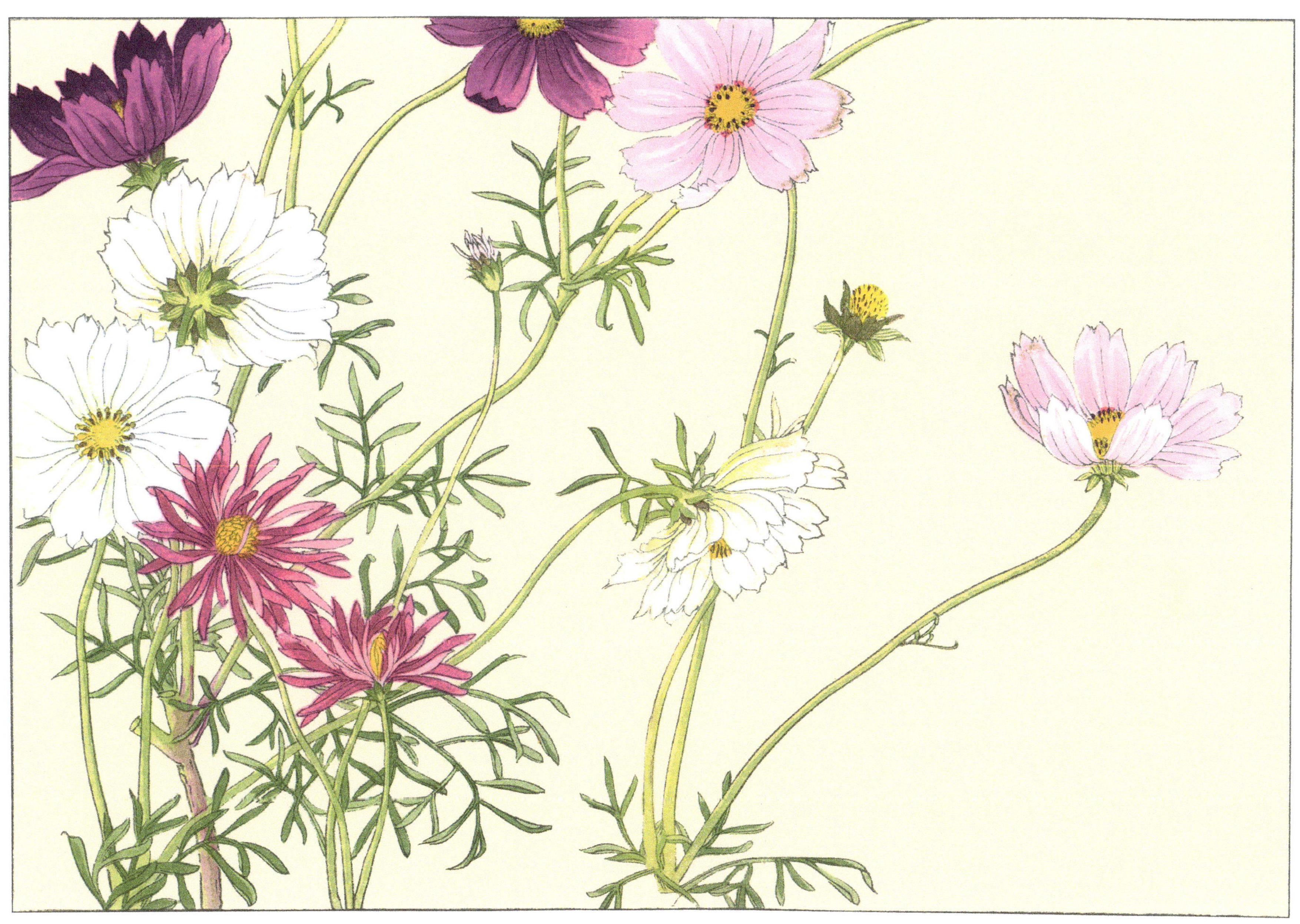

Cosmos

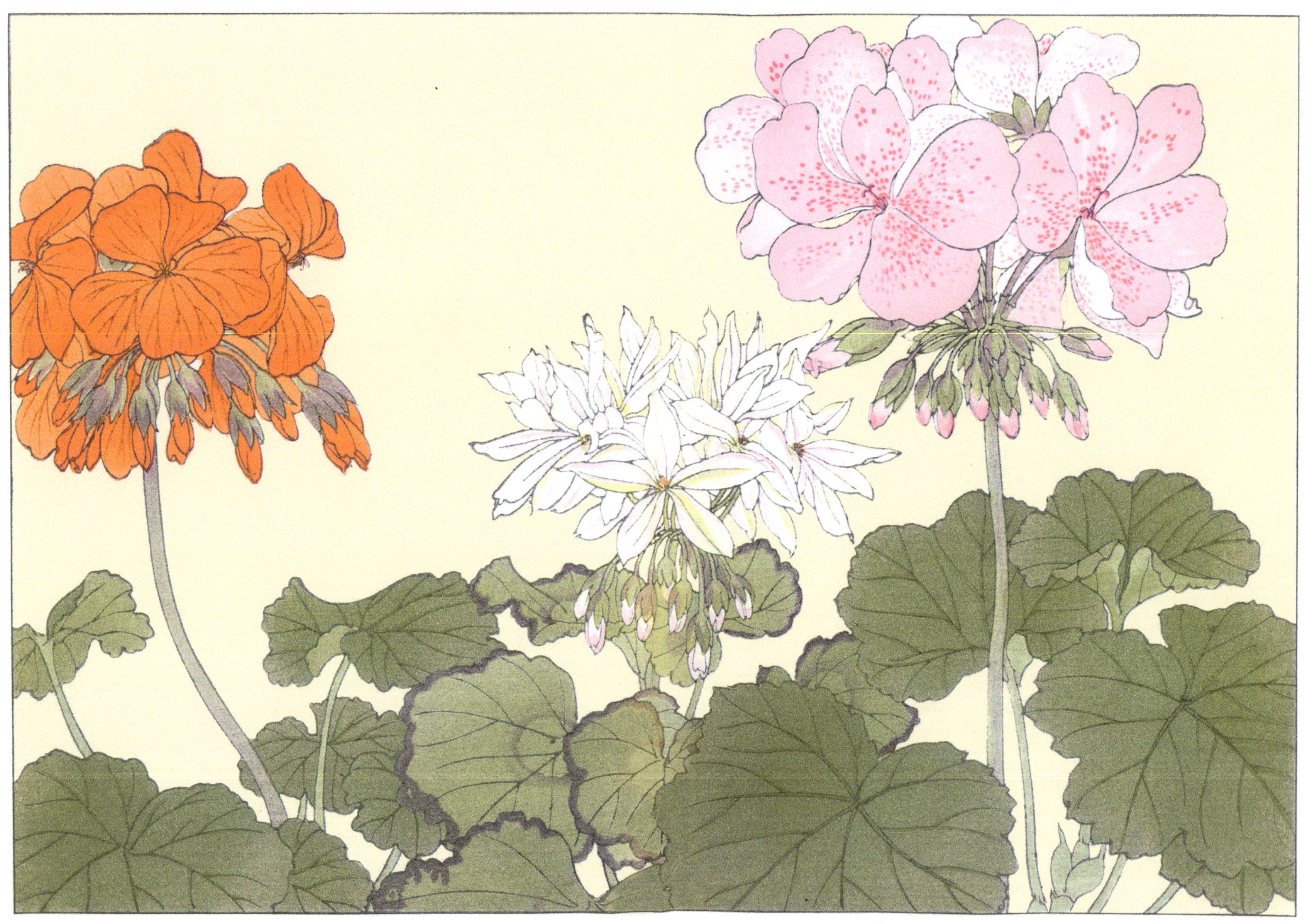

Pelargonium

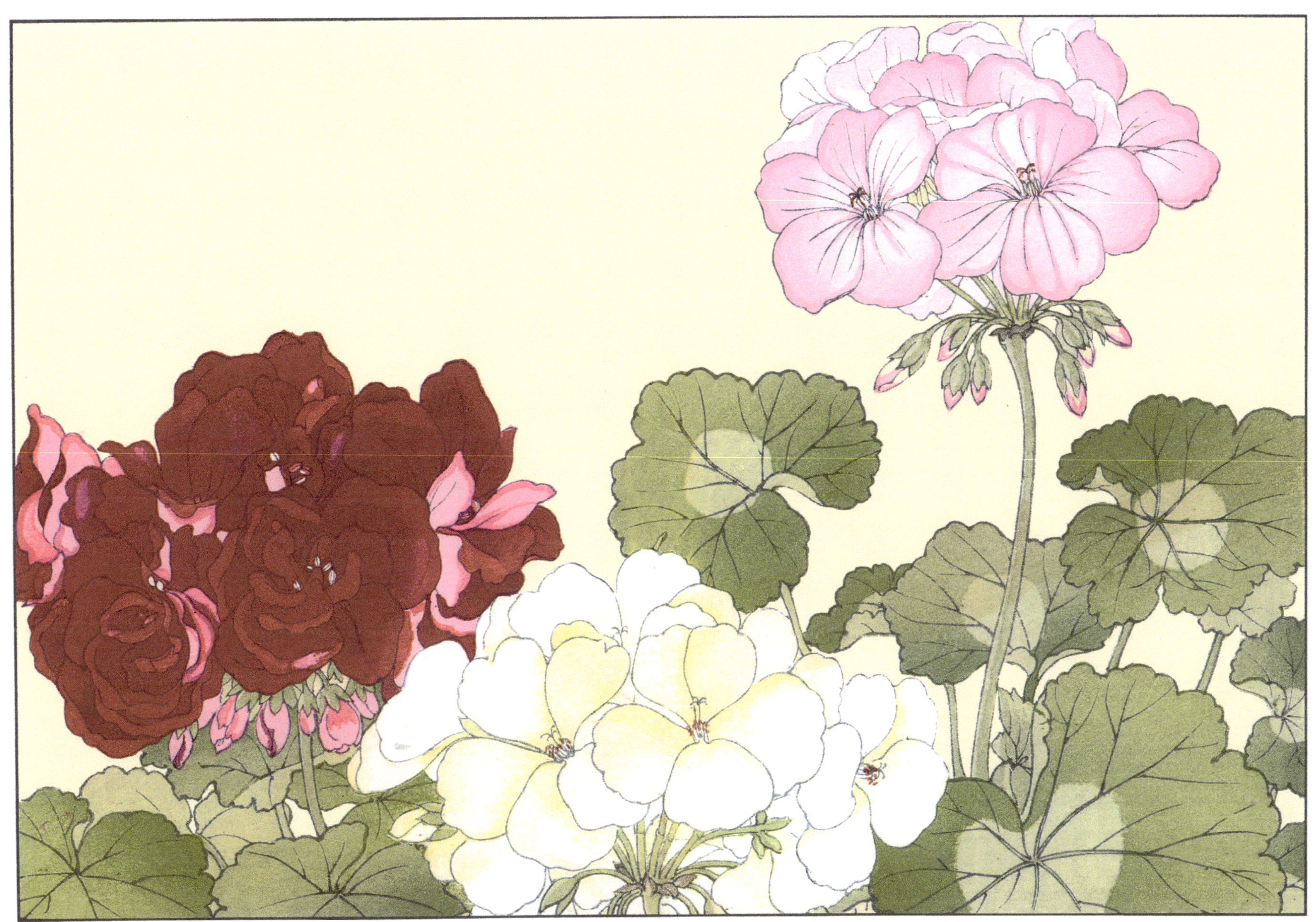

Geranium

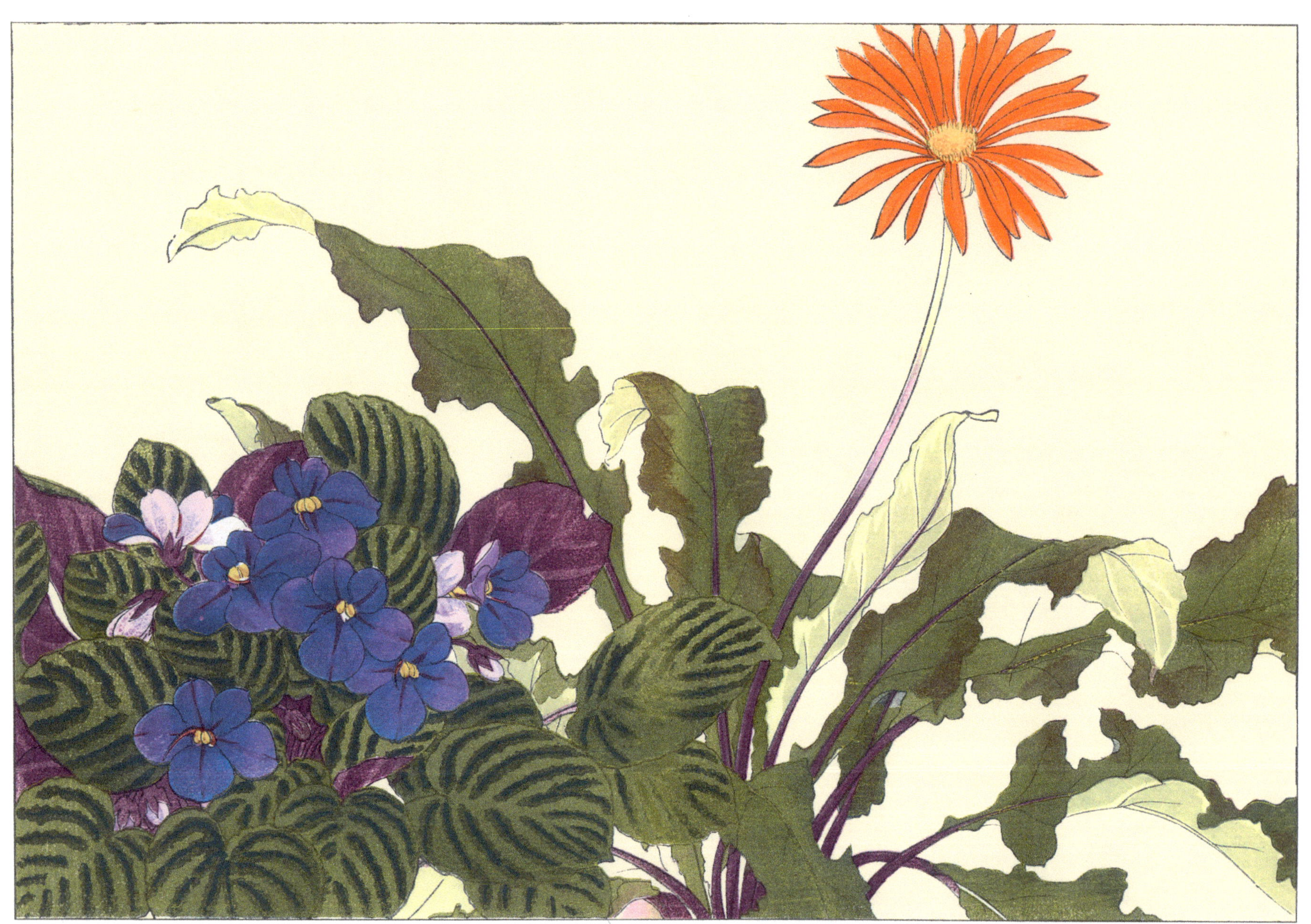

Gerber Daisy and Saintpaulia (or African Violet)

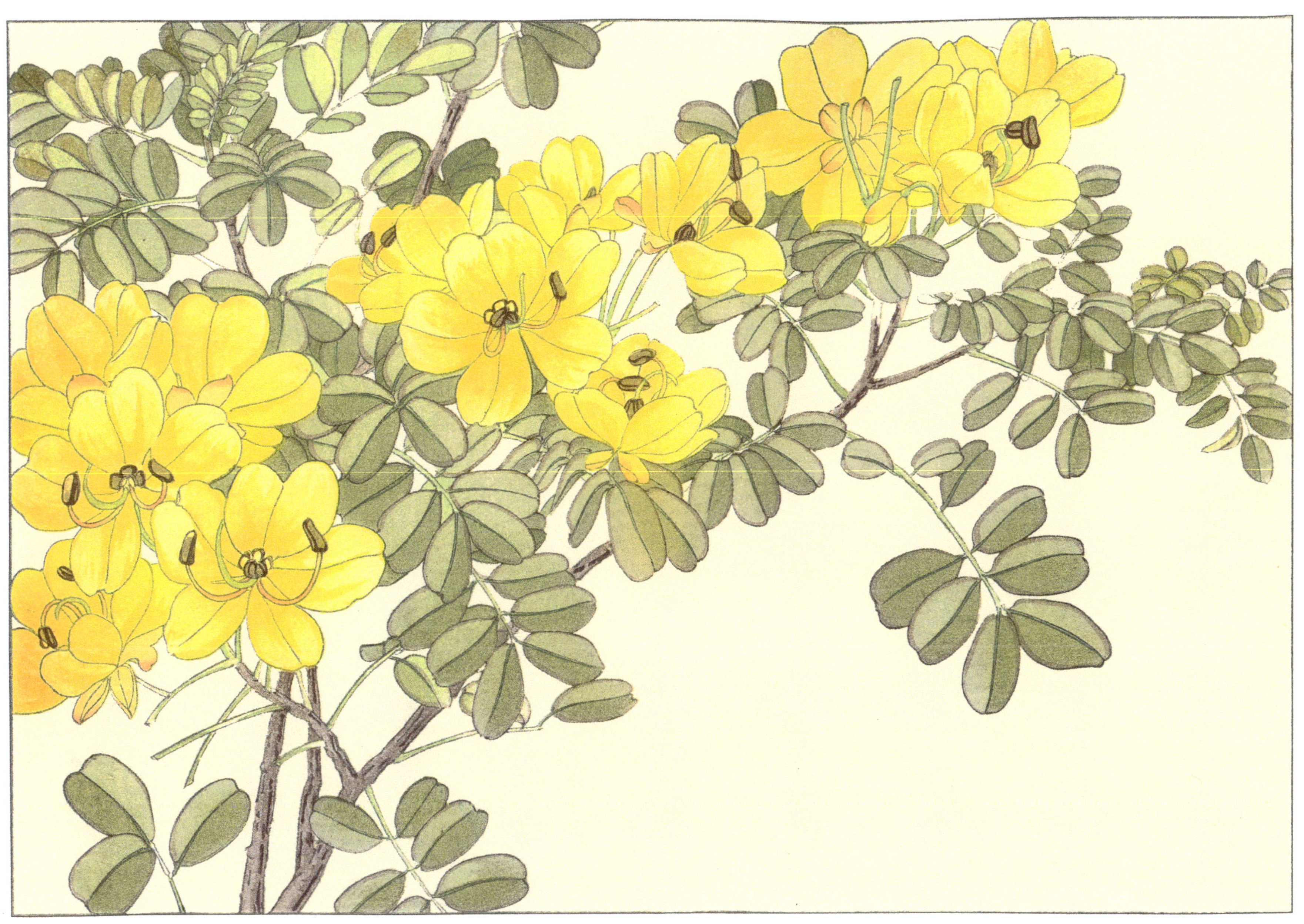

Allamanda

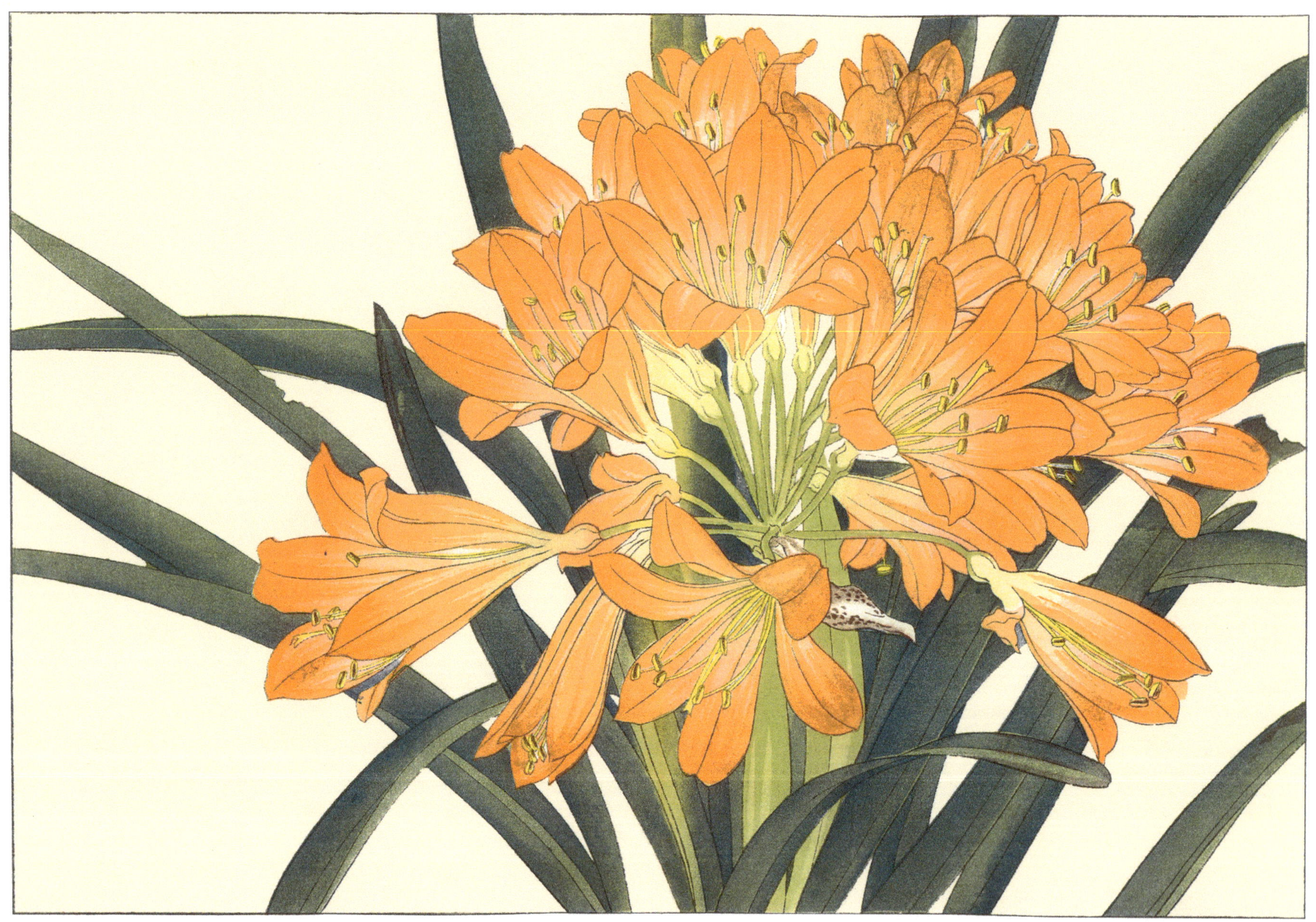

Clivia

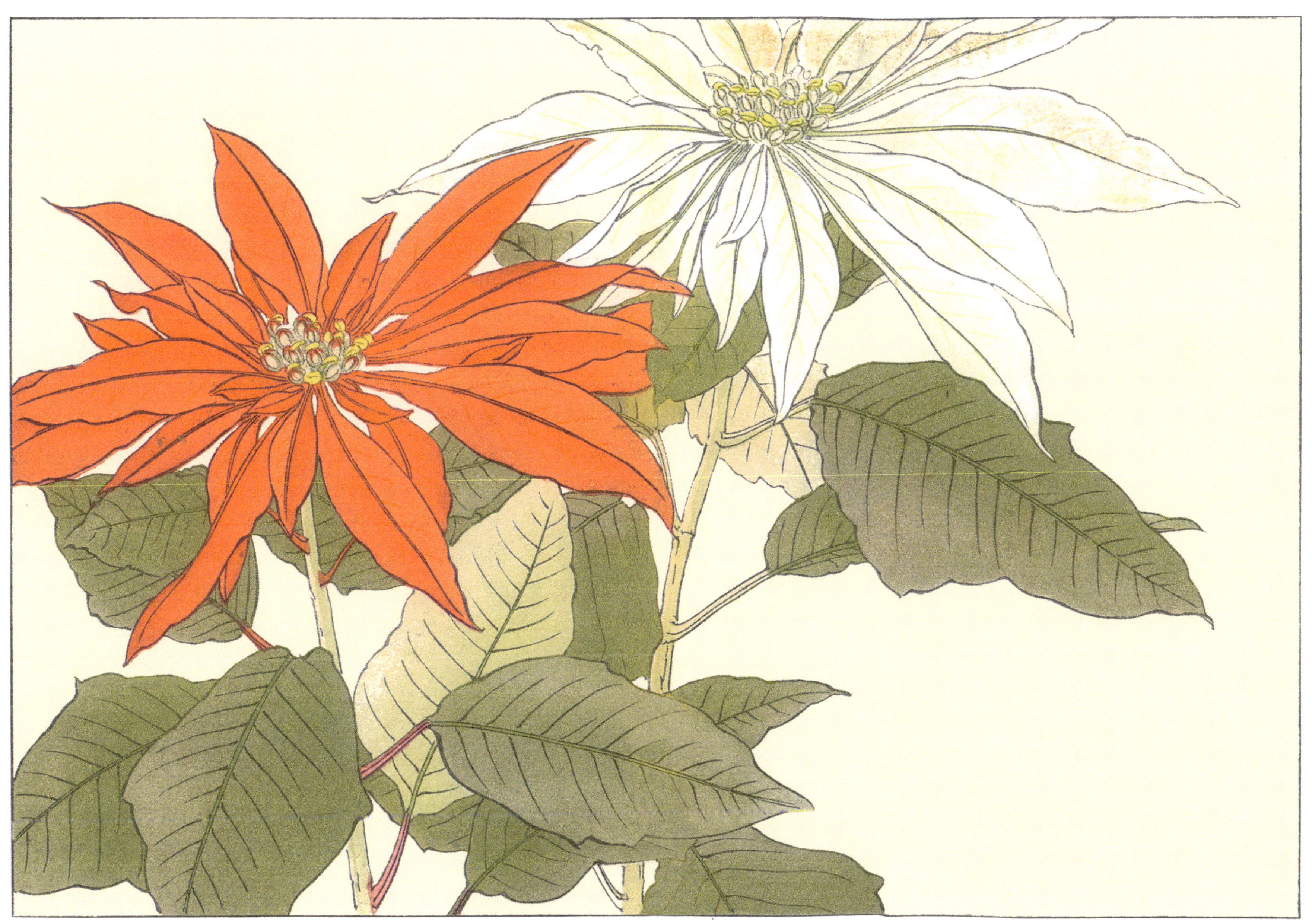

Poinsettia

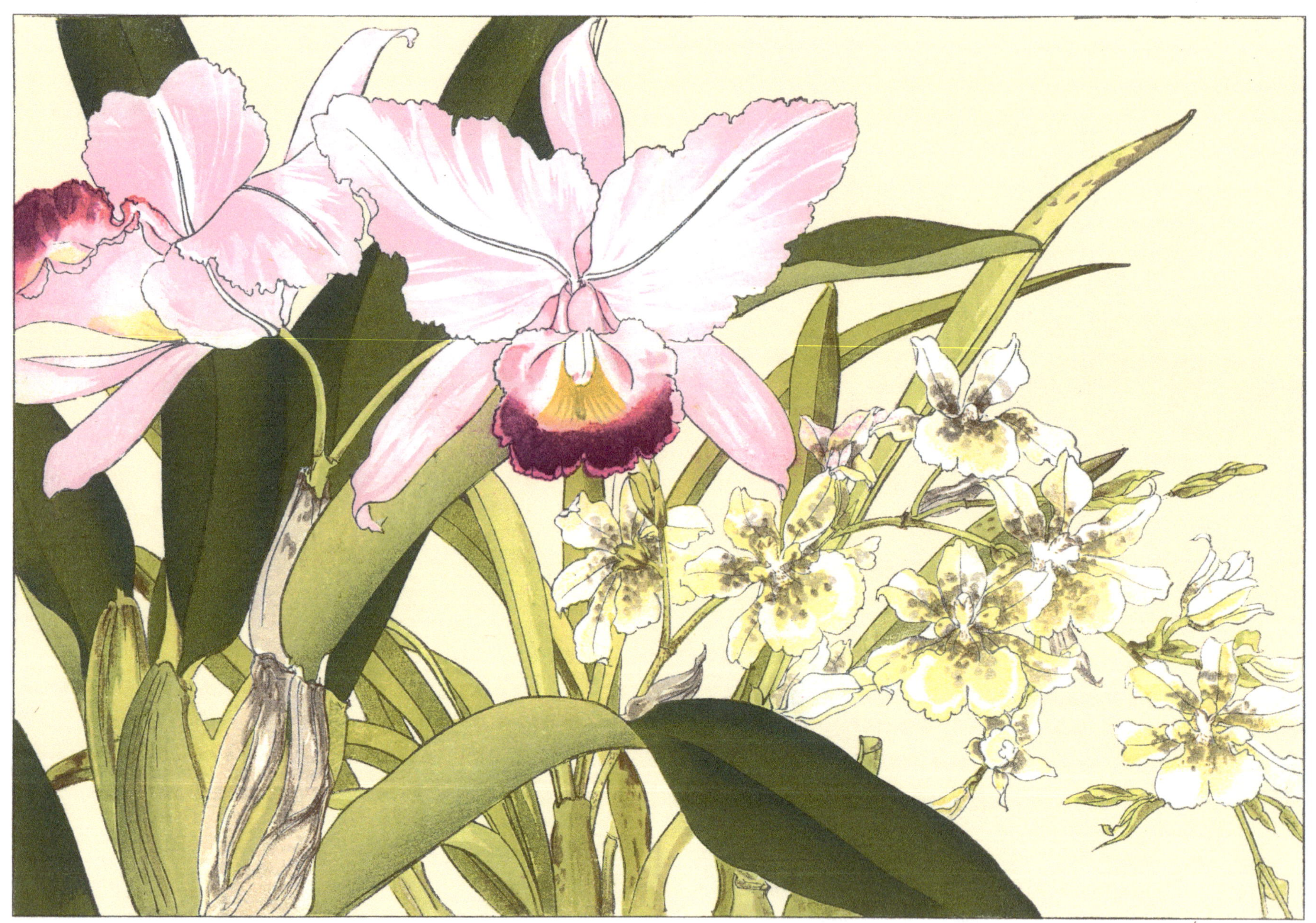

Oncidium and Cattleya Orchids

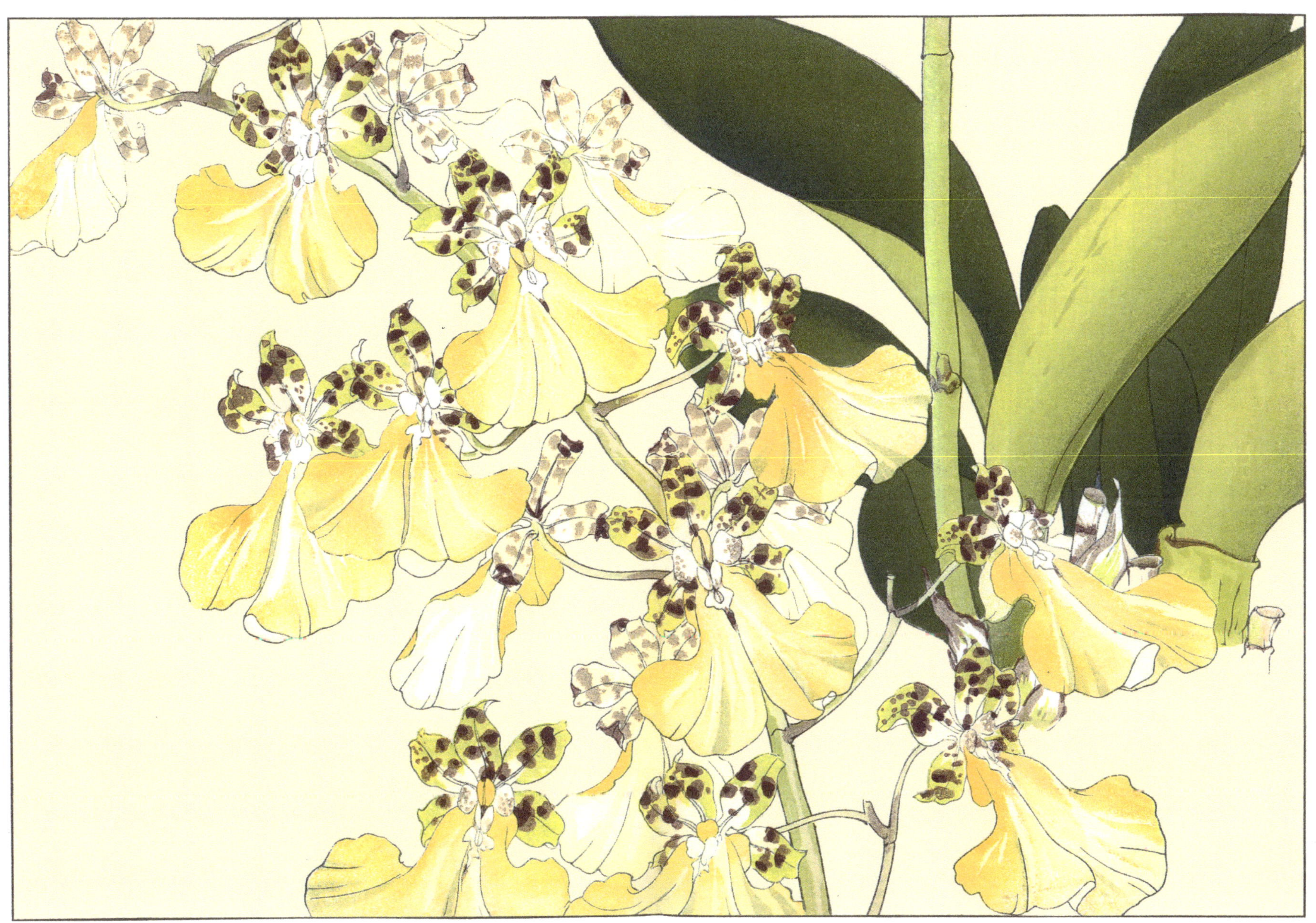

Oncidium Orchid

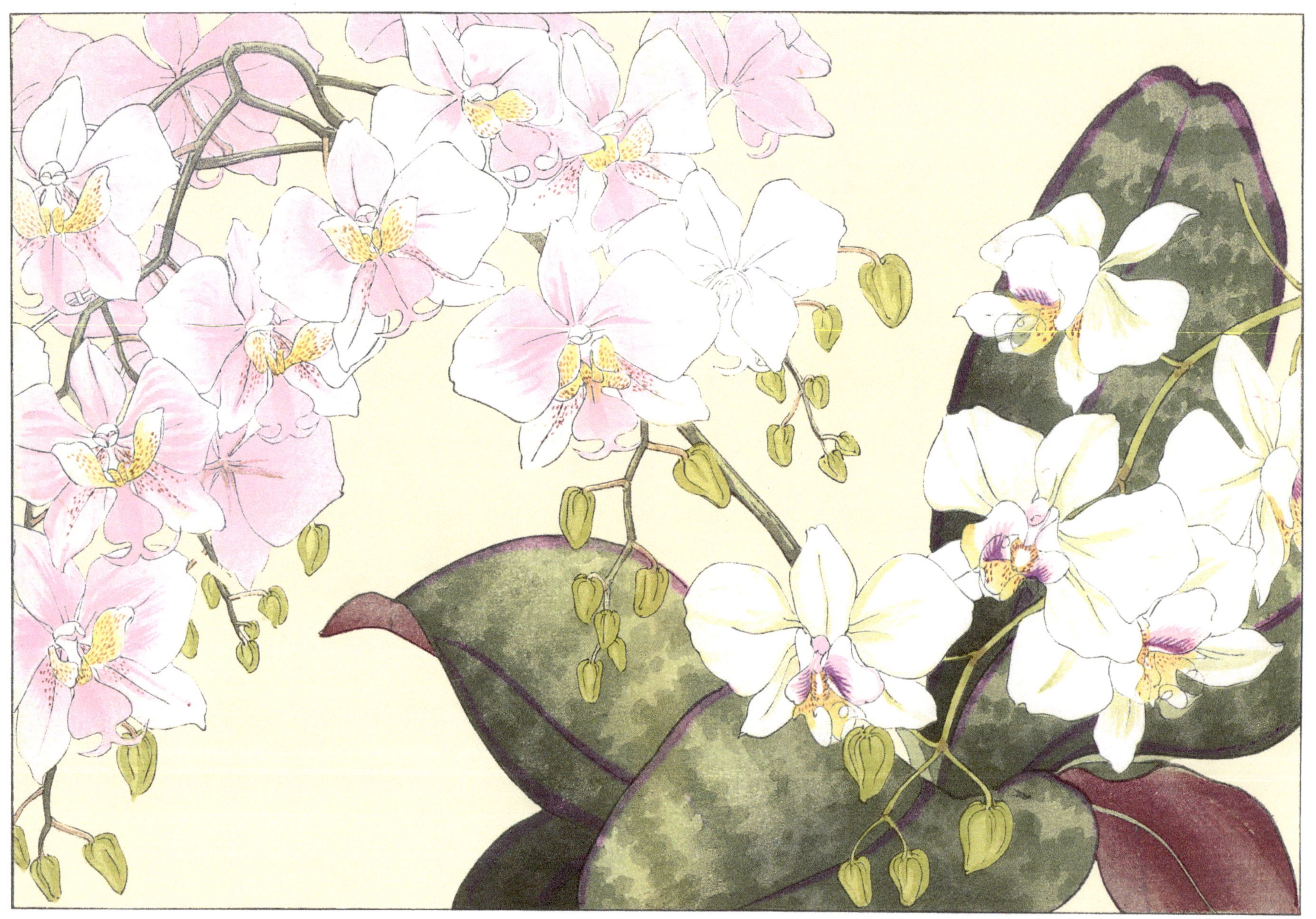

Phalaenopsis Orchid

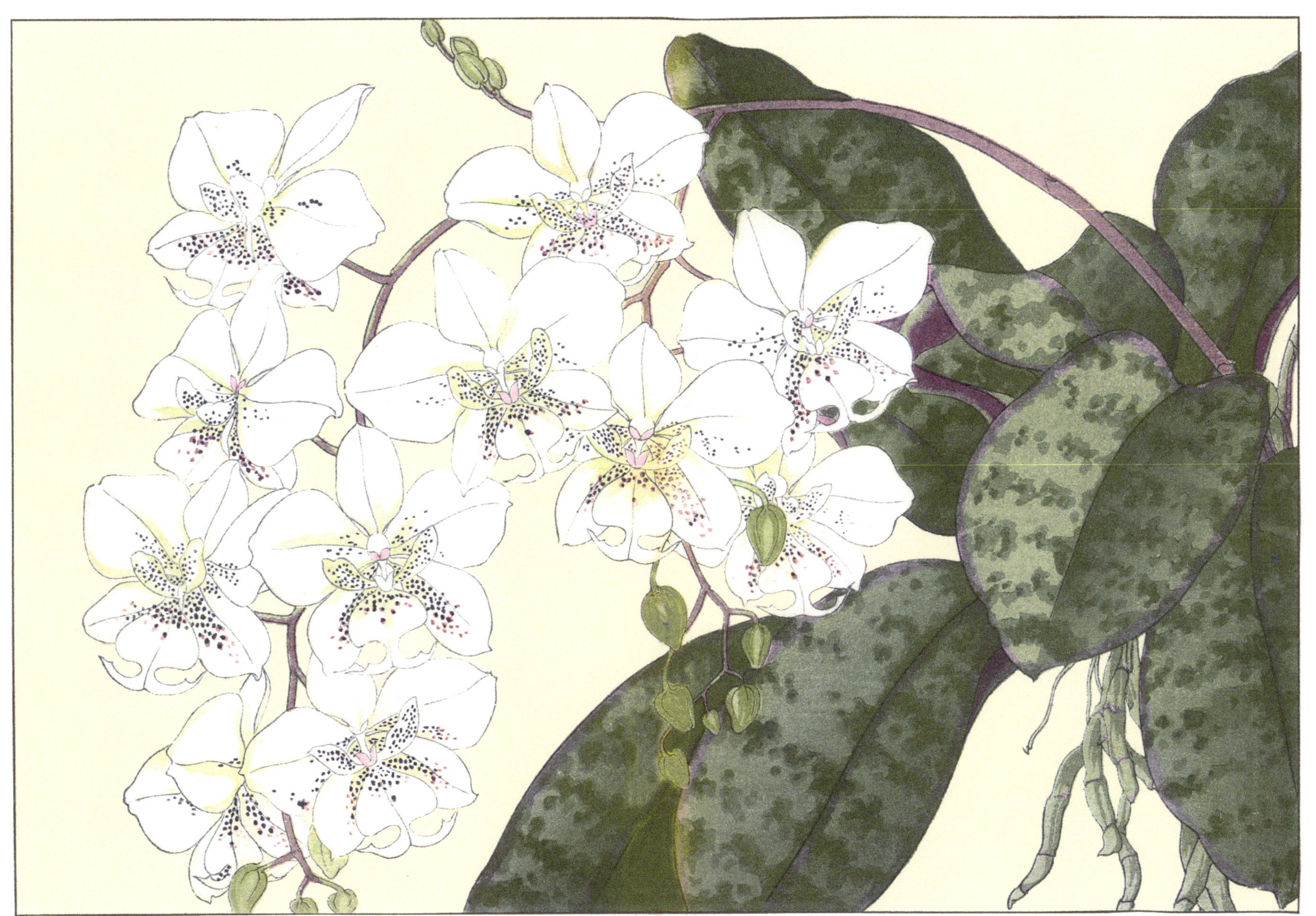

Phalaenopsis Orchid

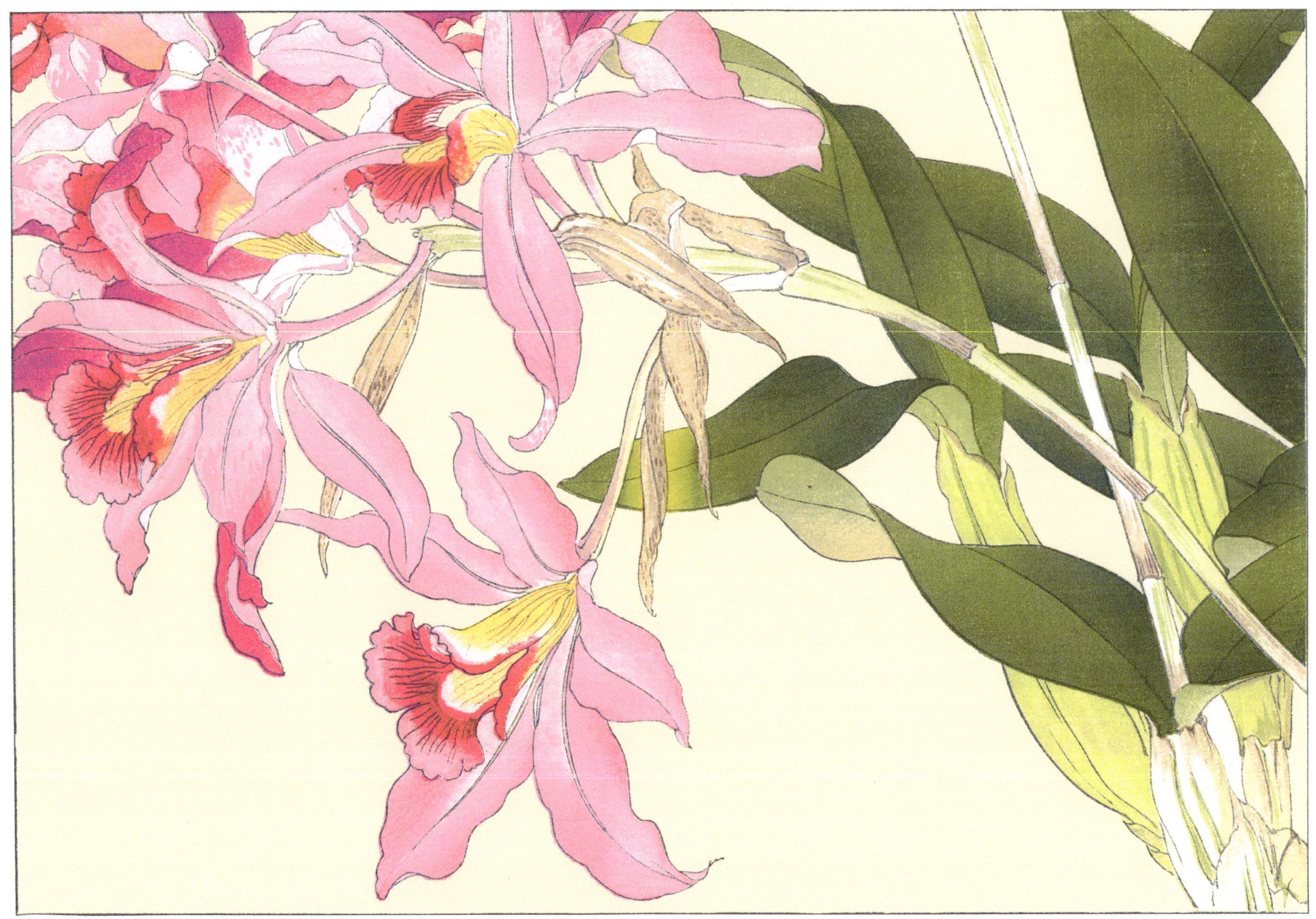

Laelia Orchid

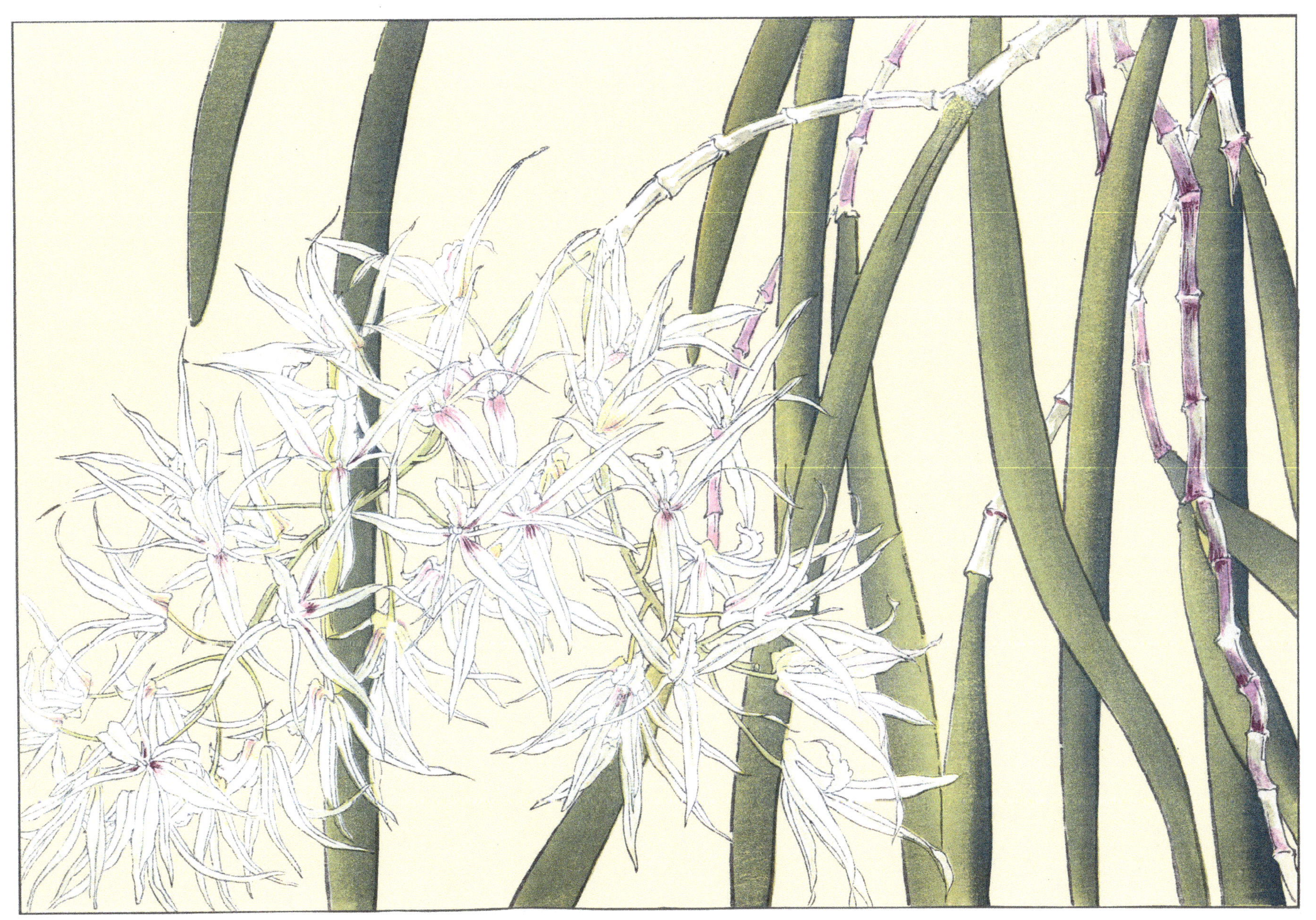

Dockrillia Teretifolium (or Bridal Veil Orchid)

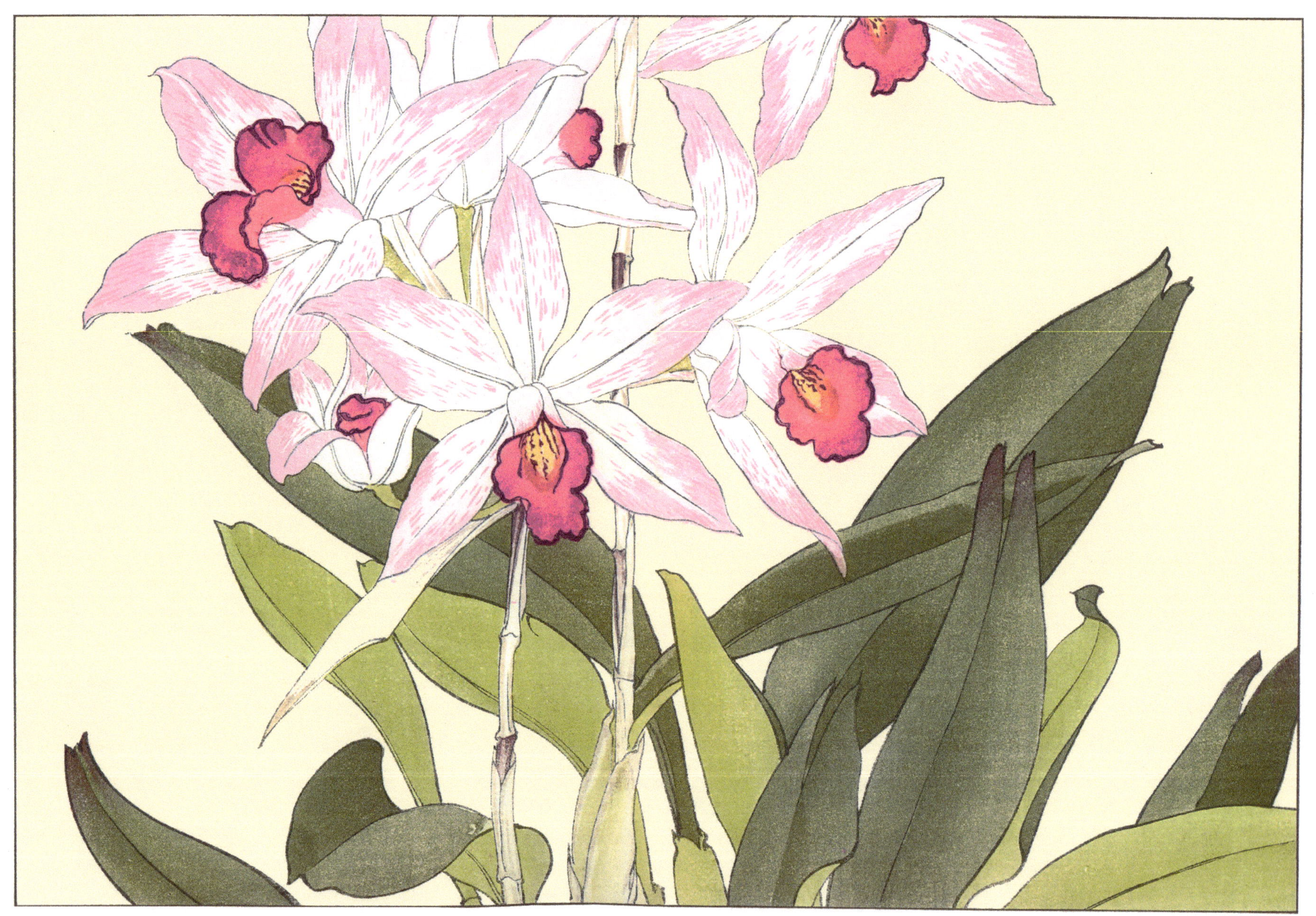

Laelia Anseps Orchid

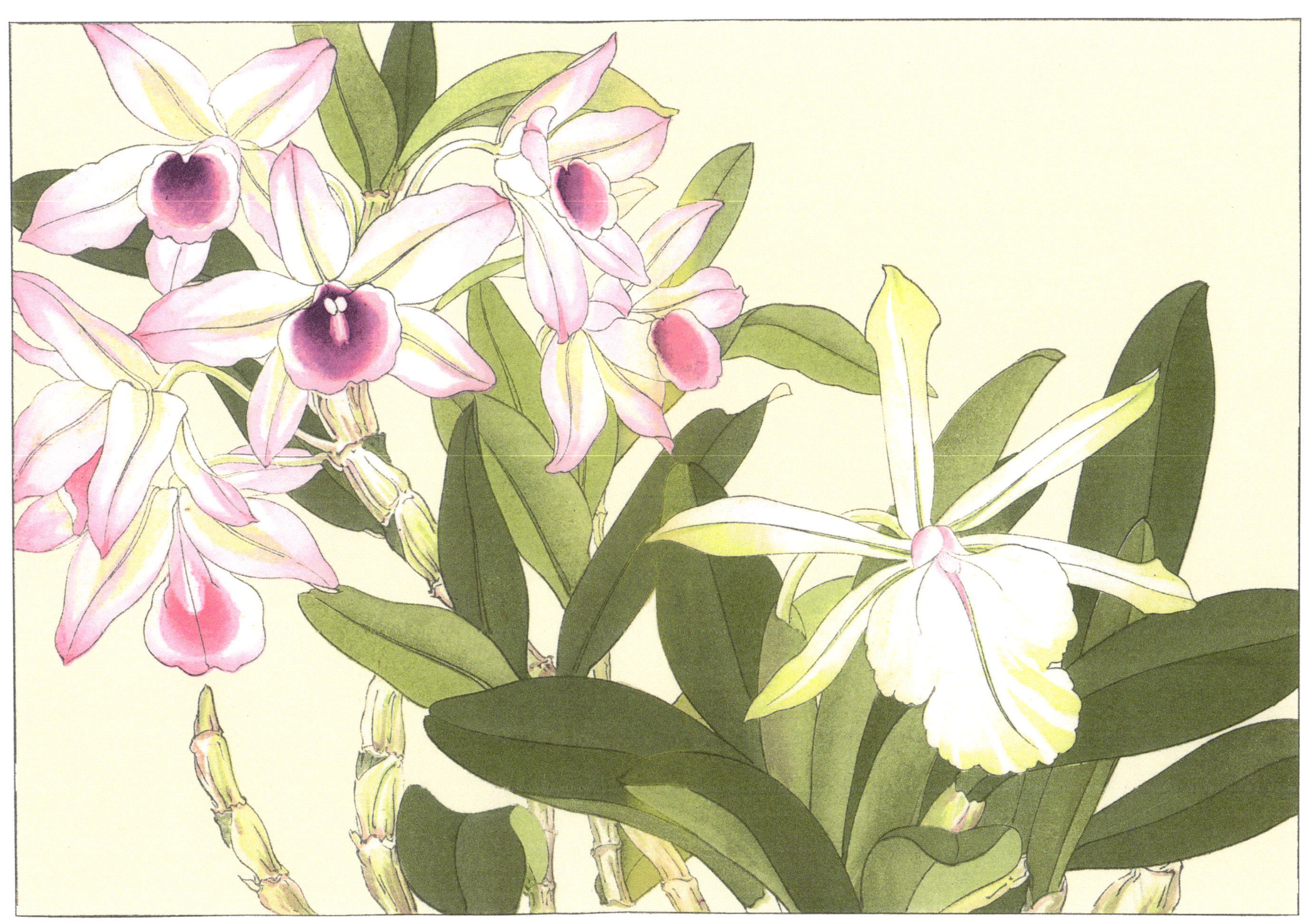

Laelia and Dendrobium Orchids

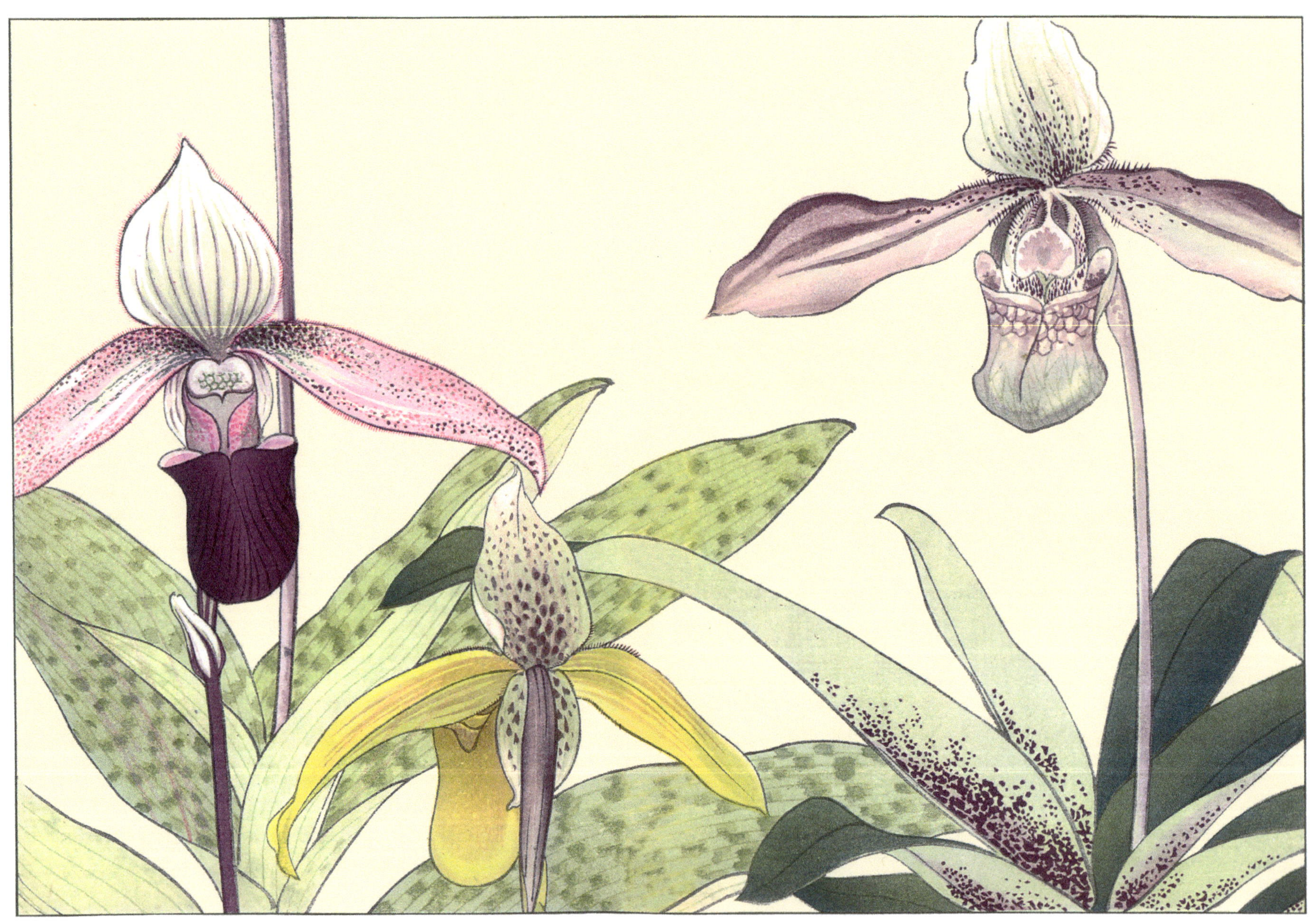

Cypripedium Orchid

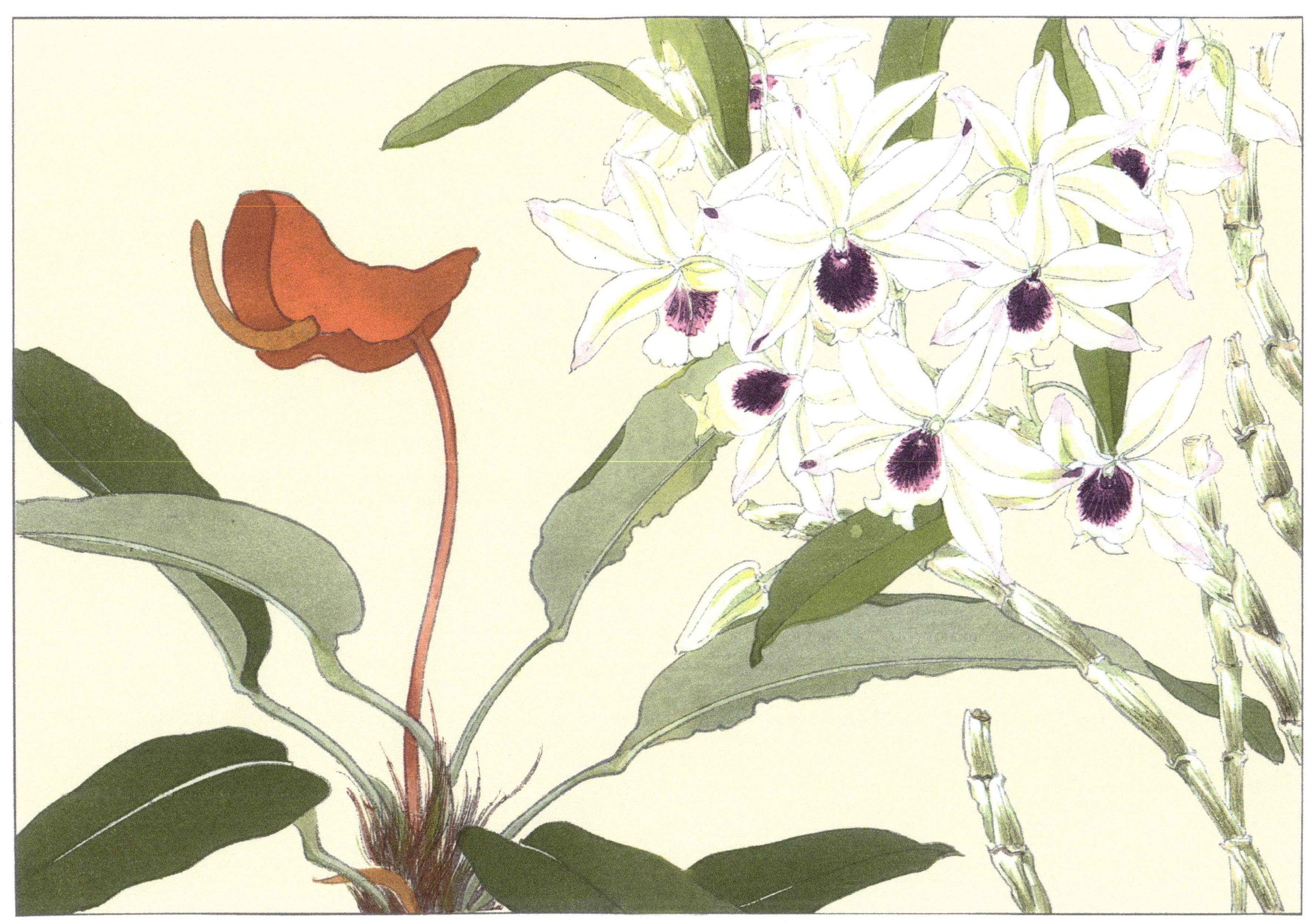

Dendrobium Orchid and Anthurium

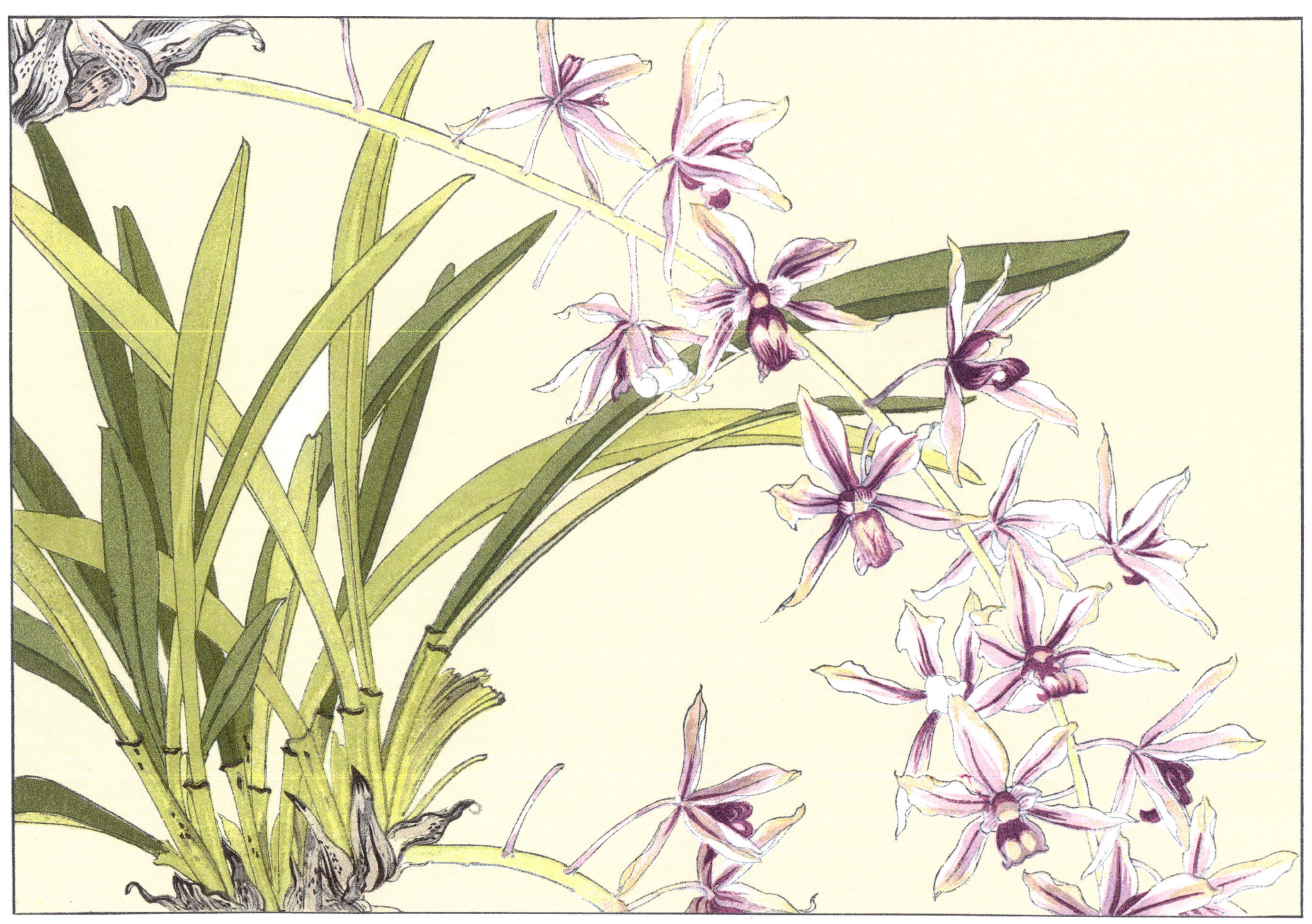

Cymbidium Orchid

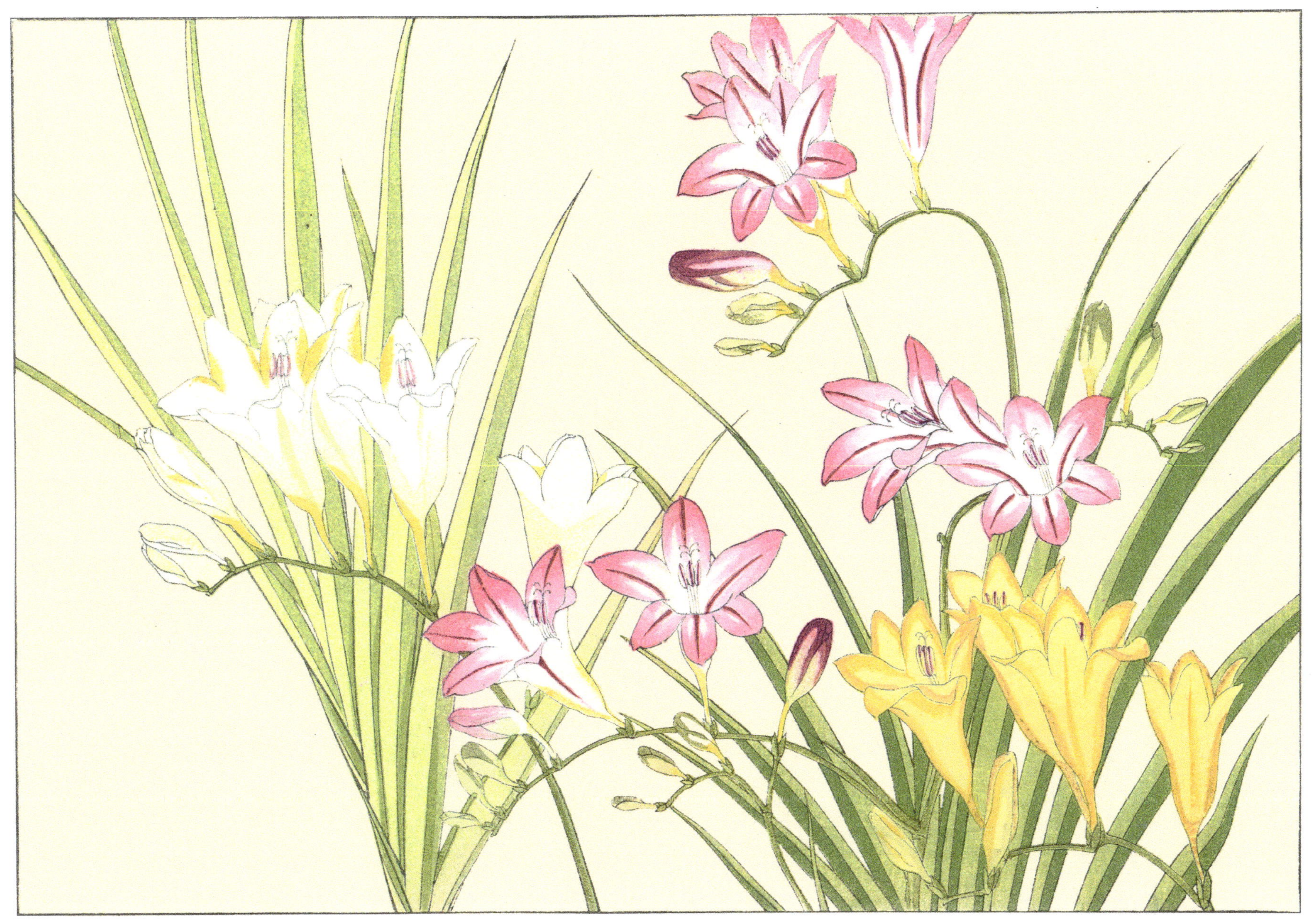

Freesia

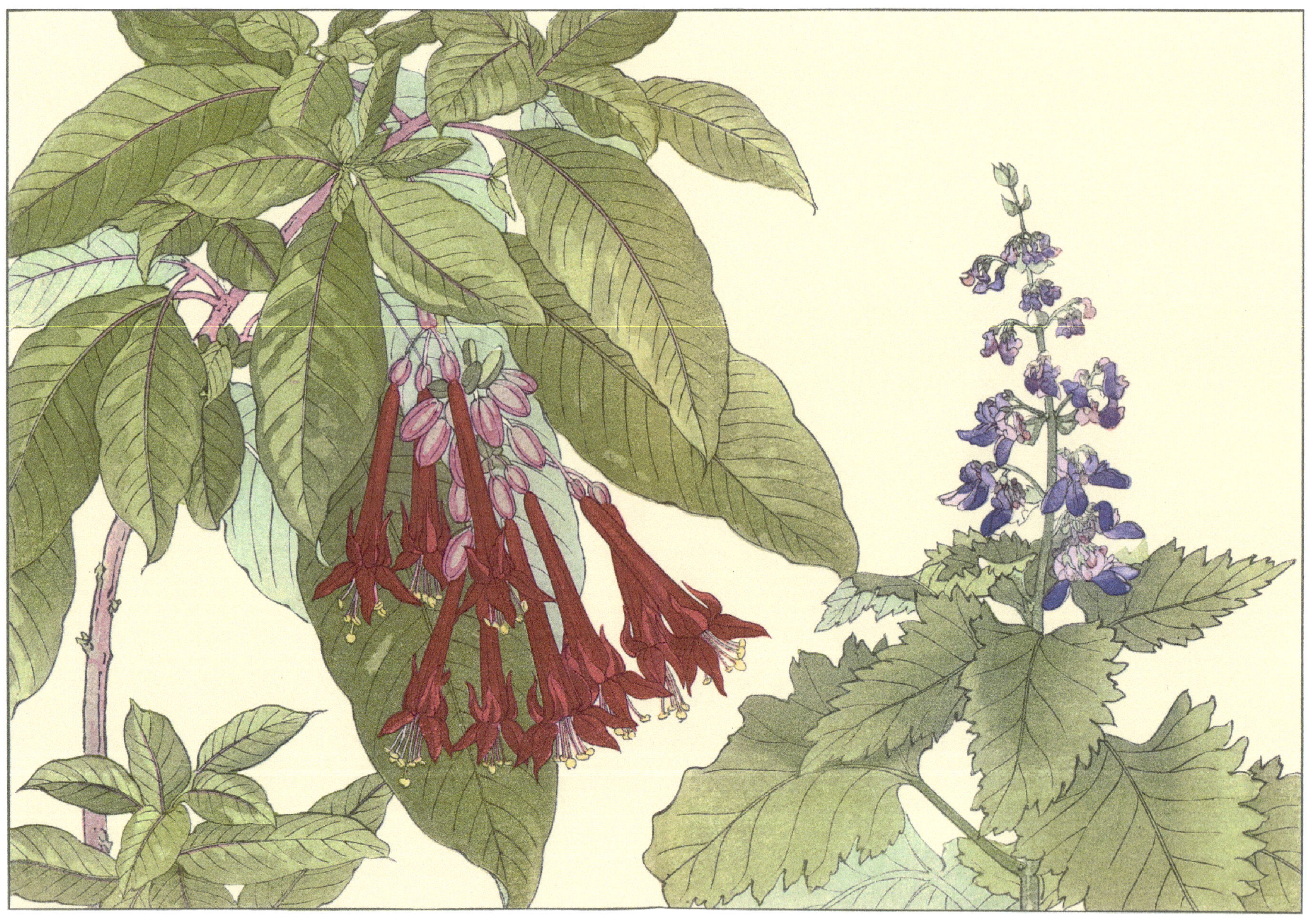

Coleus and Fuchsia

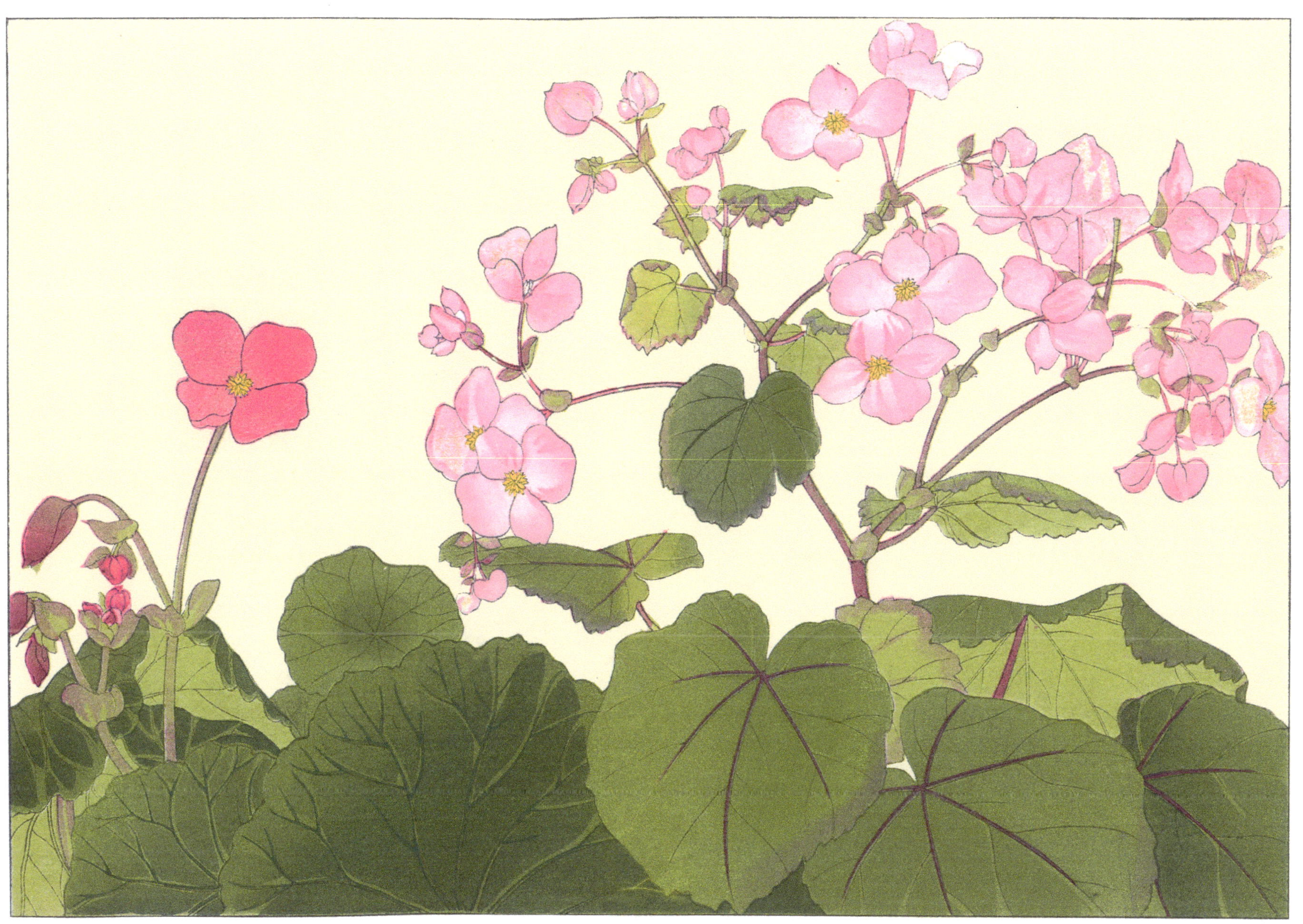

Begonia

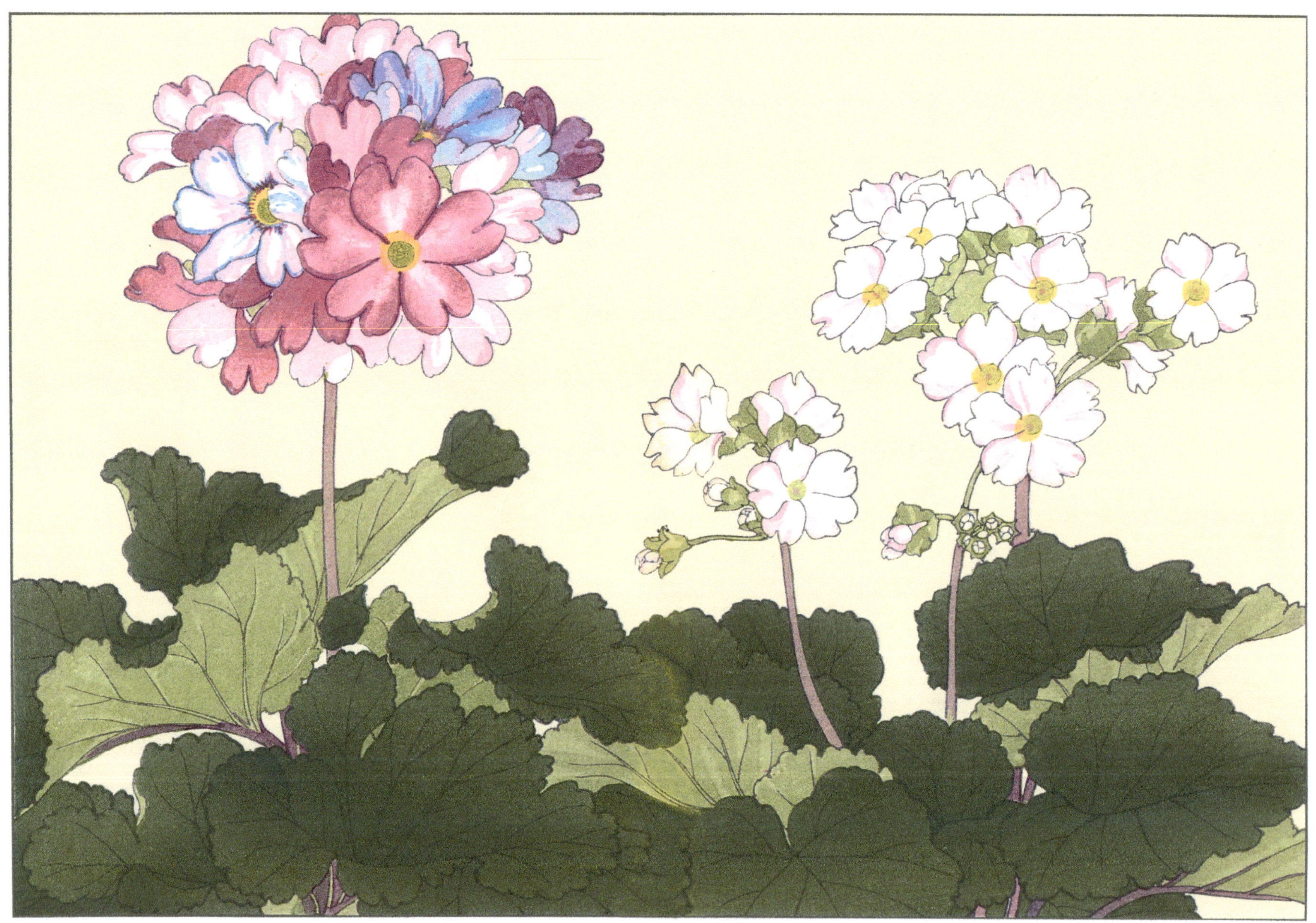

Primula

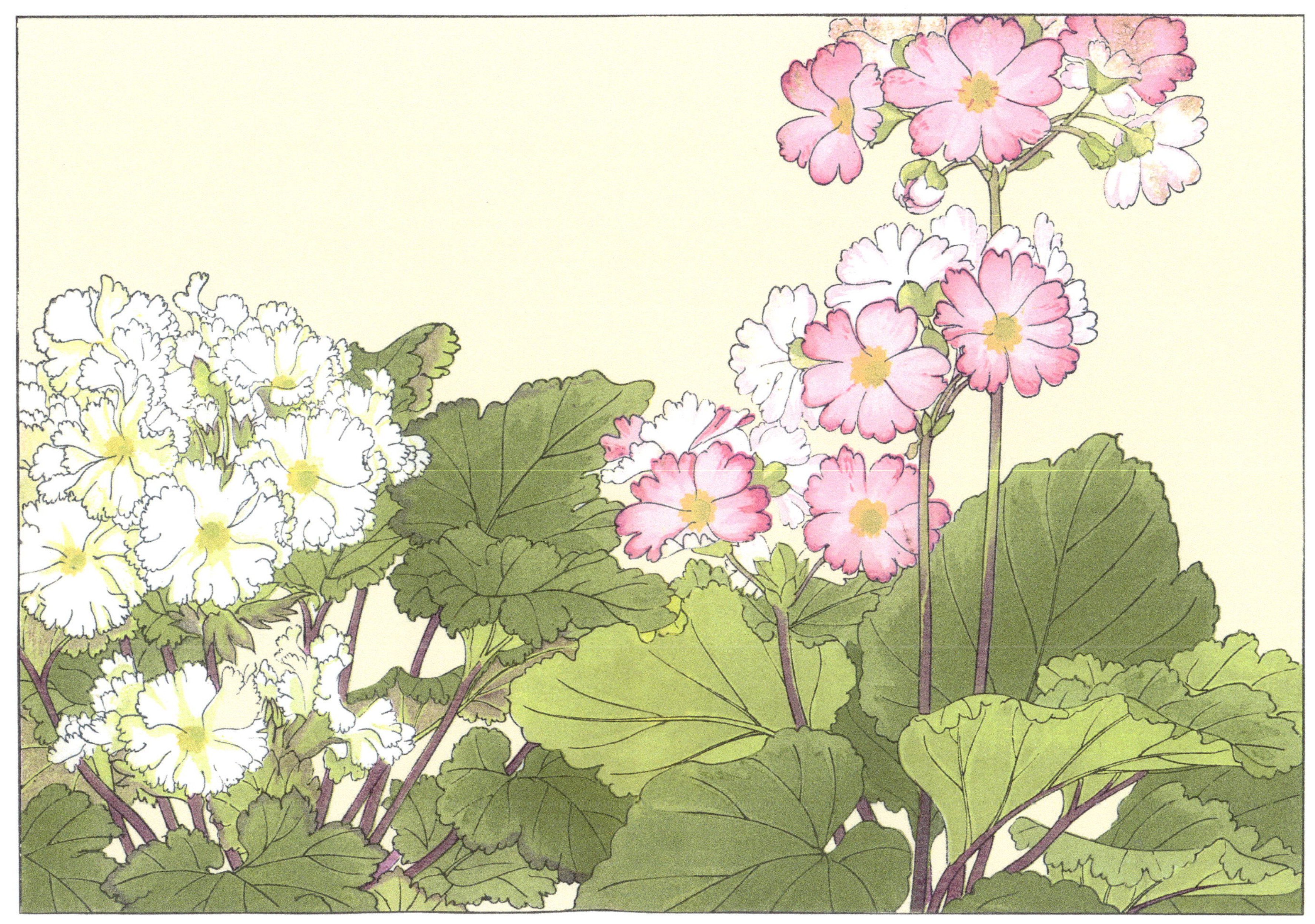

Primula

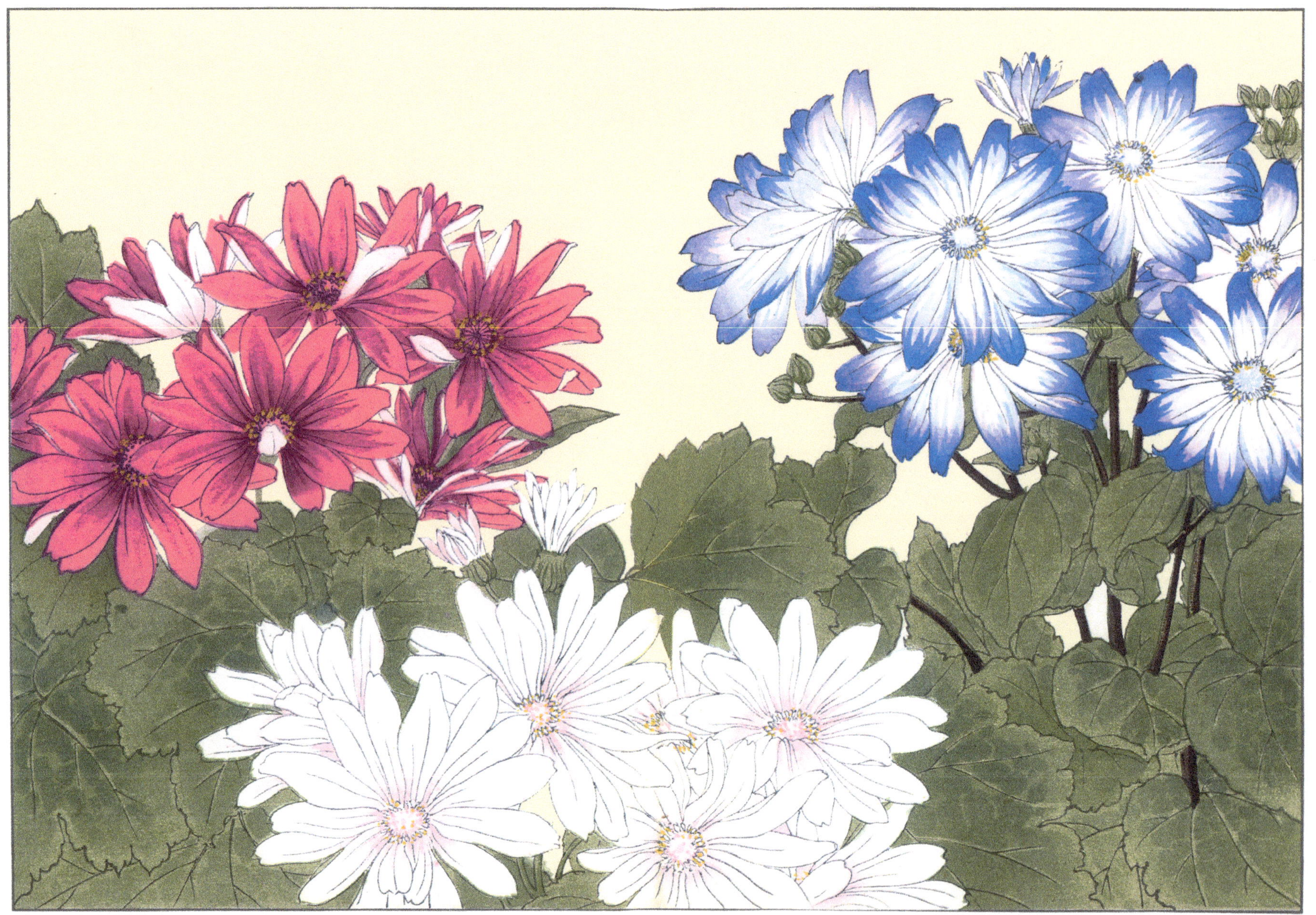

Cineraria

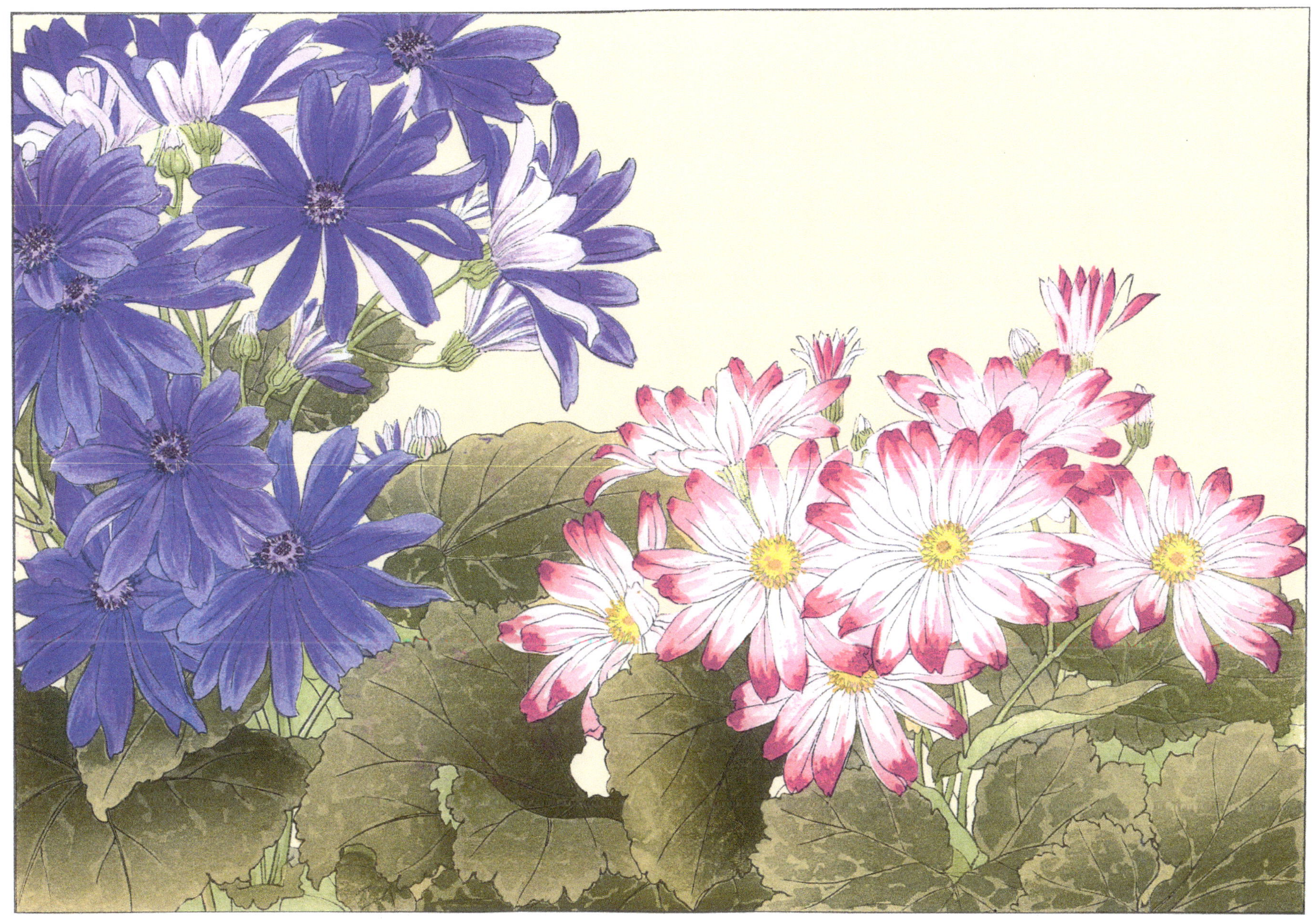

Cineraria

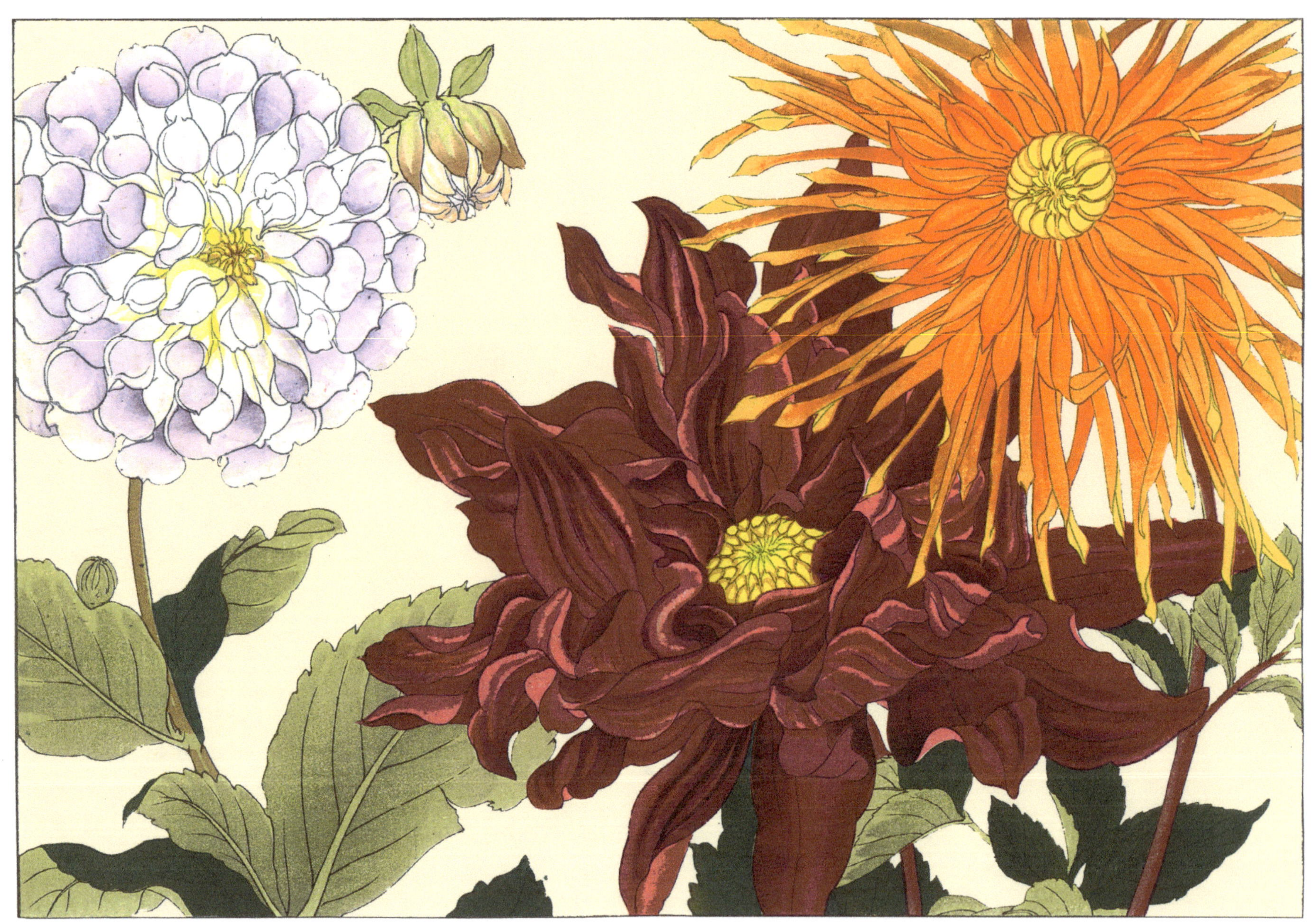

Dahlia